EDUGORILLA™
PUBLICATION

AF647739

KVS TGT

Science

Latest Edition
Practice Kit

05 Tests
05 Mock Test

Based On Real Exam Pattern

✓ Thoroughly Revised and Updated
✓ Detailed Analysis of all MCQs

Title	: KVS TGT Science
Author Name	: Mr. Rohit Manglik
Published By	: EduGorilla Community Pvt. Ltd.
Publishers Address	: 12/651, First Floor Opp. Arvindo Park, Near Jama Masjid, Indira Nagar, Lucknow, Uttar Pradesh-226016, India

Copyright EduGorilla

ISBN : 978-93-55565-60-0

First Edition

Disclaimer EduGorilla

Compiled and created by EduGorilla Community Pvt. Ltd

ROHIT MANGLIK
CEO, EduGorilla

Dear Applicants,

People say *"Success comes to those who work hard."* But I've seen people working hard for their exams day in and day out for marginal success. While others succeed in their examinations by putting in just half the work. So are they God Gifted? No! I believe that it's because they work *smart* and not just *hard*. Similarly, for your exams, you should strategize your preparation so as to increase the likelihood of success. Well with EduGorilla get ready to increase your *chances of selection* in your exam by *16x*.

EduGorilla helps you in not only working *hard* but also working in a *smart and strategic* manner. With EduGorilla's preparation package, you get a chance to make your exam preparation easy, and a fun learning path towards selection. Finding the right path to your preparations can be difficult if you don't know in which direction to head. Don't worry, we have you covered! EduGorilla will be your guide to success in your journey. With our Preparation Package, you can prepare strategically and beat the exam in just one attempt.

EduGorilla's Preparation Package includes-

- **Test Series**
- **Books**

Our preparation package is handcrafted as per the latest changes, expert opinions, and students' discretion. Thus, enabling you to get through each stage of the selection process for your exam.

Our Books are designed by the teachers and experts of the respective exam with a combined 150+ years of experience; to provide you with easy, efficient, and effective learning. Our books are smart, in the sense that not only do they give you the answers to the questions but also provide similar questions for practice.

EduGorilla's competent Test Series gives you real-time experience and confidence through which you can clear your offline or online exam in just one attempt. We currently host 84,000+ mock tests for 1,440+ competitive and academic exams.

Thus, EduGorilla misses no chance to assist you in your preparation and covers all stages of the exam, so that you don't have to look anywhere else.

We provide complete preparation packages for defense, banking, teaching, and other National & State-Level exams. Hence, it doesn't matter which exam you aspire to because you will reach your success.

ALL THE BEST !

Let **EduGorilla** be your Guide to Success.

Rohit Manglik,
Founder and CEO, EduGorilla

Editor's Note

INTRODUCTION

EduGorilla focuses on guiding students to succeed in their examinations. With that in mind, our book, titled "KVS TGT : Science", has been drafted through the collective efforts of our distinguished experts with 150+ years of combined experience. This book consists of questions that are created following the latest changes in the syllabus and exam pattern. We compiled the book on the basis of questions that are most likely to appear in the KVS TGT Science. Through EduGorilla's "KVS TGT : Science" your chances of success will increase 16x.

EduGorilla does this through our Complete Preparation Package. This package consists of well-conceptualized and structured content in the form of questions that are tailor-made according to your needs and will help you practice for exams in a smart way by pinpointing all the necessary information. It also provides hints and solutions, along with a smart answer sheet for your self-evaluation. You can assess your shortcomings and work accordingly on areas that may require more of your attention.

EduGorilla promises to help you succeed in your examination and accomplish your dream goals. We believe in our aspirants and see them at the top of the merit list. And the first step towards the top is to start preparing with us. EduGorilla's "KVS TGT : Science" includes the following attributes.

➤ Well-Researched Content

➤ Top-Notch Quality

➤ Detailed Answers and Analysis

➤ Smart Answer Sheet

➤ Exam Relevant Questions

Therefore, EduGorilla fortifies your preparation and makes it durable enough to help you stand tall and beat the examination.

KVS TGT Science

Scan QR code for Eligibility, Exam Pattern, Syllabus and more.

Book ID: 1230

TABLE OF CONTENTS

Mock Test 01

Q.1 The substance formed by the combination of two or more elements in a fixed ratio is called:

A. Element **B.** Compound
C. Mixture **D.** Solid

Q.2 In the atmosphere, highest amount of ozone gas is present in:

A. Troposphere **B.** Mesosphere
C. Stratosphere **D.** Thermosphere

Q.3 If the energy of the electron in the 1st orbit of hydrogen is -13.6 eV, then how much is the energy (in eV) of an electron in the 3rd orbit?

A. -1.51 **B.** -4.53 **C.** -40.8 **D.** -122.4

Q.4 Propagation of light quanta may be described by:

A. Photons **B.** Protons
C. Neutrons **D.** Electrons

Q.5 The state of matter which consists of super energetic particles in the form of ionized gases is called:

A. Liquid state **B.** Plasma state
C. Gaseous state **D.** None of these

Q.6 Which of the following states of matter has the weakest Intermolecular forces?

A. Solids **B.** Liquids
C. Gases **D.** None of these

Q.7 In which of the following states of matter the intermolecular distance is fixed?

A. Liquids **B.** Solids
C. Gases **D.** None of these

Q.8 Outdoors on the winter, why does a piece of metal feel colder than piece of wood?

A. Metal is a good conductor of heat than wood
B. Wood is a good conductor of heat than metal
C. Wood conducts heat faster than metal
D. Both the metals and wood are bad conductors of heat

Q.9 Calculate the number of protons, neutrons and electrons in $^{80}_{35}Br$.

A. 35,45,35 **B.** 30,35,45
C. 45,35,45 **D.** 35,45,35

Q.10 Which of the following properties are similar for isotopes?

A. Physical properties
B. Chemical properties
C. Both physical and chemical properties
D. Neither physical nor chemical properties

Q.11 If Aufbau rule is violated, then Ca^{20} will be in:

A. s-block **B.** p-block **C.** d-block **D.** f-block

Q.12 Which of the following is/are true as per Thomson's model of atom?

A. An atom is not electrically neutral.
B. An atom is a positively charged sphere with electrons embedded in it.
C. Negative and positive charges in the atom are not equal in magnitude.
D. None of the above

Q.13 The number of different substitution products formed when ethane is allowed to react with bromine in sunlight is:

A. 9 **B.** 6 **C.** 8 **D.** 5

Q.14 Ether is formed when alkyl halide is heated with sodium alkoxides. This method is called:

A. Kolbe synthesis
B. Wurtz reaction
C. Perkin Reaction
D. Williamson's Synthesis

Q.15 Ethylene reacts with alkaline $KMnO_4$ to form:

A. Oxalic acid **B.** Acetic acid
C. Glycerol **D.** Glycol

Q.16 The reaction of toluene with chlorine in $FeCl_3$ gives predominantly:

A. Benzoyl Chloride
B. m-chlorotoluene
C. Benzyl Chloride
D. o and p chlorotoluenes

Q.17 Which of the following is the correct example regarding to the type of Bronsted-Lowry acids and base?

A. BF_3 – Lewis acid
B. CH_3COOH – Bronsted-Lowry base
C. H_2O – Bronsted-Lowry base
D. None of the above

Q.18 Which one of the following is formed by the reaction between a lewis acid and a lewis base?

A. Lewis base
B. Lewis acid
C. Lewis acid-base adduct
D. None of the above

Q.19 Which of the following substances cannot act as both acid as well as a base?

A. Amphoteric Solvents
B. Amphiprotic Solvents
C. Ampholyte Solvents
D. Protophilic Solvents

Q.20 pH value less than 7 indicates that the solution is ________.

A. acidic **B.** basic
C. neutral **D.** None of above

Q.21 Which of the following oxide(s) of iron would be obtained on the prolonged reaction of iron with steam?

A. FeO B. Fe_2O_3
C. Fe_3O_4 D. Fe_2O_3 and Fe_3O_4

Q.22 A metal in which even Iron can float is:

A. Sodium B. Magnesium
C. Manganese D. Mercury

Q.23 The essential constituent of an amalgam is:

[Joint Entrance Examination (Polytechnic), 2019]

A. Mercury B. An alkali metal
C. An alkali D. Silver

Q.24 Electronic configuration of copper can be represented as:

[Joint Entrance Examination (Polytechnic), 2019]

A. $[Ar]4\,s^2 3\,d^9 4p^1$ B. $[Ar]4\,s^2 3\,d^9$
C. $[Ar]4\,s^2 3\,d^{10} 4p^1$ D. $[Ar]4\,s^1 3\,d^{10}$

Q.25 An organic compound contains carbon = 38.71%, Hydrogen $= 9.67\%$ and Oxygen. The empirical formula of the compound would be:

[Joint Entrance Examination (Polytechnic), 2019]

A. CH_4O B. CH_2O C. CHO D. CH_3O

Q.26 The hydrocarbon used for welding purpose is:

[Joint Entrance Examination (Polytechnic), 2019]

A. Ethyne B. Benzene C. Ethene D. Ethane

Q.27 $F_2C = CF_2$ is a monomer of:

[Joint Entrance Examination (Polytechnic), 2019]

A. Teflon B. Buna-S C. Nylon-6 D. Glyptol

Q.28 The IUPAC name

of: $HC \equiv C - \underset{\displaystyle H}{\overset{\displaystyle C_2H_5}{\overset{|}{\underset{|}{C}}}} - CH_3$ is:

[Joint Entrance Examination (Polytechnic), 2019]

A. 3-Methyl-1-Pentyne
B. 3-Methyl-4-Pentyne
C. 2 -Ethyl-2-Propyne
D. 3 -Methyl-5-Pentyne

Q.29 The epithelial cells found in taste buds are called

A. Glandular epithelium cells
B. Pigmented epithelial cells
C. Neuroepithelial cells
D. Absorptive epithelial cells

Q.30 In which of the following is the lining of simple columnar epithelium found?

A. Lining of blood vessels
B. Lining of uterus
C. Respiratory passage of vertebrates
D. Convoluted tubules of kidney

Q.31 Which of the following statements concerning erythropoietin is true?

A. Erythropoietin is a glycoprotein hormone.
B. Hypoxia (a low level of oxygen) inhibits erythropoietin production.
C. Most erythropoietin is made in the pancreas in adults.
D. Erythropoietin stimulates white blood cell production.

Q.32 Which of the following renal cells participate(s) in acid-base homeostasis?

A. Podocytes B. Intercalated cells
C. Principal cell D. Brush border cell

Q.33 Which one of the following cell organelles may play a role in expelling excess water and wastes in the case of unicellular organisms?

[UPSC NDA, 2020]

A. Lysosome
B. Contractile vacuole
C. Golgi body
D. Endoplasmic reticulum

Q.34 In prokaryotic organisms, the nuclear region is not surrounded by a membrane. This undefined nuclear region is known as:

[UPSC NDA, 2020]

A. Nucleic acid B. Nucleoid
C. Nucleolus D. Nucleosome

Q.35 Blood is a type of:

[UPSC NDA, 2019]

A. Epithelial tissue B. Muscular tissue
C. Nervous tissue D. Connective tissue

Q.36 Movement of materials to different parts of cytoplasm and nucleus is generally carried out by:

[UPSC NDA, 2021]

A. Ribosomes
B. Mitochondria
C. Lysosomes
D. Endoplasmic reticulum

Q.37 One advantage of cleistogamy is:

A. It leads to the greater genetic diversity
B. Seed set is not dependent on pollinators
C. Seed dispersal is more eficient and widespread
D. Each visit of a pollinator result in transfer of hundreds of pollen grains

Q.38 Sucrose is converted into glucose and fructose by the enzyme:

A. Maltase B. Zymase
C. Isomerase D. Invertase

Q.39 A method in which roots are induced on the stem while it is still attached to the parent plant is called________.

A. Layering B. Cutting C. Grafting D. Budding

Q.40 Plants like Elm (Ulmus), Dandelion (Taraxacum) and members of Rose Family vegetatively reproduce by:

A. Rhizome B. Sucker C. Stolon D. Corm

Q.41 Junctions of two neurons are called _____.

A. synapse **B.** synapsis **C.** joint **D.** junction

Q.42 Which of the following is a plant hormone?

A. Insulin **B.** Thyroxin
C. Oestrogen **D.** Cytokinin

Q.43 When a person is suffering from severe cold, he or she cannot ________.

A. Differentiate the taste of an apple from that of an ice cream
B. Differentiate the smell of a perfume from that of an agarbatti
C. Differentiate red light from green light
D. Differentiate a hot object from a cold object

Q.44 The brain is lodged inside the cavity of the skull known as:

A. Piamater **B.** Duramater
C. Cranium **D.** Meninges

Q.45 Which of the following is not a part of the male reproductive system?

A. Penis **B.** Cervix
C. Spermduct **D.** Testes

Q.46 Fertilization occurs in the _______.
[RRB/RRC Group D, 2018]

A. Vagina **B.** Uterus
C. Fallopian tube **D.** Cervix

Q.47 What is the name of the muscular tube that transports sperm from the testes to the penis?

A. Fallopian tube **B.** Prostate tube
C. Urethra **D.** Vas Deferens

Q.48 Which part of the female reproductive system is known as 'Birth canal'?

A. Vagina **B.** Cervix
C. Uterus **D.** Fallopian Tube

Q.49 Name the organ analogous to the wings of birds.

A. Forelimb of human **B.** Fore-leg of horse
C. Wings of insect **D.** None of these

Q.50 What are the carriers of factor?

A. Alleles **B.** Chromosomes
C. DNA **D.** None of these

Q.51 Which plant was chosen by Mendel to work upon?

A. Gram **B.** Rose
C. Pea **D.** All of the above

Q.52 Which of these is a fossil that had wings and teeth?

A. Bird **B.** Equus
C. Archaeopteryx **D.** Reptile

Q.53 A passenger in a moving train tosses a five rupee coin. If the coin falls behind him, then the train must be moving with a uniform______.

A. acceleration **B.** deceleration
C. speed **D.** velocity

Q.54 How is temperature related to particles' motion?

A. Inversely proportional
B. Independent of each other
C. Directly proportional
D. Curvilinear relationship

Q.55 Which of the following statement is correct?

Statement (A): Newton's first law is valid from the pilot in an aircraft which is taking off.

Statement (B): Newton's first law is valid from the observer in a train moving with constant velocity.

A. (A) only
B. (B) only
C. Both (A) and (B) are correct
D. Both (A) and (B) are wrong

Q.56 Choose the correct alternative:

A. The acceleration of a moving particle is always in the direction of its velocity.
B. Velocity and acceleration vectors of a moving particle may have any angle between 0 and 360 between them.
C. Velocity and acceleration vectors of a moving particle may have any angle between 0 and 180 between them.
D. If the acceleration vector is always perpendicular to the velocity vector of a moving particle, the velocity vector does not change.

Q.57 Ranveer pulled a table cloth from a table without dislodging the dishes. This is due to ________.

A. inertia **B.** impulse
C. force **D.** momentum

Q.58 If the momentum of a body is constant, then:

A. It is in translational equilibrium
B. It is not in translational equilibrium
C. It may or may not be in translational equilibrium
D. None of these

Q.59 According to the third law of motion, action and reaction ____________.

A. always act on the same body
B. always act on different bodies in opposite directions
C. have same magnitude and directions
D. act on either body at normal to each other

Q.60 When a balloon held between the hands is pressed, its shape changes. This happens because:

A. Balanced forces acting on the balloon
B. Unbalanced forces acting on the balloon
C. Frictional forces act on the balloon
D. Gravitational force acts on the balloon

Q.61 If suddenly the gravitational force of attraction between earth and a satellite revolving around it becomes zero, then the satellite will:

A. Continue to move in its orbit with same velocity
B. Move tangentially and escape away
C. Become stationary in its orbit
D. Move towards the Earth

Q.62 A stone is thrown upward with a speed of u, find maximum height it can get with this speed. (given g is the gravitational acceleration)

A. $\frac{u^2}{2g}$ **B.** $\frac{2u^2}{g}$ **C.** $\frac{u}{g}$ **D.** $\frac{u^2}{g}$

Q.63 If g is the acceleration due to gravity on the surface of the Earth, then the gain in potential energy of an object of mass m raised from the Earth's surface to a height equal to the radius R of the earth is

A. $mg\frac{R}{4}$ **B.** $mg\frac{R}{2}$ **C.** mgR **D.** $2mgR$

Q.64 A satellite is orbiting very close to planet. Its time period depends only upon ______.

A. The density of the planet
B. Mass of the satellite
C. The radius of the planet
D. None of these

Q.65 A particle is projected vertically upwards with a speed of 16 m/s, after some time, when it again passes through the point of projection, its speed is found to be 8 m/s. It is known that the work done by air resistance is same during upward and downward motion. Then the maximum height attained by the particle is (Take $g = 10\ m/s^2$):

A. 17.6 m **B.** 12.8 m **C.** 8 m **D.** 4.8 m

Q.66 A particle of mass m is moving in a horizontal circle of radius r under a centripetal force equal to $-\frac{K}{r^2}$, where K is a constant. The total energy of the particle is:

A. $\frac{K}{2r}$ **B.** $-\frac{K}{2r}$ **C.** $-\frac{K}{r}$ **D.** $\frac{K}{r}$

Q.67 The momentum of a body is 850.00 kg m/sec and its mass is 40.00 kg. Find its kinetic energy.

A. 89031.25 J **B.** 7031.25 J
C. 9031.25 J **D.** 6031.25 J

Q.68 A 50 kg man with a 20 kg load on his head climbs up 20 steps of 0.25m height each. The work done in climbing is:

A. 5 J **B.** 350 J **C.** 100 J **D.** 3430 J

Q.69 A flying bat emits ultrasonic sound of frequency 100 KHz. If the speed of the sound in the air is 340 m/s, what is the wavelength of the sound?

A. 34000 mm **B.** 0.34 mm
C. 3.4 mm **D.** 34 mm

Q.70 Through which of the following mediums sound CANNOT travel?

A. Vacuum **B.** Milk **C.** Air **D.** Steel

Q.71 Large amplitude of sound vibrations will produce:

A. Loud sound **B.** Soft sound
C. Shrill sound **D.** Feeble sound

Q.72 What kind of sound waves does the earthquake produce before the main shocks?

A. Ultrasonics Sound Waves
B. Natural Sound Waves
C. Infra Sonics Sound Waves
D. None of the above

Q.73 'An electric current always produces a magnetic field', the above statement is:

A. Partially false **B.** False
C. Partially true **D.** True

Q.74 The lamps in household circuit are connected in Parallel because:

A. This way, they require less current
B. If one lamp fails, the other remains lit
C. This way, they require less power
D. If one lamp fails, the other also fail

Q.75 In household wiring, what is the colour of 'earth wire'?
[UPTET Science and Maths, 2022]

A. Red **B.** Green **C.** Black **D.** White

Q.76 Kirchhoff's current law is based on the conservation of:
[UPTET Science and Maths, 2022]

A. Energy **B.** Momentum
C. Charge **D.** Mass

Q.77 Which of the following is a vector quantity?

A. Magnetic field
B. Velocity, force and magnetic field
C. Force
D. Velocity

Q.78 Which of the following organs in the human body where the magnetic field produced is significant?

A. Heart, brain **B.** Heart, lung
C. Lungs, brain **D.** Liver, heart

Q.79 When a straight conductor is carrying current then________________.

A. there are circular magnetic field lines around it
B. there are magnetic field lines parallel to the conductor
C. there are no magnetic field lines
D. None of the above

Q.80 Which of the following sentences is correct about overloading?

A. Overloading can occur due to an accidental hike in the supply voltage
B. Overloading is caused by connecting too many appliances to a single socket
C. Overloading can occur when the live wire and the neutral wire wire come into direct contact
D. All of the above

Q.81 Crosses between two plants by the same variety are called:

A. Intra varietal **B.** Inter varietal
C. Inter specific **D.** None of these

Q.82 Sugarcane breeding research institute (SBRI) is situated at:

A. New Delhi **B.** Shimla
C. Coimbatore **D.** None of these

Q.83 Which district is the largest producer of wheat in Haryana?

A. Sirsa **B.** Hisar **C.** Panipat **D.** Karnal

Q.84 Which Kharif crop covers the maximum agricultural area in Haryana?

A. Rice **B.** Wheat **C.** Bajra **D.** Maize

Q.85 The process of transfer of charges from a charged object to the earth is called:

A. earthing **B.** lightning
C. oscillation motion **D.** electron movement

Q.86 Where is the lightning rod attached to protect the building from lightning?

A. On the top of the building
B. On the bottom of the building
C. In the middle of the building
D. All of these

Q.87 Which of the following is not likely to cause a tsunami?

A. A nuclear explosion undersea
B. Earthquake
C. Volcanic eruption
D. Lightning

Q.88 What Is an Aurora?

A. An interaction between Earth's magnetic field and charged particles emitted by the sun.
B. Diffraction of Earth's magnetic field and charged particles between the air and land.
C. Lights form during lightning at night while raining.
D. None of these

Q.89 In a food web, what two organism are competing for food ?

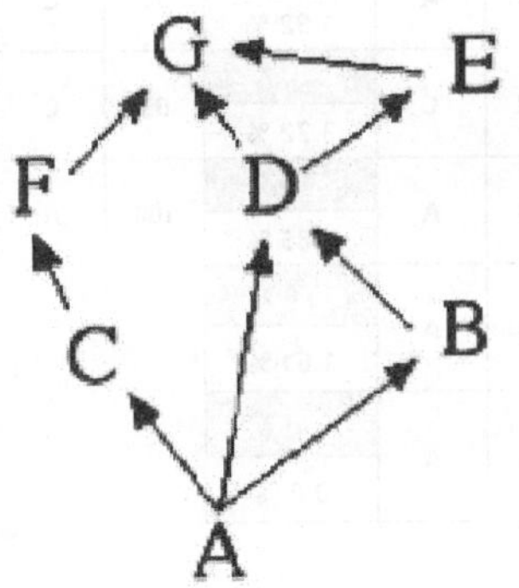

A. A and B **B.** A and C **C.** D and F **D.** B and D

Q.90 A food chain comprising birds, green plants, fish and man. The concentration of harmful chemical entering the food chain will be maximum in:

A. Green Plants **B.** Man
C. Birds **D.** Fish

Q.91 First link in any food chain is usually green plants because:

A. They are widely distributed
B. They are fixed at one place in the soil
C. They alone have the capacity to synthesize food using sunlight
D. There are more herbivores than carnivores

Q.92 Which of the following statements about food chain and energy flow through ecosystem is false?

A. Food webs include two or more food chains
B. All organisms that are not producers are consumers
C. A single organism can feed at several trophic levels
D. Detritivores feed at all trophic levels except the producer level

Q.93 Archimedes' principle is applicable to _______.

A. gases **B.** fluids
C. Both (A) and (B) **D.** None of these

Q.94 In which of the following liquids, a body will experience minimum upthrust when it is completely immersed?

A. Water **B.** Turpentine
C. Mercury **D.** Glycerine

Q.95 The relative density of a solid is 0.6. It floats in water with _________.

A. 40% of its volume inside water
B. 60% of its volume inside water
C. whole of its volume inside water
D. any fraction of its volume inside water

Q.96 What are the factors the buoyant force depends on?

A. Volume of the liquid displaced.
B. Acceleration due to gravity.
C. Density of the liquid.
D. All of the above.

Q.97 Give the compound name represented by the following formula.

Al_2O_3

A. Sodium nitrate
B. Aluminium oxide
C. Hydrogen chloride
D. Magnesium hydroxide

Q.98 After a chemical reaction, the total mass of reactants and products ________________.

A. is always increased
B. is always decreased
C. is not changed
D. is always less or more

Q.99 The law of definite proportions is not applicable to nitrogen oxide because:

A. Nitrogen atomic weight is not constant
B. Nitrogen molecular weight is variable
C. Nitrogen equivalent weight is variable
D. Oxygen atomic weight is variable

Q.100 Calculate the molecular mass of sucrose ($C_{12}H_{22}O_{11}$) molecule.

A. 342 amu **B.** 343 amu **C.** 341 amu **D.** 340 amu

// Smart Answer Sheet //

Correct — Percentage of students who answered correctly. Skipped — Percentage of students who skipped.

Q.	Ans.	Correct / Skipped	Q.	Ans.	Correct / Skipped	Q.	Ans.	Correct / Skipped	Q.	Ans.	Correct / Skipped	Q.	Ans.	Correct / Skipped	Q.	Ans.	Correct / Skipped
1	B	49.62 % / 1.38 %	18	C	79.97 % / 0.0 %	35	D	40.35 % / 1.21 %	52	C	67.93 % / 1.33 %	69	C	56.35 % / 1.33 %	86	A	56.67 % / 1.42 %
2	C	89.1 % / 0.0 %	19	D	86.34 % / 0.0 %	36	D	67.95 % / 1.01 %	53	A	46.89 % / 1.92 %	70	A	86.32 % / 0.0 %	87	D	57.85 % / 1.97 %
3	A	41.48 % / 1.03 %	20	A	77.75 % / 0.0 %	37	B	55.83 % / 1.3 %	54	C	67.87 % / 1.43 %	71	A	83.01 % / 0.0 %	88	A	55.58 % / 1.5 %
4	A	60.91 % / 1.23 %	21	C	60.13 % / 1.47 %	38	D	25.7 % / 3.62 %	55	B	59.97 % / 1.28 %	72	C	53.6 % / 1.98 %	89	D	32.85 % / 4.16 %
5	B	78.34 % / 0.0 %	22	D	81.93 % / 0.0 %	39	A	69.93 % / 1.03 %	56	C	10.68 % / 3.12 %	73	D	56.11 % / 1.25 %	90	B	53.63 % / 1.45 %
6	C	60.71 % / 1.17 %	23	A	69.91 % / 1.15 %	40	B	13.76 % / 3.43 %	57	A	57.34 % / 1.8 %	74	B	57.69 % / 1.91 %	91	C	60.34 % / 1.1 %
7	B	86.95 % / 0.0 %	24	D	25.97 % / 3.35 %	41	A	89.36 % / 0.0 %	58	A	60.76 % / 1.57 %	75	B	60.33 % / 1.94 %	92	D	30.79 % / 4.81 %
8	A	58.84 % / 1.06 %	25	D	49.0 % / 1.36 %	42	D	61.35 % / 1.71 %	59	B	77.71 % / 0.0 %	76	C	68.78 % / 1.59 %	93	C	69.43 % / 1.82 %
9	A	55.27 % / 1.24 %	26	A	62.75 % / 1.96 %	43	B	31.94 % / 4.21 %	60	A	55.6 % / 1.45 %	77	B	89.95 % / 0.0 %	94	B	52.93 % / 1.89 %
10	B	77.24 % / 0.0 %	27	A	65.02 % / 1.61 %	44	C	69.33 % / 1.34 %	61	B	53.69 % / 1.53 %	78	A	68.05 % / 1.79 %	95	B	48.66 % / 1.7 %
11	C	61.36 % / 1.21 %	28	A	83.89 % / 0.0 %	45	B	89.15 % / 0.0 %	62	A	27.96 % / 4.73 %	79	A	45.68 % / 1.63 %	96	D	52.57 % / 1.11 %
12	B	86.08 % / 0.0 %	29	C	54.76 % / 1.33 %	46	C	43.95 % / 1.69 %	63	B	22.49 % / 3.31 %	80	B	48.62 % / 1.64 %	97	B	79.54 % / 0.0 %
13	B	58.21 % / 1.3 %	30	B	58.66 % / 1.51 %	47	D	80.82 % / 0.0 %	64	A	45.55 % / 1.76 %	81	A	44.11 % / 1.92 %	98	C	65.05 % / 1.53 %
14	D	16.9 % / 4.8 %	31	A	55.4 % / 1.52 %	48	A	53.42 % / 1.69 %	65	D	40.35 % / 1.2 %	82	C	25.08 % / 3.72 %	99	C	53.08 % / 1.55 %
15	D	41.59 % / 1.6 %	32	B	41.87 % / 1.97 %	49	C	56.89 % / 1.75 %	66	B	85.06 % / 0.0 %	83	A	58.57 % / 1.85 %	100	A	47.62 % / 1.6 %
16	D	46.04 % / 1.54 %	33	B	61.86 % / 1.19 %	50	B	86.74 % / 0.0 %	67	C	45.79 % / 1.93 %	84	A	49.89 % / 1.61 %			
17	A	79.06 % / 0.0 %	34	B	86.41 % / 0.0 %	51	C	42.51 % / 1.75 %	68	D	45.06 % / 1.51 %	85	A	88.58 % / 0.0 %			

//Hints and Solutions//

1. A substance made by combining two or more elements in a fixed ratio is called a compound. In this way, the substance which is formed by the combination of two elements, that is, the compound is formed, that substance or compound is found in a stable state, but the properties of this compound are found to be different from the properties of its elements.

Example: Sulfuric acid, Common salt, etc.

Hence, the correct option is (B).

2. In the atmosphere, the highest amount of ozone gas is present in the stratosphere. Ozone layer thickness is measured in Dobson units. Ozone is an O_3 molecule. The ozone layer is present mostly in the Stratosphere and partially in the Troposphere.

Hence, the correct option is (C).

3. Concept:

- The atoms have protons and neutrons in the nucleous of the atom and electrons revolve around the nucleous in the orbits.
- For each orbits there is a certain amount of energy for the electrons.

The energy of electrons in any orbit is given by:

Energy in nth orbit $(E_n) = -13.6\frac{Z^2}{n^2}eV$

Where n is principle quantum number and Z is atomic number

For hydrogen atom:

Atomic number (Z) = 1

Given that:

Energy of electron in first orbit , E0 = -16.6

Principle quantum number of 3rd orbit, n = 3

Energy in nth orbit $(E_n) = E_0\frac{Z^2}{n^2}$

Total energy of an electron in 3 nd orbit $(E_3) = -13.6\frac{Z^2}{n^2} = -13.6\frac{1^2}{3^2} = -1.51eV$

Hence, the correct option is (A).

4. Photon: A photon is the smallest amount of electromagnetic radiation, it is called quantum.

One unit quantum is the photon.

Quanta is the plural form of quantum.

Let us see the table for electron, proton, and neutron.

Sr. No.	Electrons	Protons	Neutrons
1	Negatively charged	Positively charge d	No charge
2	Mass is negligible [1/180 0 times of proton.]	Mass is 1 a.m.u.	Mass is 1 a.m.u.
3	Get attracted to +v e charge.	Get attracted to - ve charge.	Do not get attra cted, as they are neutral.
4	Present outside the nucleus.	Presents in the n ucleus of an atom.	Present in the nu cleus of an atom.

The propagation of energy is done in the form of the photon; unit transfer of energy is called quanta.

Hence, the correct option is (A).

5. The state of matter in which there are highly energetic particles in the form of ionized gases is called plasma state.

The plasma state consists of highly energetic and highly excited particles. These particles are in the form of ionized gases. They can also be made on Earth by passing electricity through gases at very low pressures taken in a glass tube (called a discharge tube).

Hence, the correct option is (B).

6. The Intermolecular force is strongest in solids and weakest in gases.

The three states of matter varies from each other due to the following factors:

(1) The different magnitudes of the interatomic and intermolecular forces.

(2) The extent of random thermal motion of atoms and molecules of a substance (which depends upon temperature).

Hence, the correct option is (C).

7. The intermolecular distance is fixed in the case of solids. But in cases of liquids and gases, it is not fixed.

Intermolecular distance is the space between two molecule or atom. In solids it is very little, in liquids is more the solids but less than liquids and in gases its the maximum.

Hence, the correct option is (B).

8. Both are at the same temperature, the metal will feel colder than the wood because of the thermal conductivity of the metal, compared to the wood is more.

Metal will conduct the heat faster than wood. The specific heat capacity of wood is much higher than iron. So it takes time to get cooler or hotter compared to metal.

Hence, the correct option is (A).

9. In this case, ${}^{80}_{35}Br$,

$Z = 35$

$A = 80$

Number of protons $=$ number of electrons $= Z = 35$

Number of neutrons $= 80 - 35 = 45$

Hence, the correct option is (A).

10. Isotopes have same atomic numbers but different mass numbers. This also means that the isotopes have the same number of electrons.

Chemical properties are determined by electronic configuration. So, with the same electronic configuration, they have similar chemical properties.

Hence, the correct option is (B).

11. According to the Aufbau principle, electron enters into the lowest energy level (orbital), before entering into a higher energy level. Hence, according to this principle, the electronic configuration of Ca^{20} is $1\,s^2 2\,s^2 2p^6 3\,s^2 3p^6 4\,s^2$, as differentiating electron enters into the s-orbital, Ca belongs to s-block.

If we don't follow the Aufbau rule, the electronic configuration of Ca^{20} would be $1\,s^2 2\,s^2 2p^6 3\,s^2 3p^6 3\,d^2$.

So, the differentiating electron is entering in the d orbital, so it would belong to the d-block element.

Hence, the correct option is (C).

12. Thomson's model of atom states that:

- An atom consists of a positively charged sphere with electrons embedded in it.
- Total positive and negative charges in the atom are equal in magnitude. So, atom is electrically neutral.

Hence, the correct option is (B).

13. The reaction of bromine with ethane takes place as follows:

$C_2H_6 + Br_2 \rightarrow C_2H_5Br + HBr$

$C_2H_5Br + Br_2 \rightarrow C_2H_4Br_2 + HBr$

$C_2H_4Br_2 + Br_2 \rightarrow C_2H_3Br_3 + HBr$

$C_2H_3Br_3 + Br_2 \rightarrow C_2H_2Br_4 + HBr$

$C_2H_2Br_4 + Br_2 \rightarrow C_2HBr_5 + HBr$

$C_2HBr_5 + Br_2 \rightarrow C_2Br_6 + HBr$

The number of products formed are thus Six.

Hence, the correct option is (B).

14. Ethers can be prepared in the laboratory by Williamson's synthesis.

In this method, when an alkyl halide is treated with sodium alkoxide, the nucleophilic substitution of the halogen atom by the alkoxide group takes place.

The general example is given below.

Williamson Ether Synthesis

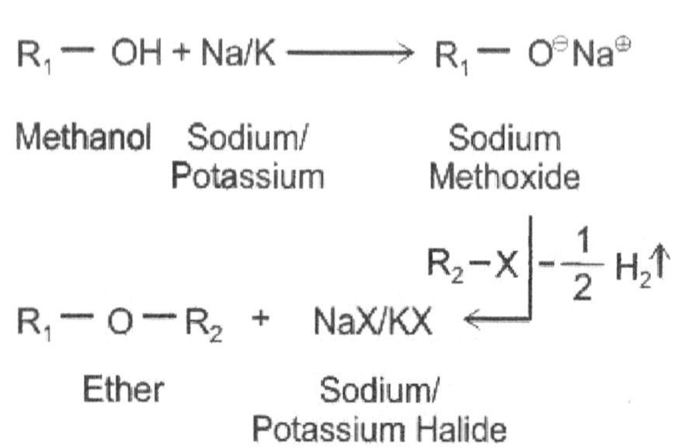

Williamson's synthesis is used to prepare symmetrical as well as unsymmetrical ethers.

As the reaction is a nucleophilic substitution reaction, the alkyl halide should be primary alkyl halide, using secondary and tertiary alkyl halide will yield alkenes due to elimination reaction and not ethers.

It is preferable to take secondary or tertiary alkoxide ion and primary alkyl halide.

Hence, the correct option is (D).

15. Ethylene on reaction with alkaline $KMnO_4$ is oxidized to Ethan-1,2-diol or Ethylene Glycol.

The pink color of Bayer's reagent is discharged in the process.

This is also proof of the presence of unsaturation in ethylene.

The reaction is as follows:

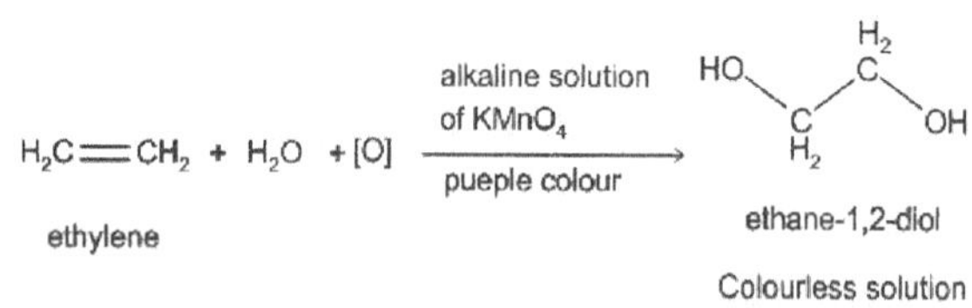

Thus, the product formed when Ethylene reacts with alkaline $KMnO_4$ is Glycol.

Hence, the correct option is (D).

16. Chlorotoluenes can be obtained by passing dry chlorine through toluene using iron or ferric chloride as catalyst.

The substitution products are ortho and para as methyl is an Electron releasing group.

The temperature of the reaction is about 310 -320K.

I_2 or $AlCl_3$ can also be used as a halogen carrier.

The function of $FeCl_3$ is to generate Cl+ which then attacks the benzene ring to form an intermediate carbocation.

The carbocation then loses a proton to form Chlorotoluene.

Formation of the intermediate carbocation is the slow rate-determining step and the halogenation of toluene is an example of electrophilic substitution reaction.

The reaction should be carried in absence of light to prevent the formation of addition products.

The net reaction is:

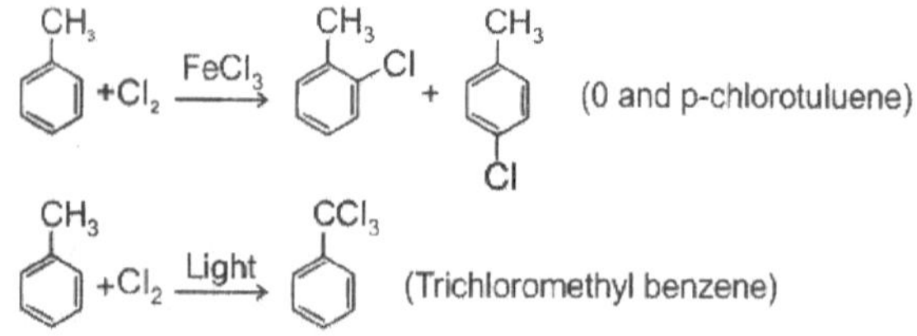

The products formed are ortho and para chloro toluenes.

Hence, the correct option is (D).

17. A Bronsted-Lowry acid is a compound that can donate a hydrogen ion while a Bronsted-Lowry base is a compound that can accept a hydrogen ion. A Lewis base is a compound that can donate a pair of electrons while a Lewis acid is a compound that can accept a pair of electrons.

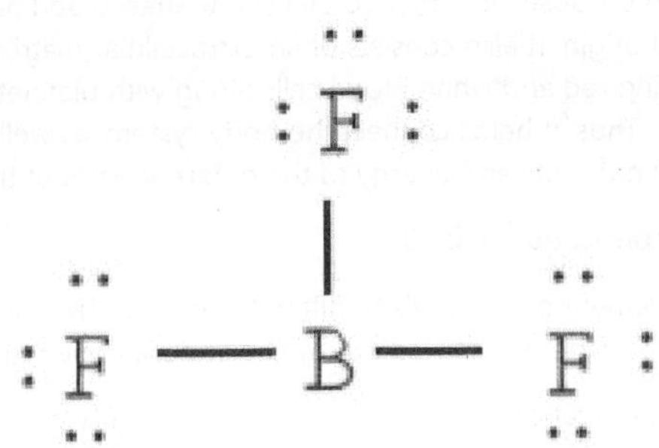

The electronic configuration of boron is $1s^2 2s^2 2p^1$. It has three electrons in its valence shell. So, it can form only three covalent bonds, which leads to only six electrons being present around the boron atom. Boron forms three covalent bonds with three Fluorine atoms. To complete the octet Boron accepts two lone electrons from Fluorine atoms. Hence, according to lewis acid-base theory, as Boron accepts lone pair of electrons, so it acts as a lewis acid.

Hence, the correct option is (A).

18. When a Lewis acid reacts with a Lewis base, then a Lewis acid-base reaction occurs in which the molecule which act as Lewis base donate its electron pair into the empty orbital of an acid, forms Lewis acid-base adduct. The adduct formed contains a covalent coordinate bond between Lewis acid and Lewis base.

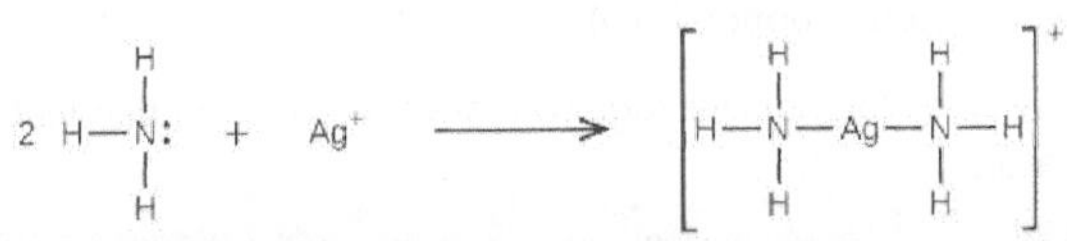

In this reaction, the two ammonia molecules reacts with silver ion. The ammonia has lone pair of electrons, so it has the ability to donate the lone pairs of electrons and acts as Lewis base. The positive charge on silver denotes its electrophilic nature that means it has an ability to accept the pairs of electrons and act as Lewis acid. When a Lewis acid reacts with a Lewis base, there is no change in the oxidation number of any of these atoms.

Hence, the correct option is (C).

19. Amphoteric or amphiprotic substance or ampholytes are the substances which act as an acid as well as a base and example for this is water. It acts as an acid with Ammonia and base with acetic acid. Protophilic solvents are the solvents which have greater tendency to accept protons, i.e. water, alcohol, liquid ammonia, etc, so they act only as an acid. A strong protophilic solvent changes the weak acids to strong acids. So protophilic solvents cannot act as both acid as well as a base. Examples of protophilic solvents are ammonia and pyridine.

Hence, the correct option is (D).

20. pH value less than 7 indicates that the solution is acidic. In an acidic solution, the concentration of hydrogen ions is greater than the concentration of hydroxide ions. If the pH is about 7 then the solution is neutral and if the pH is greater than 7 then the solution is called basic.

Hence, the correct option is (A).

21. Iron is a metal that will not directly react with cold water or hot water but forms a metal oxide when steam is passed over it. When red hot iron reacts with steam it forms iron(II, III) oxide and hydrogen, and the reaction is reversible.

$$3Fe(s) + 4H_2O(g) \rightarrow Fe_3O_4(s) + 4H_2(g)$$

Hence, the correct option is (C).

22. A metal in which even Iron can float is mercury. It is commonly known as quicksilver and was formerly named hydrargyrum. Mercury is the only metallic element that is liquid at room temperature. Iron floats on mercury but sink in water due to the density of mercury is greater than iron but less than water.

Hence, the correct option is (D).

23. The essential component of amalgam is mercury (Hg).

It may be a liquid, or a solid, depending upon the proportion of mercury.

Silver-mercury amalgams are an important dental filling material used to fill teeth cavities.

In the extraction of gold from its ore the Gold-mercury amalgam is used widely.

Hence, the correct option is (A).

24. ${}_{29}Cu = 1s^2, 2s^2, 2p^6, 3s^2 3p^6 3d^{10} 4s^1$

or $[Ar]4\,s^1 3\,d^{10}$

Hence, the correct option is (D).

25.

Element	Percentage	Nuclear filled	Number of atoms	Simplest ratio
C	$38 \cdot 71$	12	$\frac{38 \cdot 71}{12} = 3 \cdot 22$	$\frac{3 \cdot 22}{3 \cdot 22} = 1$
H	$9 \cdot 67$	1	$\frac{9 \cdot 67}{1} = 9.67$	$\frac{9 \cdot 67}{3 \cdot 22} = 3$
O	$51 \cdot 62$	16	$\frac{51 \cdot 62}{16} = 3 \cdot 22$	$\frac{3 \cdot 22}{3 \cdot 22} = 1$

$\therefore$ The proportional formula of the compound $= CH_3O$

Hence, the correct option is (D).

26. Hydrocarbon Ethine (HC = CH) used in welding.

If ethyne is burnt with oxygen, it gives a clean flame with temperature 3000°C because of complete combustion. This oxy-acetylene flame is used for welding. It is not possible to attain such a high temperature without mixing oxygen. This is the reason why a mixture of ethyne and air is not used.

Hence, the correct option is (A).

27. Tetrafluoroethylene $(F_2C = CF_2)$ is the monomer of Teflon.

$nF_2C = CF_2 \xrightarrow[High\ pressure]{(NH_4)_2S_2O_8} -(- F_2C = CF_2 -)-_n$
Tetrafluoroethylene   Teflon

Hence, the correct option is (A).

28. $\overset{1}{HC} \equiv \overset{2}{C} - \overset{H_5}{\underset{H}{\overset{3|}{C}}} - CH_3$

3-Methyl-1-Pentyne

Hence, the correct option is (A).

29. Taste buds are the receptor organs of taste. Taste pore: The opening of the taste canal at the surface of the epithelium. Neuroepithelial and supporting cells: The two types of cells are packed within the concavity of the taste bud. The neuroepithelial cells are slender, dense, and spindle-shaped.
Hence, the correct option is (C).

30. Simple columnar epithelium are found in the stomach, small intestine, large intestine, rectum, fallopian tubes, endometrium, respiratory bronchioles and lining of uterus. In essence, they are found in parts of the respiratory, digestive and reproductive tracts where mechanical abrasion is low, but secretion and absorption are important.
Hence, the correct option is (B).

31. Erythropoietin, a glycoprotein hormone, is synthesized predominantly in the kidney and secreted by renal cortical interstitial cells in response to tissue hypoxia. Erythropoietin is the main regulator of the production of red blood cells.Erythropoietin also stimulates the synthesis of hemoglobin.
Hence, the correct option is (A).

32. Intercalated cells are epithelial cells traditionally associated with the regulation of acid-base homeostasis in distal segments of the kidney tubule. These cells also participate in potassium and ammonia transport and have a role in the innate immune system.
Hence, the correct option is (B).

33. A contractile vacuole (CV) is an organelle or subcellular structure, that is involved in osmoregulation and waste removal. CVs should not be confused with vacuoles which store food or water. Contractile vacuoles absorb excess water and wastes from a microorganism's cell and excrete them into the environment by contracting.

Contractile vacuoles protect a cell from absorbing too much water and potentially exploding by excreting excess water. Wastes, such as ammonia, are soluble in water; they are excreted from the cell along with excess water by the contractile vacuoles. Contractile vacuoles function in a periodic cycle by expanding while collecting water and contracting to release the water.

Hence, the correct option is (B).

34. In prokaryotic organisms, the nuclear region is not surrounded by a membrane. This undefined nuclear region is known as Nucleoid.

Prokaryotic cells are primitive organisms. Nucleoid in a prokaryote contains all or most of the genetic material. In prokaryotic cells, the nucleus is not defined properly because it is not surrounded by a nuclear membrane.

Hence, the correct option is (B).

35. Blood is a type of connective tissue.

It is called so because like other connective tissues, blood has a mesodermal origin. It also consists of an extracellular matrix called Plasma, having red and white blood cells along with platelets floating in it. Thus, it helps connect the body system, as well as transporting nutrients and energy to the different parts of the body.

Hence, the correct option is (D).

36. The movement of materials to different parts of the cytoplasm and nucleus is generally carried out by the Endoplasmic reticulum.

Endoplasmic reticulum:

It is a network or reticulum of tiny tubular structures scattered in the cytoplasm. The important function of the ER is to serve as channels for the transport of materials (especially proteins) between various regions of the cytoplasm or between the cytoplasm and the nucleus. The ER also functions as a cytoplasmic framework providing a surface for some of the biochemical activities of the cell.

The cell has three main parts:

1. The cell membrane
2. Cytoplasm, which contains smaller components called organelles
3. Nucleus

The nucleus is separated from the cytoplasm by a membrane called the nuclear membrane.

Hence, the correct option is (D).

37. One advantage of cleistogamy is seed set is not dependent on pollinators.

Cleistogamy means self-pollination. It is seen in plants like peanuts, beans, and beans. The advantage of cleistogamy is no pollinator is required as it can propagate by using non-opening, self-pollinating flowers.

Hence, the correct option is (B).

38. Sucrose is converted into glucose and fructose by the enzyme Invertase.

Glucose and fructose are phosphorylated to give rise to glucose-6-phosphate by the activity of the enzyme hexokinase.

This phosphorylated form of glucose then isomerizes to produce fructose-6-phosphate. Subsequent steps of the metabolism of glucose and fructose are the same.

In glycolysis, a chain of ten reactions, under the control of different enzymes, takes place to produce pyruvate from glucose.

Hence, the correct option is (D).

39. A method in which roots are induced on the stem while it is still attached to the parent plant is called layering.

There are various methods used for the propagation of new plants by using the parts of the same existing plant. Layering is one of the methods of plant propagation. One of the branches of the stem of the parent plant is layered under the soil. The tip of this branch is above the ground and is attached to a rod or stick for support. The aerial branch which is layered is induced by hormones and starts producing roots and grows on its own. Later on, this new plant is separated from the mother plant. The branch which is grown underground by this method is called layer.

Hence, the correct option is (A).

40. Plants like Elm (Ulmus), Dandelion (Taraxacum) and members of Rose Family vegetatively reproduce by Sucker.

Suckers are growths that appear from the root systems of many trees and shrubs. They may appear in borders, lawns, between paving stones or through paths, and can become a nuisance. Poplars, cherries, plums, stags-horn sumac, lilacs and false acacias all sucker freely.

Hence, the correct option is (B).

41. Synapse is the junction between two neurons, a neuron and a muscle cell or a neuron and a glandular cell. Synapses help to regulate the speed and direction of nerve impulses.

Hence, the correct option is (A).

42. Cytokinin is the plant hormone which has a major role in growth and development of the plants. It helps in embryogenesis, cell division, chloroplast differentiation and many other important roles in plants. Therefore, it is clear from above the options that cytokinin is the plant hormone.

Hence, the correct option is (D).

43. The clogging of the nose with phlegm is a common problem associated with common cold. It results in the blockage of the perception of smell. The olfactory nerves will fail to send the olfactory signals and thus won't be able to differentiate between the smell of agarbatti and perfume.

So, 'Differentiate the smell of a perfume from that of an agarbatti'.

Hence, the correct option is (B).

44. The brain is lodged inside the cavity of the skull known as cranium. The cranial cavity, also known as intracranial space, is the space within the skull that accommodates the brain. The skull minus the mandible is called the cranium.

Hence, the correct option is (C).

45. The male reproductive organs include a pair of testes (singular, testis), two sperm ducts, and a penis.

The testes produce the male gametes called sperms. Millions of sperms are produced by the testes.

Though sperms are very small in size, each has a head, a middle piece, and a tail.

The male reproductive system does not include the cervix. Cervix is a part of the female reproductive tract.

The female reproductive organs are a pair of ovaries, oviducts (fallopian tubes), Cervix, Vagina, and uterus.

Ovaries produce female gametes called ova (eggs).

In human beings, a single matured egg is released into the oviduct by one of the ovaries every month.

The uterus is the part where the development of the baby takes place. Like the sperm, an egg is also a single cell.

Hence, the correct option is (B).

46. Fertilization occurs in the fallopian tube. It is a process of meeting the egg with the sperm. After this, a cell is formed which is known as zygote cell which is a fertilized egg. The fallopian tubes are the part of the female body where eggs are fertilized. It acts as a bridge through which the male spermatozoa pass.

Hence, the correct option is (C).

47. Vas Deferens is the name of the muscular tube that transports sperm from the testes to the penis.

There are two of these ducts, which are tubes surrounded by smooth muscle. They connect the left and right epididymis to the ejaculatory ducts in order to move sperm.

Hence, the correct option is (D).

48. Vagina:

- Vagina also is known as the 'Birth canal', is a canal that joins the lower part of the uterus called the cervix to the outside.

Cervix:

- The uterus opens into the vagina through a narrow called cervix.

Uterus:

- The uterus is single and it is also called the womb.
- The shape of the uterus is like an inverted pear.
- It is supported by ligaments attached to the pelvic wall.

Fallopian Tube:

- The Fallopian Tube is about 10-12 cm long and extends from the periphery of each ovary to the uterus.

Hence, the correct option is (A).

49. Wings of bird and wings of insect both are analogous as both of them perform the same function of flight while structures and origin are different. Feathers of birds originate from their forelimbs, the wings of insects originate from the inner or outer surface of the insect's body.

Hence, the correct option is (C).

50. The carriers of factor are chromosomes and transfer hereditary information from one generation to another. Genetic information is passed from generation to generation through inherited units of chemical information (in most cases, genes). Organisms produce other similar organisms through sexual reproduction, which allows the line of genetic material to be maintained and generations to be linked.

Hence, the correct option is (B).

51. Mendel selected pisum sativum (a pea plant) of his ground to observe the characteristics of progeny produced. The flowers of this pea plant are bisexual. They are self-pollinating, and thus, self and cross pollination can easily be performed. The different physical characteristics were easy to recognise and study. They have a shorter life span and are the plants are easier to maintain.

Hence, the correct option is (C).

52. Archaeopteryx had a full set of teeth and three claws on the wing which had been used to grasp prey. Archaeopteryx had toothed jaws, claws on its wings, and a long, bony tail. Other feathered dinosaurs have been found, but in Archaeopteryx the front limbs were in the form of proper wings and its feathers were the same shape as those of flying birds.

Hence, the correct option is (C).

53. A passenger in a moving train tosses a five rupee coin. If the coin falls behind him, then the train must be moving with a uniform acceleration.

Because the coin falls behind the passenger, so the train must be moving with a uniform acceleration.

As the passenger tosses the coin, it goes up and is in motion with the speed (initial) of the train but the train is accelerated, so its speed increases. But the coin is in the (initial) speed in the air, so the train slightly moves forward with the person and the coin falls behind him.

Hence, the correct option is (A).

54. Temperature is directly proportional to the speed of the particles.

The temperature of matter tells us the average kinetic energy possessed by the particles. When we apply heat to matter, it gets absorbed and results in the particles having increased kinetic energy.

This means that the particles were already in motion before, this kinetic energy results in greater motion.

Hence, the correct option is (C).

55. Newton's first law is valid for the observer in a train moving with constant velocity.

We know that,

Newton's first law is invalid in Non inertial frame of reference, since acceleration is present in the First case.

Hence, the correct option is (B).

56. Velocity and acceleration vectors of a moving particle may have any angle between 0 and 180 between them.

In circular motion, the acceleration vector is perpendicular to velocity and velocity is also changing.

So acceleration and velocity can have any angle between them.

Hence, the correct option is (C).

57. Newton's first law of motion is also called the law of inertia. Inertia is the ability of a body by virtue of which it opposes a change.

According to Newton's first law of motion, an object will remain at rest or in uniform motion in a straight line unless acted upon by an external force.

When a body is at rest, it will remain at rest until we apply an external force to move it. This property is called inertia of rest.

When a body is in a uniform motion, it will remain in motion until we apply an external force to stop it. This property is called inertia of motion.

When Ranveer pulled a table cloth from a table, at that time the dishes were at rest. Due to the inertia of rest, the dishes remain at rest because the cloth is removed soon.

Hence, the correct option is (A).

58. As we know that the momentum of a body is given as,

$P = m \times v$...(1)

Where m = mass, and v = velocity of the body

By equation (1) it is clear that if the momentum of a body is constant, then its velocity will also be constant and the acceleration will be zero.

An object is in translational equilibrium if the velocity of its translational motion is constant. To be in translational equilibrium, the net force acting on the object must be zero.

Therefore we can say that if the momentum of a body is constant, then it will be in translational equilibrium.

Hence, the correct option is (A).

59. According to the third law of motion, action and reaction always act on different bodies in opposite directions. According to Newton's third law of motion, for every action there is an equal and opposite reaction. The action and reaction forces always acts on different bodies.

Hence, the correct option is (B).

60. When we press the balloon with both hands, we are applying a balanced force because we are applying equal force with both hands. The shape of the balloon changes and that is due to the balancing forces acting on the balloon.

Hence, the correct option is (A).

61. A satellite is an object that has been placed into the orbit. This is also known as an artificial satellite.

- There is a natural satellite also. eg. Moon

Satellites orbits around the planet because they have enough speed that is fast enough to defeat the downward pull of gravity.

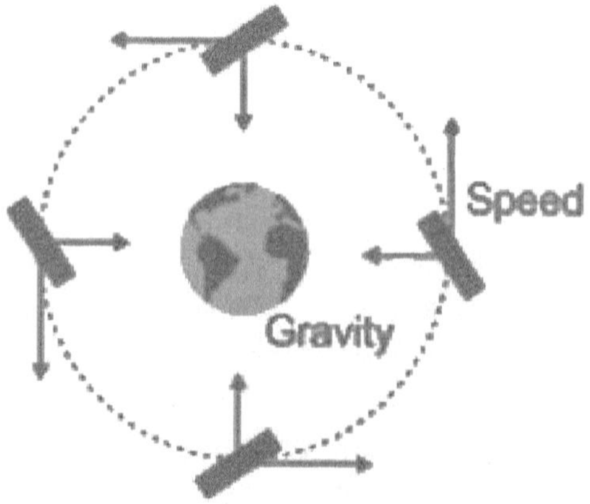

In the case of a moving satellite, the gravitational pull provides the necessary centripetal force to the satellite to move the satellite on the circular orbit.

If the gravitational pull disappears/becomes zero suddenly then there will be no centripetal force acting on the satellite. So the satellite will not move in the circular orbit.

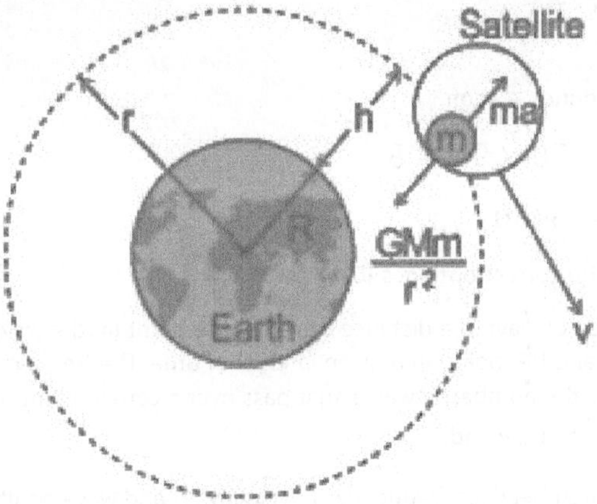

The satellite will move with the same speed and path is tangential to the circular orbit at that point where the gravitational pull disappears.

Hence, the correct option is (B).

62. When a body moves in a straight line under constant acceleration, it follows three equations of motion.

All unknowns are found by these equations.

$\Rightarrow v = u + at$

$\Rightarrow s = ut + \left(\frac{1}{2}\right)at^2$

$\Rightarrow v^2 = u^2 + 2as$

Where u = initial velocity, v = final velocity, a = constant acceleration, t = time and s = displacement.

Given that the person throws balls into the air vertically upward with speed 'u'.

The height to which the ball will rise at this initial speed (at the highest point v will be zero)

Using the 3rd equation of motion:

$v = 0; u = u; a = -g; s = h$ (downward direction)

$\Rightarrow v^2 = u^2 + 2as$

$\Rightarrow 0^2 = u^2 - 2gh$

$\Rightarrow u^2 = 2gh$

$\Rightarrow h = \frac{u^2}{2g}$

Hence, the correct option is (A).

63. As we know,

$U_i = \frac{GMm}{R}$ = Initial potential energy of the system

$U_f = \frac{GMm}{2R}$ = Final potential energy of the system

Change in potential energy, $\Delta U = U_f - U_i$

$= -GMm\left[\frac{1}{2R} - \frac{1}{R}\right] = \frac{GMm}{2R}$ ....(i)

But $g = \frac{GM}{R^2}$

$\therefore GM = gR^2$ ....(ii)

From (i) and (ii), we get

$\Delta U = \frac{gR^2m}{2R} = \frac{mgR}{2}$

Hence, the correct option is (B).

64. A time period of a satellite is the time taken by the satellite to go once around the earth.

$$T = 2\pi\sqrt{\frac{r^3}{MG}}$$

where r is the distance between the centre of the planet to the satellite revolving around the earth, M is the mass of the earth and G is the gravitational constant.

As the density of a sphere is given by,

$$\sigma = \frac{M}{V}$$

$$\sigma = \frac{M}{\left(\frac{4}{3}\pi r^3\right)}$$

Density in terms of mass,

$$\sigma = \frac{M}{\left(\frac{4}{3}\pi r^3\right)}$$

$$M = \sigma \cdot \left(\frac{4}{3}\pi r^3\right)$$

Replacing this value of mass in the formula of the time period of the satellite, we get

$$T = 2\pi \cdot \sqrt{\frac{r^3}{GM}}$$

$$T = 2\pi \cdot \sqrt{\frac{r^3}{G\left[\sigma \cdot \frac{4}{3}(\pi r^3)\right]}}$$

$$T = 2\pi \cdot \sqrt{\frac{3}{G \cdot \sigma \cdot (4\pi)}}$$

$$T = \sqrt{\frac{3 \cdot \pi}{G \cdot \sigma}}$$

So, a satellite is orbiting very close to planet. Its time period depends only upon the density of the planet.

Hence, the correct option is (A).

65. From work energy theorem:

For upward motion,

$\frac{1}{2}\ m(16)^2 = mgh + W$...(i)

For downward motion,

$\frac{1}{2}\ m(8)^2 = mgh - W$...(ii)

From equation (i) and (ii), we get

$\frac{1}{2}\ m[16^2 - 8^2] = 2\ mgh$

$\Rightarrow \frac{1}{2}[256 - 64] = 2 \times 10 \times h$

$\Rightarrow h = 4.8\ m$

Hence, the correct option is (D).

66. Centripetal force $= \frac{mv^2}{r} = \frac{k}{r^2}$... (given)

Kinetic Energy $= \frac{1}{2}mv^2 = \frac{1}{2}\frac{k}{r}$

Potential Energy $= -\int_{\infty}^{r} F\ dr$

The lower limit has been taken as ∞ because potential energyis zero at infinity

$= -\int_{\infty}^{r} \frac{k}{r^2} dr$

$= -k\int_{\infty}^{r} r^{-2}\ dr$

$= -k\left|\frac{r^{-1}}{-1}\right|_{\infty}^{r}$

$= \frac{-k}{r}$

Total energy $= \frac{k}{2r} - \frac{k}{r} = -\frac{k}{2r}$

Hence, the correct option is (B).

67. Given,

The momentum of a body $= 850.00$ kg m/sec

$m = 40.00$ kg

The momentum of a body $= mv$

$mv = 850.00$

$\Rightarrow 40.00 \times v = 850.00$

$\Rightarrow v = 21.25$ m/sec

Kinetic Energy $= \frac{1}{2}mv^2$

$= \frac{1}{2} \times 40 \times (21.25)^2$

$= 9031.25$ J

Hence, the correct option is (C).

68. Given,

Mass of load $= 20$ kg

Mass of the man $= 50$ kg

Total mass $= (50 + 20)$

$= 70$ kg

Total height $= 20 \times 0.25$

$= 5$ m

∴ Work done $=$ mgh

$\Rightarrow$ W $= 70 \times 9.8 \times 5$

$\Rightarrow$ W $= 3430$ J

Hence, the correct option is (D).

69. Speed of wave is a distance traveled by a point (in the wave say crest or another point) in a given interval of time. The frequency of a wave is the number of waves that pass over a certain point of the medium in 1 second.

The relation between frequency f, velocity v and wavelength λ of a wave is given by:

$v = f \times \lambda$

$\lambda = \frac{v}{f}$

Given that $v = 340$ m/s, Frequency $= 100$ KHz $= 100000$ Hz

Wavelength $(\lambda) =$ Velocity $(v)/$ Frequency $(f) = \frac{340}{100000}$

$\lambda = 0.0034$ meters $= 3.4$ mm

Hence, the correct option is (C).

70. Sound is a longitudinal wave that consists of compressions and rarefactions travelling through a medium.

Sound cannot travel through Vacuum.

As sound waves are longitudinal waves, the air particles vibrate to and fro in the direction of the propagation of sound.

The study of sound is called Acoustics.

Speed of sound in air $= 343$ m/s.

Unit of the frequency of sound: Hertz(Hz).

Unit of Intensity of sound: Decibels(dB).

The sound frequency at which a human can hear ranges between 20 Hz to 20 kHz.

Hence, the correct option is (A).

71. The large amplitude of sound vibrations will produce a loud sound.

The intensity of sound is identified by loudness. The loudness of sound is proportional to the square of the amplitude of the vibration producing the sound. If the amplitude of vibration is large, the sound produced is loud.

Hence, the correct option is (A).

72. Earthquakes generate these infrasonic sound waves before the main shock wave begins. Infrasonic sound waves are defined as frequencies of sound below 20 Hz, it is known as infra sound. (The deeper the frequency of the sound, the louder the sound) which we can hear.

Hence, the correct option is (C).

73. An electric current will produce a magnetic field, which can be visualized as a series of circular field lines around a wire segment. So, given statement is true.

An electric current produces a magnetic field. This is possible when an electric charge is in motion. When the electric charge is at rest, there is no production of the magnetic field. When the atom spins and orbits the nucleus there is a production of the magnetic field. Also, the direction of the magnetic field is determined by the direction of spin and orbiting of the electric charge.

Hence, the correct option is (D).

74. The lamps in household circuit are connected in Parallel because if one lamp fails, the other remains lit.

- If lamps are connected in parallel, we can have different switches for different lamps.
- Also, if one lamp fails, the current will still flow in another lamp.
- This is not possible in series, as all lamps will be connected by single path in that case.

Hence, the correct option is (B).

75. Green wire stands for grounding/ earthing in the electric circuit.

Earthing is used to protect circuits or devices from an electric shock. It does this by providing a path (a protective conductor) for a fault current to flow to earth.

Green wires are chiefly used for socket purposes. Example AC, geyser, TV, microwave, etc.

Normally, switches have only 2 wires i.e. neutral and phase.

Hence, the correct option is (B).

76. Kirchhoff's law of electricity is based on the conservation of charge and is also called current law. According to this rule, in an electric circuit, the algebraic sum of all the currents meeting at the junction is zero, that is,

$$\Sigma i = 0$$

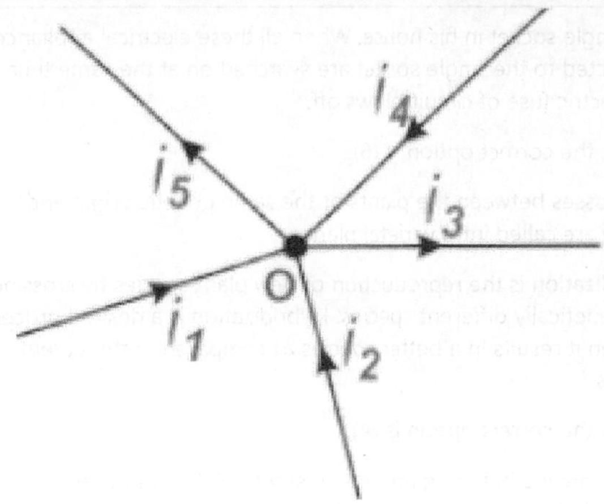

The sign convention of this rule is that the currents coming towards the junction are taken positive and the currents going away from the junction are taken negative.

So according to the diagram,

$$i_1 + i_2 - i_3 + i_4 - i_5 = 0$$

$$i_1 + i_2 + i_4 = i_3 + i_5$$

Hence, the correct option is (C).

77. Velocity, force, and the magnetic field are vector quantities.

Vector is the quantity which has both magnitude and direction. Velocity is a vector quantity because it is the speed of an object in a particular direction. Force is a vector quantity because it actually does depend on which direction you apply the force. Magnetic field is a vector quantity as it is specified by both magnitude and direction.

Hence, the correct option is (B).

78. The heart and brain are the two main organs in the human body where this magnetic field is quite significant.

The human body is an electromagnetic organism. In human body, small electric currents travels along the nerve cells due to ions, same way as electricity flows through an electric wire. This current produces a very weak magnetic field in the human body.

Hence, the correct option is (A).

79. When a straight conductor is carrying current then there are circular magnetic field lines around it. The Magnetic field lines around a straight conductor carrying current are concentric circles whose centres lie on the wire. The direction of magnetic field lines can be determined using Right-Hand Thumb Rule.

Hence, the correct option is (A).

80. Overloading is caused by connecting too many appliances to a single socket.

Overloading takes place when the live wire comes into direct contact with the neutral wire (This occurs when the insulation of wires is damaged or there is a fault in the appliance). In such a situation, the current in the circuit abruptly increases. This is called Short-circuiting.

Overloading can be avoided by connecting many appliances at a time in the circuit. A person connects too many electrical applianes to a single socket in his house. When all these electrical appliances connected to the single socket are switched on at the same time, the electric fuse of circuit blows off.

Hence, the correct option is (B).

81. Crosses between the plants of the same genetic origin and variety are called intra varietal plants.

Hybridization is the reproduction of new plant species by crossing two genetically different species. Hybridization is a desired process as often it results in a better species as compared to the parent species.

Hence, the correct option is (A).

82. Sugarcane breeding research institute (SBRI) is situated at Coimbatore.

Sugarcane breeding institute came into being in the year 1912, in Coimbatore, under the British colonial rule. Dr. C .A. Barber was the founder of this institute. Today it comes under the Indian Council of Agricultural research. The institute has built three new research centers one in Haryana and two in Kerala.

The sugarcane breeding program strives to produce better and more viable varieties of the plant. Most of the sugarcane plant varieties found in India is due to the initiative taken by this very institute. The institute follows the methods of conventional breeding as well as interventions of modern technology such as genetic analyzer and soil moisture indicator etc., to create hybrids.

Hence, the correct option is (C).

83. Sirsa district is the largest producer of wheat in Haryana.

The study also revealed that the highest growth in the production of food grains has been recorded by Sirsa (5.25) while Kurukshetra, Karnal, Panipat and Nuh districts recorded negative growth rate. Agriculture plays an essential role in the economic development of a country.

Hence, the correct option is (A).

84. Kharif crop Rice covers the maximum agricultural area in Haryana.

The major Kharif crops are rice, jowar, maize, cotton, jute, sugarcane, sesame and groundnut. These crops are sown at the commencement of rains in June and harvested by the beginning of November. Rice covers the maximum area under the Kharif crops in Haryana followed by bajra.

Hence, the correct option is (A).

85. The process of transfer of charges from a charged object to the earth is called earthing.

- An electric discharge is the transmission and release of electricity through a medium such as gas in the applied electric field.
- Lightning is caused because of the build-up of electrostatic charges in the clouds.

Hence, the correct option is (A).

86. A system of lightning protection conductors and lightning rods is installed on the roof of the building to intercept any lightning before it strikes the building.

A lightning rod is a pointed metal rod attached to the roof/top of a building because lightning tends to strike the highest object in the vicinity, rods are typically placed at the apex of a structure and along its ridges; they are connected to the ground by low-impedance cables. The rod might be an inch (2 cm) in diameter. It connects to a huge piece of copper or aluminum wire that's also an inch or so in diameter.

Hence, the correct option is (A).

87. A tsunami is caused due to disturbance caused by deep down the sea. Lightening will not cause any disturbance to the sea whereas earthquakes, A major nuclear explosion undersea, and Volcanic eruption can cause a disturbance in the sea.

Hence, the correct option is (D).

88. An aurora is the interaction between Earth's magnetic field and the charged particles emitted by the Sun. It is generally wide in latitudes from 3° to 6° and between 10° and 20° at the poles. When the rays of the Sun's electric charge collide with the Earth's magnetic field, energy is generated, which is visible to us in the form of a wavy shape in different colors in the sky, this is known as Aurora or Polar Light.

Hence, the correct option is (A).

89.

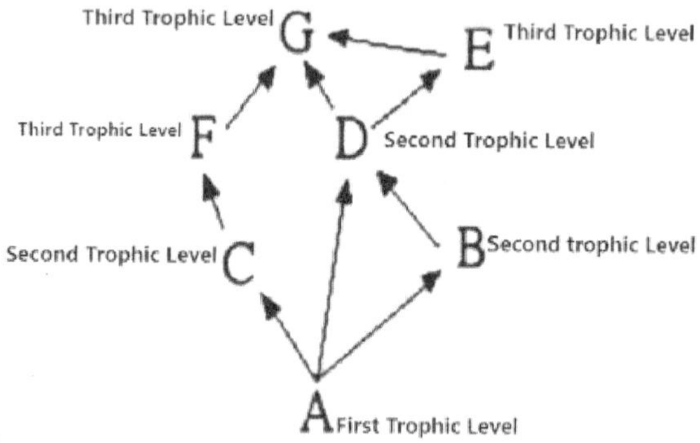

B and D are present at the same trophic level. They consume the same organisms and thus compete for food.

Hence, the correct option is (D).

90. A food chain comprising birds, green plants, fish and man. The concentration of harmful chemical entering the food chain will be maximum in man.

As these chemicals are not degradable, these get accumulated progressively at each trophic level. As human beings occupy the top level in any food chain, the maximum concentration of these chemicals get accumulated in human's bodies. This phenomenon is known as biological magnification.

So in the given food chain, the concentration of harmful chemical order is given in increasing order below:

Green plants → Fish → Man.

Hence, the correct option is (B).

91. First link in any food chain is usually green plants because they alone have the capacity to synthesize food using sunlight.

In all the ecosystems, the sun is the ultimate source of energy. Green plants trap solar energy and convert it into a usable form, which can be used by other organisms at successive trophic levels. Nearly all autotrophs use photosynthesis to make food (glucose) from sunlight, CO_2, and water.

Hence, the correct option is (C).

92. There are many food chains which are interconnected to form the food web and so one organism can feed at different trophic levels in the different food chain. There is a gradual decrease in the energy of the increasing trophic levels due to the loss of energy with each transfer.This is explained by the 10% energy law given by Lindman.

The producers are the organisms which can synthesize food and the organisms which feed on the other sources are known as consumers. The detritivores are the organisms which feed on the dead matter of the organisms which belong to all the trophic levels.

Hence, the correct option is (D).

93. Archimedes' principle is applicable to both gases and fluids.

Archimedes' principle is applicable to all fluids. Fluids are those substances that can flow, so gases are also fluids. Thus, Archimedes' principle can be applied to gases as well.

Hence, the correct option is (C).

94. Lesser the density of the liquid, lesser the upthrust experienced by a body. Amongst these, turpentine has the least density.

Density is main factor for the liquid upthrust action.
So, turpentine will face minimum upthrust.

Hence, the correct option is (B).

95. Relative density (RD) of a substance is defined as the ratio of the density of the substance to the density of water at $4°C$.

$$RD = \frac{\text{density of a substance}}{\text{density of water at } 4°C}$$

The relative density of solid is 0.6, which means that the solid is 60% more dense for an equal volume of water.

So, 60% of the volume of the solid is inside the water.

Hence, the correct option is (B).

96. The buoyant force is the upward force exerted on an object wholly or partly immersed in a fluid. This upward force is also called Upthrust. Due to the buoyant force, a body submerged partially or fully in a fluid appears to lose its weight, i.e. appears to be lighter. Buoyant force on a body depends on the following factors:

- Volume of the liquid displaced.
- Volume of the body submerged in liquid.
- Density of the liquid.
- Acceleration due to gravity.

Hence, the correct option is (D).

97. The compound name of Al_2O_3 is Aluminium oxide.

Sodium nitrate : $NaNO_3$

Hydrogen chloride : HCl

Magnesium hydroxide : $Mg(OH)_2$

Hence, the correct option is (B).

98. After a chemical reaction, the total mass of reactants and products is not changed as law of conservation of mass states Mass is never lost or gained in chemical reactions. It can be say that mass is always conserved.

Hence, the correct option is (C).

99. The law of definite proportions is not applicable to nitrogen oxide because nitrogen equivalent weight is variable. Nitrogen forms multiple compounds with oxygen. The law of definite proportions states that a given chemical compound always contains the same elements in the exact same proportions by mass.

Hence, the correct option is (C).

100. As we know,

The individual mass of carbon = 12 amu

The individual mass of hydrogen = 1 amu

The individual mass of oxygen = 16 amu

But sucrose has 12 carbon atoms, 22 hydrogen atom and 11 oxygen atom.

So for sucrose, molecular mass = 12 × 12 + 22 × 1 + 11 × 16

= 144 + 22 + 176

= 342 amu

Hence, the correct option is (A).

Mock Test 02

Q.1 The statement "Any given compound has a fixed proportion by mass of its constituents" is related to the:

A. First law of Dalton's atomic theory
B. Second law of Dalton's atomic theory
C. Avogadro's law
D. None of these

Q.2 The smell of perfume spreads out by a process known as:

A. Evaporation **B.** Diffusion
C. Condensation **D.** Fusion

Q.3 According to the Dalton's atomic theory the smallest constituents of an element are:

A. Molecules
B. Atoms
C. Electron, proton and neutron
D. None of these

Q.4 The melting point of ice is:

A. -273 C **B.** 273 K **C.** 273 C **D.** -273 K

Q.5 Which of these states of matter has the maximum density?

A. Liquids **B.** Solids
C. Gases **D.** None of these

Q.6 On heating, solid is directly converted into a gaseous state. This process is called ______.

A. Sublimation **B.** Evaporation
C. Diffusion **D.** Condensation

Q.7 When a teaspoon of solid sugar is dissolved in a glass of liquid water, what is the state of the mixture?

A. Solid state only
B. Solid and liquid state
C. Liquid state only
D. None of these

Q.8 When 1 liter of water is cooled from $4^{\circ} C$ to $0^{\circ} C$, its volume ________.

A. First decreases and then increases
B. Remains the same
C. Increases
D. Decreases

Q.9 The number of electrons, protons and neutrons in a species are equal to 18, 16 and 16 respectively. Assign the proper symbol to the species.

A. ${}^{32}_{18}S^{2-}$ **B.** ${}^{32}_{16}Ca^{2-}$ **C.** ${}^{32}_{16}P^{2-}$ **D.** ${}^{32}_{16}S^{2-}$

Q.10 The Vividh Bharati station of All India Radio, Delhi, broadcasts on a frequency of 1368 kHz. Calculate the wavelength of the electromagnetic radiation emitted by transmitter.

A. $319.3\ m$ **B.** $219.3\ m$ **C.** $200\ m$ **D.** $220.3\ m$

Q.11 The wavelength range of the visible spectrum extends from violet $(400\ nm)$ to red ($750\ nm$). Express these wavelengths in frequencies (Hz). (1nm $= 10^{-9}\ m)$

A. 7.50×10^{14} Hz, 4×10^{14} Hz
B. 5.50×10^{14} Hz, 4×10^{14} Hz
C. 6.50×10^{14} Hz, 5.00×10^{14} Hz
D. 8.50×10^{14} Hz, 3×10^{14} Hz

Q.12 Calculate energy of one mole of photons of radiation whose frequency is $5 \times 10^{14}\ Hz$.

A. $199.51\ kJ\ mol^{-1}$ **B.** $201.51\ kJ\ mol^{-1}$
C. $193.51\ kJ\ mol^{-1}$ **D.** $199.51\ J\ mol$

Q.13 Which of the following are false with respect to substitution reactions of Benzene?

A. Benzene reacts with the Nitric acid to produce Nitrobenzene
B. Benzene reacts with the Sulfuric acid to produce benzenesulphonic acid
C. Benzene acts with bromine water to produce phenyl bromide
D. None of the above

Q.14 The major product of the following reaction is:

$$CH_3CH = CHCO_2CH_3 \xrightarrow{LiAlH_4}$$

A. $CH_3CH_2CH_2CO_2CH_3$
B. $CH_3CH = CHCH_2OH$
C. $CH_3CH_2CH_2CH_2OH$
D. $CH_3CH_2CH_2CHO$

Q.15 Which one of these is an example of displacement reaction?

A. $Fe(s) + CuSO_4(aq) = FeSO_4(aq) + Cu(s)$
B. $2FeSO_4(s) = Fe_2O_3(s) + SO_2(g) + SO_3(g)$
C. $CaO(s) + H_2O(L) = Ca(OH)_2(aq)$
D. $C(s) + O_2(g) = CO_2(g)$

Q.16 What is the product of polymerization of phenol and formaldehyde?

A. PVC **B.** Bakelite
C. Polyester **D.** Teflon

Q.17 When hydrogen chloride gas is prepared on a humid day, the gas is usually passed through the guard tube containing calcium chloride. The role of calcium chloride taken in the guard tube is to:

A. Absorb the evolved gas
B. Moisture the gas
C. Absorb moisture from the gas
D. None of the above

Q.18 In which of the following reactions does conc. H_2SO_4 act as an oxidizing agent?

A. $ZnO + H_2SO_4$ **B.** $KBr + H_2SO_4$

C. $NaCl + H_2SO_4$ D. None of the above

Q.19 Calcium phosphate is present in tooth enamel. The nature of the calcium phosphate is:

A. Acidic B. Basic
C. Neutral D. Amphoteric

Q.20 A sample of soil is mixed with water and allowed to settle. The clear supernatant solution turns the pH paper yellowish-orange. Which of the following would change the colour of this pH paper to greenish-blue?

A. Lemon juice B. Vinegar
C. Common salt D. Antacid

Q.21 Silver articles become ________ after some time, when exposed to air.

A. black B. yellow C. brown D. red

Q.22 Which of the following is a dehydrating agent?

A. Anhydrous calcium chloride
B. Aqueous calcium chloride
C. Calcium hydroxide
D. Aqueous calcium hydroxide

Q.23 The reaction between ________ is called thermite reaction.

A. aluminum oxide and iron
B. iron oxide and aluminum
C. manganese oxide and aluminum
D. zinc oxide and carbon

Q.24 Copper reacts with moist carbon dioxide in the air to form ________.

A. copper oxide
B. basic copper carbonate
C. copper carbide
D. copper hydride

Q.25 Which gas is used for the artificial ripening of fruits?

A. Acetylene B. Propane
C. Methane D. Ethane

Q.26 What is the main component of biogas and CNG?

A. Propane B. Hydrogen sulfide
C. Methane D. Ethane

Q.27 What is the chemical formula of glucose?

A. $C_{12}H_{22}O_{11}$ B. $C_6H_{10}O_5$
C. $C_6H_{12}O_6$ D. $C_6H_6O_6$

Q.28 Which of the following chemicals are used in the manufacture of Refrigerators?

A. Hexachloro carbons
B. H_2SO_4
C. Chlorofluoro carbons
D. Sulfur hexafluoride

Q.29 Paneth cells are found in:

A. Crypts of Lieberkuhn
B. Peyer's patches
C. Islet of Langerhans
D. Gastric glands

Q.30 Which of the following is not a property of lymph?

A. It is a carrier of hormones
B. Prevention of infection due to microbes.
C. It contains lymphocytes that are responsible for the immune response of the body
D. It is an important carrier of nutrients

Q.31 An antigen is a substance that causes the immune system to produce antibodies against itself. Which type of cells are known to be involved in the initial presentation of antigen to T lymphocytes?

A. Dendritic cells
B. Plasma cells
C. Neutrophil polymorphonuclear leucocytes
D. Erythrocytes

Q.32 The term 'sarcode' was coined by

A. Robert Hooke B. Robert Brown
C. Durjarden D. Purkinje

Q.33 In mitochondria, ATP synthesizing chemical reactions takes place in the:

A. Outer membrane
B. Matrix
C. Inner membrane
D. DNA of mitochondria

Q.34 Which one of the following cell organelles does NOT possess its own genetic material encoding proteins?

A. Ribosome B. Nucleus
C. Mitochondria D. Chloroplast

Q.35 Which one of the following organelles of mammalian cells is rich in hydrolytic enzymes?

[UPSC NDA, 2019]

A. Mitochondria B. Ribosomes
C. Lysosome D. Nucleus

Q.36 Which one of the following groups of cellular organelles contains DNA?

A. Mitochondria, nucleus, chloroplast
B. Mitochondria, Golgi bodies, nucleus
C. Mitochondria, plasma membrane, nucleus
D. Chloroplast, nucleus, ribosomes

Q.37 A major application of embryo culture is in:

A. Clonal propagation
B. Production of alkaloids
C. Overcoming hybridization barriers
D. Induction of lethal mutations

Q.38 Root pressure occurs:

A. When rate of transpiration is low during the day
B. When soil moisture is high at the night
C. When rate of transpiration is high during the day
D. Both (A) and (B)

Q.39 The rupture or fractionation do not usually occur in the water column in vessels/tracheids during the ascent of sap because of:

A. Lignified thick walls
B. Cohesion and adhesion
C. Weak gravitational pull
D. Transpiration pull

Q.40 The overall goal of glycolysis, Krebs' cycle and the electron transport system is the formation of:
A. ATP in small stepwise units
B. ATP in one large oxidation reaction
C. Sugars
D. Nucleic acids

Q.41 The electrical impulse travels in a neuron from ________.
A. Dendrite → Axon → Axonal end → Cell body
B. Cell body → Dendrite → Axon → Axonal end
C. Dendrite → Cell body → Axon → Axonal end
D. Axonal end → Axon → Cell body → Dendrite

Q.42 Which hormone brings about the development of the mammary gland?
A. Estrogen B. Progesterone
C. Relaxin D. Oxytocin

Q.43 Which one of the endocrine glands is known as the master gland?
A. Pituitary B. Adrenal
C. Thyroid D. Parathyroid

Q.44 The growth of tendrils in pea plants is due to ________.
A. effect of light
B. effect of gravity
C. rapid cell division in tendrilled cells in contact with the support
D. rapid cell divisions in tendrilled cells that are away from the support

Q.45 Withdrawal of which hormone is the immediate cause of menstruation?
A. Estrogen B. FSH
C. FSH-RH D. Progesterone

Q.46 Signals for parturition originate from:
A. Fully developed foetus only
B. Placenta only
C. Oxytocin released by maternal pituitary
D. Both A and B

Q.47 In mammals, the testes occur in scrotal sacs outside the viscera because of the:
A. Presence of urinary bladder
B. Presence of rectum
C. Long vas deferens
D. Requirement of low temperature for spermatogenesis

Q.48 Hormones secreted by the placenta to maintain pregnancy are:

[NEET UG, 2018]

A. hCG, progestogens, estrogens, glucocorticoids
B. hCG. hPL, progestogens, prolactin
C. hCG, hPL, progestogens, estrogens
D. hCG, hPL, estrogens, relaxin, oxytocin

Q.49 'The use and disuse of an organ by an organism leads to acquiring 'variation' in the features of that organ' was proposed by ______.
A. Darwin
B. gregor Mendel
C. jean Baptist Lamarck
D. weismann

Q.50 One of the examples of two analogous organs can be the wing of parrot and ______.
A. front leg of frog B. foreleg of horse
C. wing of housefly D. flipper of whale

Q.51 Find the correct statement.
A. Chromosomes are the bearers of hereditary factors
B. J. B. S. Haldane, suggested that life have evolved from the simple organic molecules
C. The wing of a bird and the bat are homologous organs
D. A child who inherits an X – chromosome from his father will be a boy

Q.52 An example of homologous organs is-
A. Our hand and dog's forelimbs
B. Our teeth and elephant teeth
C. Potato and Grass Uplands
D. All of the above

Q.53 Force exerted on a body changes its______:
A. Direction of motion B. Momentum
C. Kinetic energy D. All the above

Q.54 There are two statements:

Statement A: Rate of change of momentum is proportional to force.

Statement B: Rate of change of momentum is proportional to kinetic energy.

Which one of the following is correct?
A. A only
B. B only
C. Both A and B are correct
D. Both A and B are wrong

Q.55 The distance- time graph for a body moving at uniform speed is:
A. A hyperbola B. A straight line
C. An ellipse D. A parabola

Q.56 An athlete diving off a high springboard can perform a variety of exercises in the air before entering the water.

Which one of the following parameters will remain constant during the fall?
A. The athlete's linear momentum
B. The athlete's moment of inertia
C. The athlete's kinetic energy
D. The athlete's angular momentum

Q.57 A passenger in a moving train tosses a five rupee coin. If the coin falls behind him, then the train must be moving with a uniform______:
A. Acceleration B. Deceleration
C. Speed D. Velocity

Q.58 Out of the given options which of the following has more inertia?

A. A rubber ball
B. A stone of the same size as of a ball
C. Both will have same inertia
D. Cannot be determined

Q.59 A block A of mass m_1 is released from the top of the smooth inclined plane and it slides down the plane. Another block B of mass $m_2 (m_2 > m_1)$ is dropped from the same point and falls vertically downwards.
Which one of the following statements will be true if the friction offered by air is negligible?

A. Both blocks will reach the ground at the same time
B. Both blocks will reach the ground at the same speed
C. Speed of both the blocks when they reach the ground will depend on their masses.
D. Block A reaches the ground before block B.

Q.60 When the motion of a body is confined to only one plane, the motion is said to be:

A. Plane motion **B.** Rectilinear motion
C. Curvilinear Motion **D.** None of the above

Q.61 If the orbital velocity of the satellite revolving around the earth is 7 km/sec, then its escape velocity will be:

A. 11.2 km/sec **B.** 8 km/sec
C. 9.9 km/sec **D.** 10.2 km/sec

Q.62 What is the intensity of the gravitational field at the center of a spherical shell of mass 'm' and radius 'r' ?

A. $\frac{Gm}{r^2}$ **B.** $\frac{Gm}{r}$
C. Zero **D.** None of these

Q.63 Which of the following laws says that "Every object in the universe attracts every other object with a force which is proportional to the product of their masses and inversely proportional to the square of the distance between them?"

A. Universal Law of gravitation
B. Kepler's Law
C. Newton's third Law of motion
D. Newton's first Law of motion

Q.64 An astronaut on a strange planet finds that acceleration due to gravity is twice as that on surface of Earth. Which of the following could explain this?

A. Both the mass and radius of the planet are twice as that of Earth.
B. Mass of the planet is half as that of Earth, but radius is same as that of Earth.
C. Both the mass and radius of the planet are half as that of Earth.
D. Radius of the planet is half as that of Earth, but the mass is the same as that of Earth.

Q.65 The device used for converting mechanical energy into electrical energy is called a/an?

A. Transformer **B.** Dynamo
C. Cell **D.** Electric motor

Q.66 When a force of 50 N is applied on an object of 5 kg, it covers a horizontal distance of 5 m. Calculate the amount of work done in this case.

A. 150 J **B.** 0 J **C.** 1250 J **D.** 250 J

Q.67 Suresh purchases a table lamp for study. The table lamp consumes 960 J of electrical energy in 16 s. What is its power?

A. 60W **B.** 45W **C.** 50W **D.** 48W

Q.68 Find the work done (in kJ) if a force of 750 N pushes a cart of mass 30 kg by 16 m.

A. 24 **B.** 12 **C.** 36 **D.** 48

Q.69 A sound can be identified with its ________.

A. Amplitude
B. Frequency
C. Amplitude and frequency
D. Speed and Frequency

Q.70 An object is vibrating at 1000 Hz. The time period of the sound produced is:

A. 0.001 second **B.** 10 second
C. 100 seconds **D.** 0.01 second

Q.71 For hearing distinct echoes the minimum distance of the obstacle from the source of sound must be:

A. $34.4\ m$ **B.** $17.2\ m$ **C.** $3.44\ m$ **D.** $1.72\ m$

Q.72 What do dolphins, bats, and porpoises send out:

A. Ultrasound **B.** Infrasound
C. Both (A) and (B) **D.** None of them

Q.73 If the resistor follows Ohm's law, what is it called?

A. Linear resistor
B. Parasitic resistor
C. Non-linear resistor
D. Non-parasitic resistor

Q.74 If $1\mu A$ current is flowing across a wire having potential difference $2V$, then the heat generated in 2 minutes will be (Considering the circuit to be pure resistive).

A. 2.4×10^{-2} Joule **B.** 2.4×10^{-4} Joule
C. 2.4 Joule **D.** 1.2×10^{-4} Joule

Q.75 If three resistors of equal resistance R is in parallel and this combination is in series with another resistance R, then the equivalent resistance across the circuit will be ________.

A. $\frac{4R}{3}$ **B.** $\frac{3R}{4}$ **C.** $\frac{R}{3}$ **D.** $\frac{2R}{3}$

Q.76 When a glass rod is rubbed with silk, the glass rod ________.

A. Loses electrons
B. Gains electrons
C. Both gain and lose of electrons
D. None of these

Q.77 Find the incorrect statement:

A. A wire with a red insulation is usually the neutral wire of an electric supply
B. Field lines emerge from the south pole and merge at north pole

C. Magnetic field lines can intersect each other
D. All of the above

Q.78 The right-hand thumb rule is used to find:
A. Force on a charged particle passing through the magnetic field
B. Force on a current-carrying conductor placed in a magnetic field
C. Direction of induced current
D. Direction of the magnetic field around a current-carrying straight conductor

Q.79 What are the factors affecting the strength of the magnetic field at a point due to a straight conductor carrying current?
A. Distance of the point from the wire only
B. Current, length and distance of the wire
C. Current only
D. Length of the wire only

Q.80 You have a coil and a bar magnet, you can produce an electric current by moving ______.
A. The magnet, but not the coil
B. Neither the magnet nor the coil
C. The coil, but not the magnet
D. Either the magnet or the coil or both

Q.81 There crops that contribute maximum to global food grain production are:
A. Wheat, rice and maize
B. Wheat rice and barley
C. Wheat, maize and sorghum
D. Rice, maize and sorghum

Q.82 Which city is known as the "Rice Bowl of Haryana"?
A. Karnal B. Ambala C. Sirsa D. Hisar

Q.83 Haryana ranks first in the production of ______.
A. Mushrooms B. Wheat
C. Rice D. None of these

Q.84 Which district of Haryana ranks first in the production of mustard?
A. Rewari B. Mahendragarh
C. Hisar D. None of these

Q.85 Which is the surest test of charge on a body?
A. Repulsion B. Lightning
C. Combustion D. Insulation

Q.86 The epicenter of an earthquake is:
A. in the core of the earth
B. on the surface of the earth
C. in the middle of the earth
D. None of these

Q.87 Benjamen Franklin showed lightening in:
A. 1750 B. 1752 C. 1740 D. 1753

Q.88 A rainbow is a meteorological phenomenon that is caused by:
A. Reflection B. Refraction
C. Dispersion D. All of the above

Q.89 Which of the following is a logical sequence of food chain?
A. Producer → Consumer → Decomposer
B. Producer → Decomposer → Consumer
C. Consumer → Producer → Decomposer
D. Decomposer→ Producer → Consumer

Q.90 Which one of the following is an artificial ecosystem?
[Jharkhand PSC (JPSC), 2014]
A. Pond B. Crop field
C. Lake D. Forest

Q.91 An ecosystem includes:
A. All living organisms
B. Non-living objects
C. Both living organisms and non-living objects
D. Sometimes living organisms and sometimes nonliving objects

Q.92 Excessive exposure of humans to UV-ray s results in:
(i) Damage to immune system
(ii) Damage to lungs
(iii) Skin cancer
(iv) Peptic ulcer
A. (i) and (ii) B. (ii) and (iv)
C. (i) and (iii) D. (iii) and (iv)

Q.93 6.022×10^{23} atoms of Helium contains:
A. 1 mole B. 2 mole C. 3 mole D. 4 mole

Q.94 How many basic laws are required to govern the combination of elements to form compounds?
A. 6 B. 5 C. 4 D. 1

Q.95 $NaHCO_3$ is chemical formula for:
A. Borax B. Vinegar
C. Lime D. Baking soda

Q.96 What's the molecular mass of carbon dioxide?
A. 43 B. 28 C. 44 D. 40

Q.97 All objects experience buoyancy when they are immersed in a fluid. Buoyancy is:
A. A downward force
B. A downward pressure
C. An upward force
D. An upward pressure

Q.98 An object is floating in water with $\left(\frac{1}{4}\right)^{th}$ of its volume above the surface of water. Which of the following statements is true?
A. The buoyant force on the object is greater than the weight of the object.
B. The buoyant force on the object is less than the weight of the object.
C. The buoyant force on the object is equal to the weight of the object.
D. No buoyant force is acting on the object.

Q.99 Calculate the pressure (in Pa) if a thrust of $1000N$ is applied to an area of $5m^2$.

A. 200 **B.** 50 **C.** 100 **D.** 25

Q.100 A body of dimensions $1.5m \times 1.0m \times 2m$, weighs $1962N$ in water. What is the weight of the body in the air? (Take acceleration due to gravity as $9.81m/s^2$)

A. $31392N$ **B.** $23392N$ **C.** $14392N$ **D.** $46392N$

// Smart Answer Sheet //

Correct: Percentage of students who answered correctly. Skipped: Percentage of students who skipped.

Q.	Ans.	Correct	Skipped	Q.	Ans.	Correct	Skipped	Q.	Ans.	Correct	Skipped	Q.	Ans.	Correct	Skipped	Q.	Ans.	Correct	Skipped	Q.	Ans.	Correct	Skipped
1	A	65.88 %	1.31 %	18	D	42.25 %	1.98 %	35	C	11.99 %	3.67 %	52	D	52.42 %	1.72 %	69	C	55.33 %	1.3 %	86	B	56.61 %	1.51 %
2	B	84.03 %	0.0 %	19	B	77.14 %	0.0 %	36	A	47.94 %	1.28 %	53	D	80.96 %	0.0 %	70	A	58.35 %	1.87 %	87	B	66.95 %	1.55 %
3	B	66.17 %	1.75 %	20	D	60.64 %	1.62 %	37	A	40.55 %	1.03 %	54	A	60.6 %	1.08 %	71	B	48.69 %	1.84 %	88	D	43.61 %	1.19 %
4	B	62.4 %	1.7 %	21	A	65.72 %	1.95 %	38	D	63.14 %	1.42 %	55	B	66.05 %	1.23 %	72	A	53.61 %	1.06 %	89	A	88.39 %	0.0 %
5	B	66.28 %	1.44 %	22	A	60.13 %	1.66 %	39	B	17.56 %	3.07 %	56	D	56.48 %	1.66 %	73	A	49.19 %	1.51 %	90	B	86.29 %	0.0 %
6	A	88.78 %	0.0 %	23	B	86.45 %	0.0 %	40	A	67.59 %	1.16 %	57	A	45.57 %	1.59 %	74	B	61.0 %	1.41 %	91	C	83.79 %	0.0 %
7	C	48.93 %	1.8 %	24	B	59.56 %	1.33 %	41	C	14.48 %	4.88 %	58	B	54.09 %	1.49 %	75	A	50.6 %	1.29 %	92	C	57.39 %	1.94 %
8	C	67.36 %	1.18 %	25	A	67.24 %	1.24 %	42	A	40.7 %	1.8 %	59	B	27.07 %	4.35 %	76	A	64.1 %	1.96 %	93	A	67.23 %	1.13 %
9	D	54.54 %	1.61 %	26	C	76.11 %	0.0 %	43	A	62.84 %	1.97 %	60	A	85.3 %	0.0 %	77	D	14.94 %	3.3 %	94	B	65.83 %	1.87 %
10	B	40.96 %	1.19 %	27	C	81.58 %	0.0 %	44	D	64.92 %	1.63 %	61	C	59.46 %	1.51 %	78	D	60.02 %	1.45 %	95	D	41.9 %	1.27 %
11	A	81.02 %	0.0 %	28	C	52.76 %	1.44 %	45	D	50.47 %	1.23 %	62	C	17.81 %	4.81 %	79	B	69.02 %	1.77 %	96	C	53.91 %	1.46 %
12	A	47.82 %	1.95 %	29	A	69.06 %	1.53 %	46	D	53.81 %	1.89 %	63	A	55.35 %	1.35 %	80	D	89.75 %	0.0 %	97	C	59.65 %	1.22 %
13	D	63.31 %	1.94 %	30	C	57.94 %	1.89 %	47	D	45.11 %	1.05 %	64	C	54.03 %	1.08 %	81	A	83.7 %	0.0 %	98	A	41.18 %	1.99 %
14	B	40.9 %	1.76 %	31	A	58.31 %	1.84 %	48	C	62.27 %	1.45 %	65	B	76.19 %	0.0 %	82	A	66.18 %	1.0 %	99	A	56.09 %	1.43 %
15	A	50.81 %	1.69 %	32	C	68.82 %	1.23 %	49	C	29.36 %	4.42 %	66	D	65.56 %	1.76 %	83	A	83.15 %	0.0 %	100	A	55.73 %	1.86 %
16	B	88.37 %	0.0 %	33	C	54.22 %	1.5 %	50	C	68.18 %	1.83 %	67	A	68.55 %	1.67 %	84	B	60.08 %	1.5 %				
17	C	19.76 %	3.64 %	34	A	45.41 %	1.59 %	51	A	13.55 %	3.7 %	68	B	58.67 %	1.98 %	85	A	50.42 %	1.35 %				

//Hints and Solutions//

1. Dalton's atomic theory:

The scientific 'Atomic Theory' is usually credited to John Dalton.

He proposed the atomic theory to explain the laws of definite and multiple proportions obeyed by elements when they combine into compounds.

- The first law says that any given compound has, a fixed proportion by mass of its constituents.
- The second law says that when two elements form more than one compound, for a fixed mass of one element, the masses of the other elements are in ratio of small integers.

To explain the laws Dalton suggested, about 200 years ago, that the smallest constituents of an element are atoms.

Atoms of one element are identical but differ from those of other elements. A small number of atoms of each element combine to form a molecule of the compound.

Hence, the correct option is (A).

2. Diffusion is the tendency of gas molecules to occupy the entire volume available to them. In other words, we can say it's the mixing of two substances on their own. The molecules of perfume diffuse with air and reach us with the movement of air particles.

Hence, the correct option is (B).

3. Dalton's atomic theory:

- The scientific 'Atomic Theory' is usually credited to John Dalton.
- He proposed the atomic theory to explain the laws of definite and multiple proportions obeyed by elements when they combine into compounds.
- The first law says that any given compound has, a fixed proportion by mass of its constituents.
- The second law says that when two elements form more than one compound, for a fixed mass of one element, the masses of the other elements are in the ratio of small integers.
- To explain the laws, Dalton suggested, about 200 years ago, that the smallest constituents of an element are atoms.
- Atoms of one element are identical but differ from those of other elements. A small number of atoms of each element combine to form a molecule of the compound.

Hence, the correct option is (B).

4. The melting point of ice is 273 K.

Water can exist in all three forms, i.e., solid, liquid, and gas. Solid in the form of ice, liquid in the form of water, and gas in the form of water vapours.

The melting point is the temperature at which a substance changes its state from solid into liquid. For ice, the temperature in degree Celcius is 0 and in kelvin, it is 273.

Hence, the correct option is (B).

5. The density is maximum in case of solids. In the case of liquids, the density is less than solids but more than gases. In gases, the density is minimum.

In liquid form, water has strong hydrogen bonding between molecules but when water freezes into ice, the hydrogen bonds that form allow the molecules to be spaced further apart by locking them into fixed positions, hence making them take more space. That is why overall density decreases and making ice float on the water.

Hence, the correct option is (B).

6. The direct transformation of a solid into vapor on heating is called sublimation. Sublimation is the process of transformation directly from the solid phase to the gaseous phase, without passing through an intermediate liquid phase.

Hence, the correct option is (A).

7. When a teaspoon of solid sugar is dissolved into a glass of water then it means a homogeneous mixture or solution has formed as the sugar has completely mixed into the water. Therefore, we can conclude that there exists only liquid state as the solid state of sugar has also turned into liquid by dissolution.

Hence, the correct option is (C).

8. When 1 liter of water is cooled from $4°C$ to $0°C$, its volume Increases.

When water reaches $4°C$ the molecules have been pushed as close to one another as possible and the density of water becomes precisely 1.00 g/cm ^{3}

When water freezes at $0°C$ due to the crystal structure the molecules arranged in some structured fashion so a little far apart ended up less dense -0.93 g/cm ^{3}, and so floats due to buoyancy.

As density decreases the volume increases.

Volume $=$ mass /density.

Hence, the correct option is (C).

9. The atomic number is equal to number of protons $= 16$. The element is sulphur (S).

Atomic mass number $=$ number of protons $+$ number of neutrons

$= 16 + 16 = 32$

Species is not neutral as the number of protons is not equal to electrons. It is anion (negatively charged) with charge equal to excess electrons $= 18 - 16 = 2$

Thus symbol is $^{32}_{16}S^{2-}$.

Hence, the correct option is (D).

10. Given,

$\nu = 1368$ kHz $= 1368 \times 10^3$ Hz

As we know,

The speed of light, $c = 3 \times 10^8$ m/s

The wavelength is,

$$\lambda = \frac{c}{\nu}$$

$$= \frac{3.00 \times 10^8}{1368 \times 10^3}$$

$$= 219.3\ m$$

Hence, the correct option is (B).

11. Given,

Wavelength of violet light $= 400\ nm = 400 \times 10^{-9}\ m$

Wavelength of red light $= 750\ nm = 750 \times 10^{-9}\ m$

As we know,

The speed of light,

$c = 3 \times 10^8$ m/s

Frequency of violet light is given as,

$$\nu = \frac{c}{\lambda}$$

$$= \frac{3.00 \times 10^8}{400 \times 10^{-9}}$$

$= 7.50 \times 10^{14}$ Hz

Frequency of red light is given as,

$$\nu = \frac{c}{\lambda}$$

$$= \frac{3.00 \times 10^8}{750 \times 10^{-9}}$$

$= 4 \times 10^{14}$ Hz

Hence, the correct option is (A).

12. Given,

Frequency, $\nu = 5 \times 10^{14}\ Hz$

As we know, Planck constant is given as,

$h = 6.626 \times 10^{-34} Js$

Energy of one photon is given by the expression,

$E = h\nu$

$E = (6.626 \times 10^{-34}\ J\ s) \times (5 \times 10^{14}\ s^{-1})$

$= 3.313 \times 10^{-19}\ J$

As we know,

Avogadro's number $= 6.022 \times 10^{23}\ mol^{-1}$

Energy of one mole of photons,

$= (3.313 \times 10^{-19}\ J) \times (6.022 \times 10^{23}\ mol^{-1})$

$= 199.51\ kJ\ mol^{-1}$

Hence, the correct option is (A).

13. Benzene is an aromatic hydrocarbon with the chemical formula C_6H_6

In the substitution reaction of Benzene, hydrogen atoms are replaced by one or more atoms.

With concentrated nitric acid, the substitution reaction takes place and Benzene produces nitrobenzene and water.

$$C_6H_6 + HNO_3 \rightarrow C_6H_5NO_2 + H_2O$$

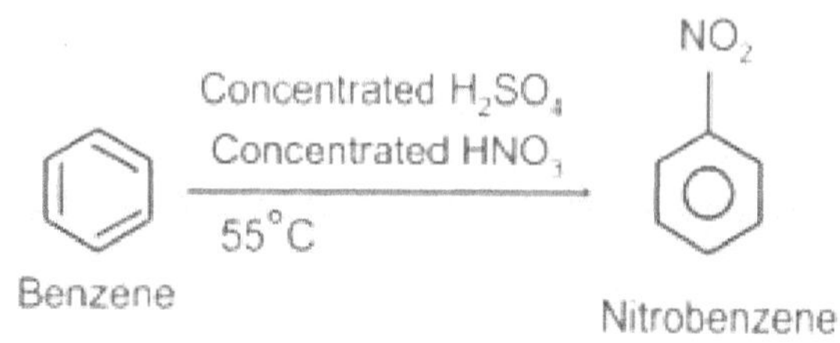

In the sulphonation, the substitution reaction takes place and Benzene reacts with concentrated sulphuric acid to produce benzene sulphonic acid and water.

$$C_6H_6 + H_2SO_4 \rightarrow C_6H_5SO_3H + H_2O$$

Bromine reacts with Benzene under substitution reaction to form phenyl bromine and bromine water.

$$C_6H_6 + Br_2 \rightarrow C_6H_5Br + HBr$$

Hence, the correct option is (D).

14.

- $LiAlH_4$ is used as a reducing agent in organic synthesis, especially for the reduction of esters, carboxylic acids, and amides.
- The solid is dangerously reactive toward water, releasing gaseous hydrogen (H_2).
- $LiAlH_4$ does not reduce double bond $(C = C$ bond $)$ but it reduces ester into alcohol.
- $LiAlH_4$ reduces a C-C double bond which is in conjugation i.e., resonance.
- $LiAlH_4$ reduces double bond in case of only when it is conjugation with phenyl ring but "cinnamic acid" is an exception because it has both carbonyl carbon as well as phenyl ring in its conjugation.

Here, it reduces an ester given above into alcohol.

$$CH_3CH = CH - CO_2CH_3 \xrightarrow{LiAlH_4} CH_3CH = CHCH_2OH$$

Hence, the correct option is (B).

15. A displacement reaction is a type of reaction in which part of one reactant is replaced by another reactant.

There are two types of displacement reactions.

- Single displacement reactions: These are those reactions in which one reactant replaces part of the other.
- Eg: Fe + $CuSO_4$ → $FeSO_4$ + Cu

- Double displacement reactions: These are those reactions in which the cations and anions in the reactants switch partners to form products.
- Eg: $AgNO_3$ + NaCl → AgCl + $NaNO_3$
- A displacement reaction is also known as a replacement reaction or a metathesis reaction.

Hence, the correct option is (A).

16. A polymer is a large molecule that is made up of repeating subunits called monomers, connected to each other by chemical bonds.

Polymerization is the process by which monomers are linked together to generate long chains composed of repeated units.

Bakelite is a Polymer, made up of the monomer of Formaldehyde + Phenol.

PVC Polyvinylchloride is formed by the polymerization of ethylene in which one of the four atoms is replaced by a Hydrogen atom.

Polyester forms by the reaction between dimethyl terephthalate and ethylene glycol.

Teflon is formed by the polymerization of tetrafluoroethylene monomer.

Hence, the correct option is (B).

17. Calcium chloride is used as an absorbent in the guard tube while hydrogen chloride is being formed on a humid day as it can absorb the moisture from the gas. Hydrochloric acid corrosively reacts with water leading to the formation of hydrochloric acid as it is strongly acidic in nature. It gives out white fumes on reacting with moisture.

Hence, the correct option is (C).

18. The oxidizing agent increases the oxidation state of the other substance in the chemical reaction. Conc. Sulphuric acid is a strong oxidizing reagent, but when it reacts with salts it either does not give reaction or shows displacement reaction. The reactions are as follows:

1. When zinc oxide reacts with conc. Sulphuric acid, zinc displaces hydrogen due to high reactivity.

$$\Rightarrow ZnO + H_2SO_4 \rightarrow ZnSO_4 + H_2O$$

The oxidation number of zinc in zinc oxide is $+2$ as the oxygen atom has -2 state in oxides so the molecule is neutral. In zinc sulphate the oxidation number of zinc is:

$$\Rightarrow x + (-2) = 0 \Rightarrow x = +2 \Rightarrow x + (-2) = +2$$

2. When potassium bromide reacts with conc. Sulphuric acid, potassium displaces hydrogen to form potassium sulphate as it is more reactive than hydrogen.

$$\Rightarrow 2KBr + H_2SO_4 \rightarrow K_2SO_4 + 2HBr$$

The oxidation number of potassium does not change and remains $+1$ after the reaction.

The oxidation state of potassium in potassium bromide is: $\Rightarrow$
$2x + 2(-1) = 0 \Rightarrow x = +1$

The oxidation state of potassium in potassium sulphate is: $\Rightarrow$
$2x + (-2) = 0 \Rightarrow x = +1$

3. When sodium chloride is reacted with conc. Sulphuric acid, it gives no reaction as sodium chloride is neutral salt.

$$\Rightarrow NaCl + H_2SO_4 \rightarrow \text{no reaction}$$

Since no reaction happens so the oxidation state of sodium does not change.

Hence , in the above reactions the sulphuric acid does not act as an oxidizing agent.

Hence, the correct option is (D).

19. Calcium phosphate is present in tooth enamel. The nature of the calcium phosphate is basic.

Calcium phosphate is basic salt since it is a source of weak phosphoric acid and a slightly stronger base of calcium hydroxide. Calcium phosphate is a mineral comprising calcium ion (Ca^{2+}) and phosphate ion which is inorganic in nature. It is present in the crown area of the tooth and also in bones.

Hence, the correct option is (B).

20. According to the question the solution of water and soil is acidic in nature as it is able to turn the litmus paper into yellow-orange colour. As we know lemon is a rich source of vitamin C, which is known as citric acid. Being a weak acid it will be able to turn the litmus to red. Vinegar is a combination of water and acetic acid. It acts as a mild acid and it also turns the litmus paper to red. Common salt includes the sodium and chloride ions and is not able to turn the litmus to blue as it is not a basic compound.

Antacid has its neutralizing property for acids and it reduces the acidity with the alkaline nature of its compounds such as aluminium and sodium carbonate. So antacid would change the pH paper from yellow-orange to greenish-blue while others are acidic in nature.

Hence, the correct option is (D).

21. When silver articles are exposed to air it becomes black after some time because the silver metal reacts with hydrogen sulphide present in the atmosphere that leads to the formation of silver sulphide (Ag_2S) because of which they appear dull and black. This is a kind of corrosion of silver metal.

$$Ag + H_2S \rightarrow Ag_2S + H_2$$

Hence, the correct option is (A).

22. Anhydrous calcium chloride is known as "hygroscopic". This means that it draws in water molecules and moisture from its environment and thus acts as a dehydrating agent. The anhydrous calcium chloride will absorb any water (including condensation, vapour etc.,) in its environment. It effectively traps that water by changing its molecular make-up.

Hence, the correct option is (A).

23. The reaction between iron oxide and aluminum is called a thermite reaction. A thermite reaction is an exothermic oxidation-reduction reaction.

In this process elemental aluminum reduces the oxide of another metal. For example iron oxide, because aluminum forms stronger and more stable bonds with oxygen than iron:

$$Fe_2O_3 + 2Al \rightarrow 2Fe + Al_2O_3$$

Hence, the correct option is (B).

24. When a copper vessel is exposed to moist air for a long time it develops a green layer on its surface. Copper corrodes by oxidation in which it reacts with oxygen in the air to form copper oxide.

Copper oxide then combines with carbon dioxide to make copper carbonate, which gives it a green colour. This process is called corrosion of copper.

The green material is a mixture of copper hydroxide $(Cu(OH)_2)$ and copper carbonate $(CuCO_3)$.

Hence, the correct option is (B).

25. Acetylene is used to artificially ripen fruits.

Raw fruit is sprayed with calcium carbide, which reacts with water and produces acetylene (C_2H_2).

$CaC_2 + 2H_2O \rightarrow C_2H_2 + Ca(OH)_2$

It only helps in changing the color and external appearance of the fruits, not changing the taste and quality of the fruits.

Hence, the correct option is (A).

26. The main component of both biogas and CNG is methane.

The major components of biogas are methane and carbon dioxide, while H2S and ammonia are also found in it.

The major components of CNG (compressed natural gas) are methane and ethane. It can be used in place of gasoline, diesel fuel and liquefied petroleum gas (LPG).

Hence, the correct option is (C).

27. The chemical formula of glucose is $C_6H_{12}O_6$. Glucose is the simplest carbohydrate. It is soluble in water. It is sweet in taste and is the main source of energy for living cells.

Hence, the correct option is (C).

28. Chlorofluoro carbons are used in the manufacture of Refrigerators.

CFC stands for chlorofluorocarbons. CFCs are compounds having carbon, chlorine, and fluorine in them. CFCs are prepared by partial or complete halogenation of the paraffin or alkanes. The CFCs are also known commonly as Freons.

Hence, the correct option is (C).

29. Paneth cells are highly specialized secretory epithelial cells located in the small intestinal crypts of Lieberkühn. The dense granules produced by Paneth cells contain an abundance of antimicrobial peptides and immunomodulating proteins that function to regulate the composition of the intestinal flora.

Hence, the correct option is (A).

30. The primary parts of the immune system include the bone marrow and thymus. The bone marrow is extremely important to the immune system because all the body's blood cells (including T and B lymphocytes) originate in the bone marrow. B lymphocytes remain in the marrow to mature, while T lymphocytes travel to the thymus. Therefore it is not the property of lymph.

Hence, the correct option is (C).

31. Dendritic cells are known as the most efficient antigen-presenting cell type with the ability to interact with T cells and initiate an immune response. Dendritic cells are receiving increasing scientific and clinical interest due to their key role in the immune response and potential use with tumor vaccines.

Hence, the correct option is (A).

32. Protoplasm or living matter is a polyphasic crystallo-colloidal complex that possesses all the properties of life and is found inside living cells. It was called a sarcode by Dujarden in 1835. The term protoplasm was coined by Purkinje in 1839.

Hence, the correct option is (C).

33. Mitochondria are made up of two membranes: the outer and inner mitochondrial membranes. The inner mitochondrial membrane is folded several times to form cristae and contains F_0-F_1 particles, which are the electron transport system's particles. The inner membrane is likewise densely packed with proteins involved in ATP generation, and here is frequently where ATP is produced. Adenosine triphosphate (ATP) is the energy currency for cellular processes. ATP provides energy for both energy-consuming endergonic reactions and energy-releasing exergonic reactions, which require a small input of energy.

Hence, the correct option is (C).

34. Ribosomes don't have their own genetic material or DNA as apart from the Nucleus, Mitochondria, and Chloroplast, all the other cell organelles are considered to be non-living.

- Ribosomes are the cellular machines that assemble proteins.
- The nucleus houses the cell's genetic material or DNA.
- The genetic materials of mitochondria and chloroplast are circular double-stranded. This kind of material is found in the prokaryotes.
- Examples of prokaryotes are bacteria and archaea.
- Examples of eukaryotes are protists, fungi, plants, and animals.

Hence, the correct option is (A).

35. Lysosomes are formed by the Golgi apparatus and are membrane-bound structures. This organelle in the mammalian cell is rich in all types of hydrolytic enzymes. These hydrolytic enzymes include hydrolase, lipases, carbohydrases, proteases. They help in digesting carbohydrates, lipids, proteins, nucleic acids at acidic Ph. They are also called the suicidal bags.

Mitochondria are also known as the powerhouse of the cell.

Ribosomes are a cell structure that makes protein

Nucleus stores the cell's hereditary material, or DNA, and coordinates the cell's activities.

Hence, the correct option is (C).

36. The three organelles that contain DNA are the nucleus, mitochondria, and chloroplasts.

- Organelles are those subunits in the cell which are membrane-bound performing specific functions.
- Thus, in a way, they are analogous to body organs.
- The Nucleus is the control center of the cell housing the genetic information.
- Mitochondria are known as the powerhouse of the cell.
- Chloroplasts both produce energy in plant cells.
- The Golgi apparatus is responsible for the transportation of proteins, lipids into the vesicles. It is near the cell nucleus and located in the cytoplasm next to the endoplasmic reticulum.

Hence, the correct option is (A).

37. A major application of embryo culture is in clonal propagation.

Clonal propagation helps to produce the genetically identical copies of individual plants. It is a mode of asexual reproduction. The vegetative propagation of plants is labour-intensive, low in productivity and seasonal. The tissue culture methods of plant propagation, known as micropropagation where the explant is taken from apical shoots, axillary buds, and meristems on suitable nutrient medium.

Hence, the correct option is (A).

38. Root pressure occurs when rate of transpiration is low during the day and when soil moisture is high at the night.

The root pressure is the osmotic pressure within the cells of a root system that generates due to the difference in the pressure gradient. This difference results in the flow of water from high water potential to low water potential and water is absorbed by the root from the soil. According to root pressure theory, hydrostatic pressure is generated in the root system due to accumulation of water absorbed by the roots, which is responsible for the ascent of sap. Root pressure is created due to gain of water whereas, transpiration is loss of water in the form of water vapour. Therefore, root pressure is inversely proportional to the rate of transpiration and that's why, it occurs when the rate of transpiration is low during the day or when the soil moisture level is high at night. At night, the temperature is low and humidity (moisture) level is comparatively high which would slow the rate of transpiration.

Hence, the correct option is (D).

39. The rupture or fractionation do not usually occur in the water column in vessels/tracheids during the ascent of sap because of cohesion and adhesion.

This is because continuity of water column is maintained by cohesion and adhesion. The conduction of water from root to aerial parts of plants is called ascent of sap. The water molecules remain attached to each other by cohesion force. The magnitude of this force is very high. This helps in the continuous water column in the xylem. The adhesive force is present between the water molecules and the walls of xylem. This also helps in continuous water column in the xylem.

Hence, the correct option is (B).

40. The overall goal of glycolysis, Krebs' cycle and the electron transport system is the formation of ATP in small stepwise units.

In glycolysis, the glucose is broken down into pyruvate and forms energy in the form of ATP. At the end of glycolysis, 2 ATP molecules are produced, or we can say the net gain of ATP is 2. This process takes place in the cytoplasm. In the oxidative decarboxylation of pyruvate, NADH+H+ is produced which helps in the production of 3 molecules of ATP. In Krebs cycle, the Acetyl CoA that is formed in the oxidative decarboxylation step reacts with oxaloacetate to form citric acid this leads to the beginning of Krebs cycle. The Krebs cycle produces 34 molecules of ATP and NADH. This biochemical reaction takes place in the matrix of mitochondria. The NADH that is produced in the glycolysis, oxidative decarboxylation and Krebs cycle, enters the electron transport chain that takes place in the inner mitochondrial membrane and produces ATP by ATP synthase.

So, we can clearly see that the overall goal of glycolysis, Krebs cycle and the electron transport system is the formation of ATP by small stepwise reactions.

Hence, the correct option is (A).

41. The electrical impulse travels in a neuron from Dendrite → Cell body → Axon → Axonal end.

The electrical impulse travels in a neuron from Dendrite to cell body to axon end to axonal end. Dendrites are tree-like extensions at the beginning of a neuron that help increase the surface area of the cell body.

Hence, the correct option is (C).

42. The ovarian hormone, estrogen, is another critical regulator of pubertal mammary development and is responsible for the tremendous surge in growth occurring during this period that generates a functional mammary gland.

Estrogen, a membrane-soluble ligand, is released from the ovary and activates gene expression through intracellular receptors. For a long time, it was unclear whether hormones such as estrogen had direct effects on mammary gland development or whether, instead, they functioned indirectly to stimulate the release of hormones such as prolactin from the pituitary.

Hence, the correct option is (A).

43. The pituitary gland is sometimes called the "master" gland of the endocrine system because it controls the functions of many of the other endocrine glands. The pituitary gland is no larger than a pea, and is located at the base of the brain. Oxytocin, ADH/vasopressin hormone, prolactin hormone, growth hormone are secreted by this. These are collectively called pituitary hormones.

Hence, the correct option is (A).

44. The growth of tendril in pea plants is due to rapid cell divisions in tendril cells that are away from the support. A tendril is a slender stem- or petiole-like structure that is used by vines and lianas (climbing plants) to wrap around or to hook a support.

Hence, the correct option is (D).

45. After ovulation, the pituitary hormones FSH and LH cause the remaining parts of the dominant follicle to transform into the corpus luteum, which produces progesterone. The increased progesterone in the adrenals starts to induce the production of estrogen. The hormones produced by the corpus luteum also suppress production of the FSH and LH that the corpus luteum needs to maintain itself. Consequently, the level of FSH and LH fall quickly over time, and the corpus luteum subsequently atrophies.

Falling levels of progesterone trigger menstruation and the beginning of the next cycle.

Hence, the correct option is (D).

46. Parturition is an induced Complex neuroendocrine mechanism. In this signals are originated from a fully developed fetus and placenta. This leads to mild uterine contractions and hence fetal ejection reflex. Then oxytocin is released from the maternal pituitary and it acts on uterine muscles leading to strong uterine contractions. This further continues to stronger and stronger contractions. As a result, the baby is expelled out of the uterus with the placenta through the birth canal.

Hence, the correct option is (D).

47. In mammals, the testes occur in scrotal sacs outside the viscera because of the requirement of low temperature for spermatogenesis. The testes are situated outside the abdominal cavity within a pouch called scrotum. The scrotum helps in maintaining the low temperature of the testes (2–2.5°C lower than the normal internal body temperature), which is necessary for spermatogenesis. The slightly cooler temperature of the scrotum is necessary for the development of normal sperm. So, the testes start their development in the abdominal cavity and descend into the scrotal sacs during the 7th month of the fetal life, in presence of testosterone hormone.

Hence, the correct option is (D).

48. Placenta releases human chorionic gonadotropic hormone (hCG) which stimulates the Corpus luteum during pregnancy to release estrogen and progesterone and also rescues corpus luteum from regression. Human placental lactogen (hPL) is involved in growth of body of mother and breast. Progesterone maintains pregnancy, keeps the uterus silent by increasing uterine threshold to contractile stimuli.

Hence, the correct option is (C).

49. The use and disuse of an organ by an organism leads to acquiring 'variation' in the features of that organ' was proposed by Jean Baptist Lamarck.

Individual efforts during the lifetime of the organisms drive species to adaptation, as they supposedly would acquire adaptive changes and pass them on to offspring i.e.., by selective use and disuse of an organ, organisms acquire or loose certain traits during their lifetime.

Hence, the correct option is (C).

50. Wings of parrot and wings of a housefly perform the function of flying. But the parrot's wings are originated from the mesoderm and are supported by bones while the housefly's wings are ectodermal in origin are supported by the chitinous structures.

Hence, the correct option is (C).

51. This statement is correct that chromosomes are bearers of hereditary units or genes and each chromosome carries hundreds or thousands of genes. Chromosomes contain basic hereditary units called Genes. A gene is a segment of DNA that carries information from parents to children and determines the heredity characters in the offspring.

Hence, the correct option is (A).

52. Such parts of the body of living beings which are similar in origin and structure, but differ in functions, are called homologous organs.

Example:

- Our hand and dog's forelimbs
- Our teeth and elephant teeth
- Potato and Grass Uplands

Human hands and dog feet are homologous structures. They have a different purpose, but they are similar and share common traits. Elephants have specialized rodents for digging and fighting food. They are structures homologous to human teeth, inherited from a common ancestor with incisor teeth. The corm of the colocasia, the tuber of the potato and the epiphysis of the grass are all homologous structures.

Hence, the correct option is (D).

53. Force exerted on a body changes its direction of motion, momentum and kinetic energy.

When a body acted upon by a certain force produces acceleration i.e. it undergoes change in its velocity and momentum and kinetic energy of a moving body depends on the velocity of the body.

Hence, the correct option is (D).

54. Rate of change of momentum is proportional to force.

We know that,

$F = \frac{dp}{dt}$ (which is the rate of change of momentum with time)

and

$$KE = \frac{p^2}{2m}$$

Therefore the rate of change of momentum is not proportional to the kinetic energy.

Hence, the correct option is (A).

55. The distance-time graph for a body moving with uniform speed is a straight line.

Uniform motion is defined as the speed where the speed does not change with time, only distance and time change.

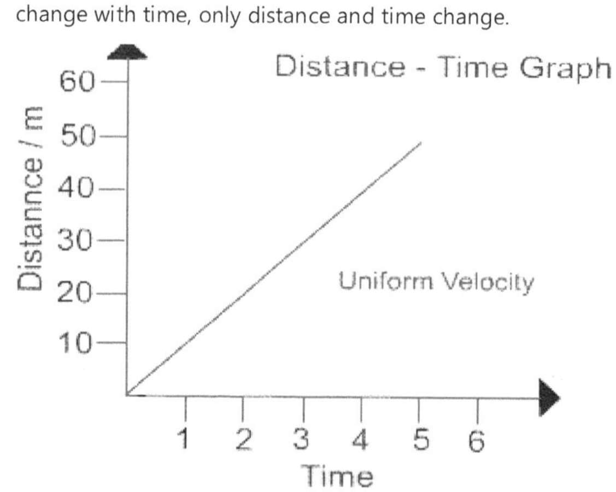

We know that,

$$speed = \frac{distance}{time}$$

Since, speed remains constant, we can conclude that distance and time are directly proportional to each other.

Therefore the graph between distance and time is a straight line.

Hence, the correct option is (B).

56. The athlete's angular momentum will remain constant during the fall.

When a diver jumps off a springboard, he or she rotates their body by moving their arms and legs. By doing so, it reduces its moment of inertia and increases angular momentum to maintain angular momentum.

Hence, the correct option is (D).

57. A passenger in a moving train tosses a five rupee coin. If the coin falls behind him, then the train must be moving with uniform acceleration. Because the coin falls behind the passenger, the train must be moving with uniform acceleration.

As the passenger tosses the coin, it goes up and is in motion with the speed (initial) of the train but the train is accelerated, so its speed increases. But the coin is at the (initial) speed in the air, so the train slightly moves forward with the person and the coin falls behind him.

Hence, the correct option is (A).

58. A stone of the same size as of ball has more inertia.

Mass is a measure of inertia. The more the mass, the more inertia. The mass of a stone is more than the mass of a plastic ball of the same size. Therefore, the inertia of the stone is greater than that of the plastic ball.

Inertia is defined as the natural tendency of an object to resist the change in its state of motion or rest. The mass of an object is a measure of its inertia. The mass of the stone is more than the mass of the rubber ball. Therefore, stones of the same size as of ball have more inertia.

Hence, the correct option is (B).

59. Both blocks will reach the ground at the same speed.

As we know:

$$v^2 = u^2 + 2gh$$

Here $u = 0$ for both m_1 and m_2

So the velocity of each block when it reaches the ground:

$$v^2 = 0 + 2gh$$

$$v = \sqrt{2gh}$$

And it is independent of the mass.

Hence, the correct option is (B).

60. When the motion of a body is confined to only one plane, the motion is said to be plane motion. The plane motion may be either rectilinear or curvilinear.

Motion in a plane is also referred to as a motion in two dimensions. For example, circular motion, projectile motion, etc. For the analysis of such type of motion, the reference point will be made of an origin and the two coordinate axes X and Y.

Hence, the correct option is (A).

61. Given, $v_\circ = 7\ km/sec$

We know that the relation between the orbital velocity and the escape velocity is given as,

$$v_e = \sqrt{2}v_\circ$$

Where v_e = escape velocity and $v_\circ$ = orbital speed of the satellite

So the escape velocity of the satellite is given as,

$$v_e = \sqrt{2}v_\circ$$

$$v_e = \sqrt{2} \times 7$$

$$v_e = 9.9\ km/sec$$

Hence, the correct option is (C).

62. Gravitational potential: Gravitational potential at any point inside the gravitational field is equal to work done in bringing a unit mass from infinite distance to a certain distance r from its center.

Thus, it can be expressed as:

$$V = -\frac{GM}{r}$$

Here V is gravitational potential, G is gravitational constant, M is mass of the planet and r is the distance between Mass M and some other object brought from an infinite distance.

- Inside the hollow sphere, the potential is equally distributed at every point of the surface in the gravitational field. So at any point, the potential will be zero.

Hence, the correct option is (C).

63.

- The universal law of gravitation was proposed by Sir Isaac Newton In the year 1686.
- Newton's law of gravitation: Every particle in the universe attracts every other particle with a force, which is directly proportional to the product of their masses and inversely proportional to the square of the distance between them.

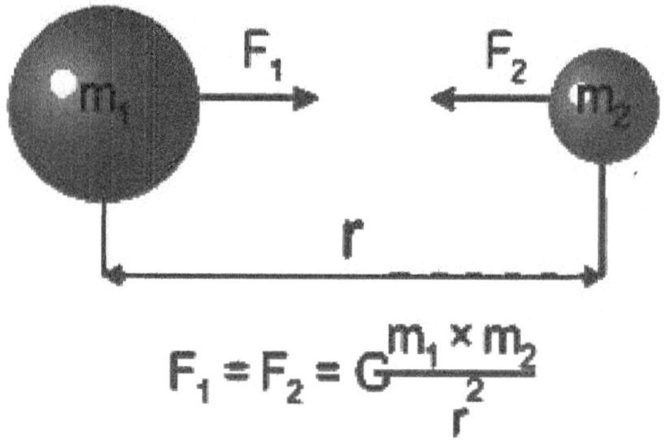

- If two bodies with mass m_1 and m_2, where r be the distance between two masses, then gravitational force,

$F_1 = F_2 = F \propto \frac{m_1 m_2}{r^2}$

Where, $F =$ force of attraction, $G = 6.67 \times 10^{11}\ N - m^2/kg^2$ (gravitational constant) m_1 and $m_2 =$ mass of bodies, $r =$ distance between them.

Universal Law of gravitation says that "Every object in the universe attracts every other object with a force which is proportional to the product of their masses and inversely proportional to the square of the distance between them".

Hence, the correct option is (A).

64. Given that in the strange planet acceleration due to gravity is twice as that on the surface of Earth
The expression for acceleration due to gravity on the surface of a planet is given by $g = \frac{GM}{r^2}$

Let g ' is gravitational acc on the strange planet. The mass of it is M_S and the radius is R_S so

$g' = \frac{GM_S}{R_S^2}$

Let g is gravitational acc on earth. The mass of the earth is M and the radius is R so

$g = \frac{GM}{R^2}$

$\frac{g'}{g} = \frac{\frac{GM_S}{n_S^2}}{\frac{GM}{n^2}}$

$\frac{g'}{g} = \frac{M_S}{M}\frac{R^2}{R_S^2}$

The value of g on the other planet is double then this will be satisfied by the only condition in option 3 .

$\frac{g'}{g} = \frac{M_S/2}{M}\frac{R^2}{(R_S/2)^2}$

$\frac{g'}{g} = 2$

$g' = 2g$

Hence, the correct option is (C).

65. Dynamo converts mechanical energy into electrical energy.

Its work is based on Faraday's law of Induction. The stator provides a magnetic field and armature (rotating windings) turns in a magnetic field. This magnetic field produces an electromotive force that pushes electrons thus generating current.

Hence, the correct option is (B).

66. Given that:

Force (F) = 50 , Displacement (s) = 5 m and θ = 0 (because the force is in the direction of motion)

To find the amount of work done in this case, we must apply the following formula:

⇒ W = Fs cosθ

⇒ W = 50 × 5 = 250 J

Hence, the correct option is (D).

67. Power – It is defined as the rate of doing work.

$\therefore P = \frac{W}{t}$

Where, P = power, W = work done, and t = time.

Now,

Time = 16 s

Work done = Energy consumed by the lamp = 960 J

Power = $\frac{960}{16}$ = 60 Js^{-1}

= 60 W

Hence, the correct option is (A).

68. Given that:

Force, F = 750 N

Displacement, s = 16 m

Work done, w = Fs Cos θ

Here θ is zero degree so Cos θ = 1

⇒ W = 750 × 16

⇒ W = 12000 J

To convert Joule into Kilo Joule divide by 1000

⇒ w $= \frac{12000}{1000}$

⇒ Work done, W = 12 KJ

Hence, the correct option is (B).

69. The sound is produced by vibrations. The pitch of the sound is determined by its frequency. Frequency is the number of vibrations taking place in one second. It is having SI unit Hertz. The amplitude of the sound determines its loudness. Amplitude in the case of sound is the maximum displacement of the particles from the mean position. A sound is identified by both its loudness and pitch.

So, Amplitude and frequency is the correct option.

Hence, the correct option is (C).

70. $T = \frac{1}{f}$

The frequency of the vibrating object in the given question is $-1000Hz$.

So, the time period will be -

$$T = \frac{1}{1000}$$

$T = 0.001$ second

So, the time period of the sound produced is 0.001 Seconds.

Hence, the correct option is (A).

71. The human ear can distinguish between two sounds if they came at an interval of a minimum of 0.1 seconds.

So, to hear the sound, and its reflection, the reflected sound must strike our ear at least after 0.1second.

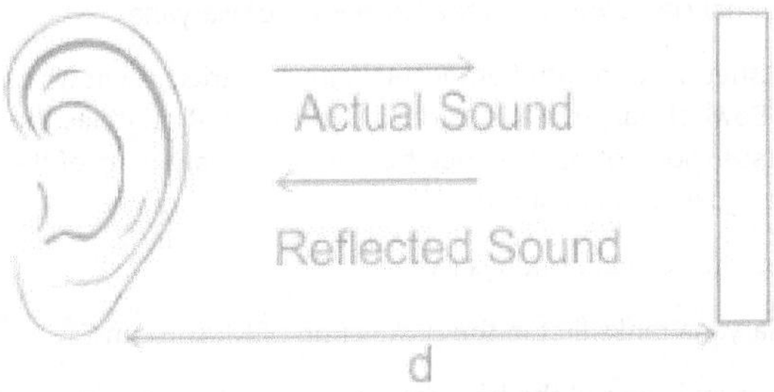

Let, the minimum distance required to hear echo d. (Obstacle is kept at distance d).

Now, distance travelled by sound to reach the obstacle and come back be .

(distance travelled by sound) $+$ (distance travelled by reflected sound) $= d + d = 2d$

Speed of sound $v = 343\ m/s$

The minimum time required to hear an echo is $t = 0.1$ second (Persistance of hearing of human ear)

distance travelled $=$ speed $\times$ time

$$\Rightarrow 2\ d = 343\ m/s \times 0.1\ s$$

$$\Rightarrow d = \frac{34.3}{2}\ m = 17.2\ m$$

So, minimum the distance at which the obstacle must be kept is 17.2 m

Hence, the correct option is (B).

72. Animals such as bats and dolphins send out ultrasound waves and use their echoes, or reflected waves, to identify the locations of objects they cannot see. This is called echolocation. Animals use echolocation to find prey and avoid running into objects in the dark.

Hence, the correct option is (A).

73. If an element follows the ohm's law, then the element is known as a linear element.

Ex: Resistor

Limitations of ohms law:

- Ohm's law is not applicable to unilateral networks. Unilateral networks allow the current to flow in one direction. Such types of networks consist of elements like a diode, transistor, etc.
- Ohm's law is also not applicable to non – linear elements. Non-linear elements are those which do not have current exactly proportional to the applied voltage that means the resistance value of those elements' changes for different values of voltage and current. An example of a non-linear element is thyristor.
- Ohm's law is also not applicable to vacuum tubes.

Hence, the correct option is (A).

74. Joules Heating:

The current flowing through a resistor generates heat due to resistances offered by it.

The heat energy generated is given by $H =$ V.I.t

V is the potential difference, I is current, t is the time

Calculation:

Given,

Potential difference $V = 2V$

Current $I = 1\mu A = 1 \times 10^{-6} A$

Time $t = 2$ minutes $= 2 \times 60s = 120s$

$H = VIt = 2V \times 1 \times 10^{-6} A \times 120s = 240 \times 10^{-6}$ Joule $= 2.4 \times 10^{-4}$ Joule.

Hence, the correct option is (B).

75. Equivalent Resistance:

- Equivalent Resistance between two Points is the ratio of Potential Difference between them and the amount of current passing through them.
- Equivalent Resistance can also be defined as the resistance of the resistor which will replace all the resistors between two points and will draw the same current between these two points as it was flowing Earlier.

The Circuit diagram according to the solution can be drawn as shown in the figure.

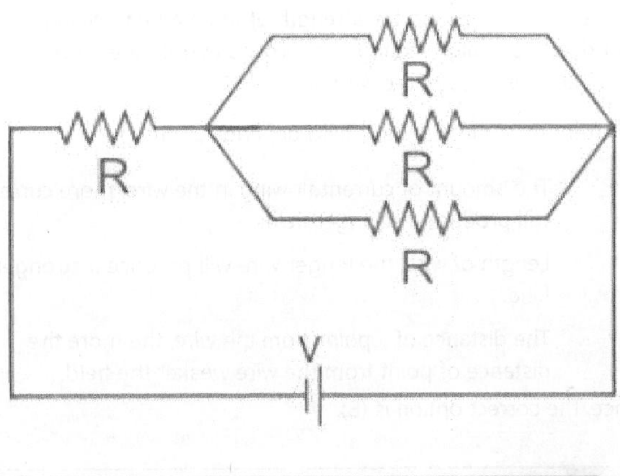

The three resistors are in series, So, the equivalent resistance across them will be:

$$\frac{1}{R_{eq}} = \frac{1}{R} + \frac{1}{R} + \frac{1}{R}$$

$$\Rightarrow \frac{1}{R_{eq}} = \frac{3}{R}$$

$$\Rightarrow R_{\text{eq}} = \frac{R}{3}$$

Now this R_{eq} is in series with another resistance R.

The Net equivalent resistance will be,

$$\Rightarrow R'_{eq} = \frac{R+R}{3} = \frac{4R}{3}$$

Hence, the correct option is (A).

76. During the process of charging by friction, the electrons are transferred from one material to another material.

If a dry glass rod is rubbed with silk cloth the glass rod gives out negative electrons, and therefore, becomes positively charged.

The silk cloth receives negative electrons and therefore it becomes negatively charged.

So, When a Silk cloth is rubbed with a glass rod, the glass rod Loses electrons.

Hence, the correct option is (A).

77. Magnetic field emerges from north pole to south pole and have only one direction, thus no two field lines overlap. A wire with a red insulation is usually the live wire of an electric supply. In old convention, the red wire is the live wire, the black wire is neutral and the earth wire is given green insulation. So, all sentence are incorrect.

Hence, the correct option is (D).

78. The right-hand thumb rule is used to find the direction of the magnetic field around a current-carrying straight conductor.

Right-hand rules states that "If the current carrying conductor is held in the right hand by pointing thumb finger towards the direction of current flow and the other fingers curled around the conductor then the curled fingers indicate the direction of the magnetic field due to the current carrying conductor". This rule only gives the direction of the magnetic field of the current carrying conductor.

Hence, the correct option is (D).

79. The factors affecting the strength of the magnetic field at a point due to a straight conductor carrying current are current, length, and distance of the wire.

The strength of the magnetic field depends upon:

- The amount of current flowing in the wire, more current will produce a stronger field.
- Length of wire, the longer wire will produce a stronger field.
- The distance of a point from the wire, the more the distance of point from the wire weaker the field.

Hence, the correct option is (B).

80. You have a coil and a bar magnet, you can produce an electric current by moving either the magnet or the coil or both.

Moving a magnet around a coil of wire, or moving a coil of wire around a magnet, pushes the electrons in the wire and creates an electrical current.

Hence, the correct option is (D).

81. There crops that contribute maximum to global food grain production are wheat, rice and maize.

Wheat, rice and maize are the three crops that contribute maximum to the global food grain production. These three crops form the base of grain requirement across the world. This is mainly responsible for the high production rates of these food crops across the world.

Hence, the correct option is (A).

82. Karnal city is known as the "Rice Bowl of Haryana".

Kurukshetra along with Karnal and Kaithal districts is known as the 'Rice Bowl of Haryana' and famous for Basmati Rice. It has the highest exports of basmati rice from India. A major part of the export goes to Gulf countries.

Hence, the correct option is (A).

83. Haryana ranks first in the production of Mushrooms.

Mushroom is one of the best diets, which contains protein, minerals, and vitamins like Nutritive material in a sufficient quantity.

It is having less quantity of fats due to this reason it is a very good diet for heart patients and due to the very fewer carbohydrates mushroom is the most suitable diet for diabetic patients.

About one dozen mushroom spaces are commercially grown in the world but in Haryana mainly two spaces are cultivated.

Hence, the correct option is (A).

84. Mahendragarh district of Haryana ranks first in the production of mustard.

In Haryana, Mahendragarh district takes lead in growing mustard followed by Rewari, Hisar, Sirsa, Jhajjar, Mewat and others. In Haryana, sowing period for mustard varies from last week of September to the last week of October.

Hence, the correct option is (B).

85. Repulsion is being considered as the sure test of charge on the body as the induction of charge is possible between an uncharged body and charged body when brought close together.

Hence, the correct option is (A).

86. The epicenter, epicenter n seismology is the point on the Earth's surface directly above a hypocenter or focus, the point where an earthquake or an underground explosion originates. In most earthquakes, the epicenter is the point where the greatest damage takes place, but the length of the subsurface fault rupture may indeed be a long one, and damage can be spread on the surface across the entire rupture zone.

Hence, the correct option is (B).

87. Benjamen Franklin showed lightning in 1752.

On June 10, 1752, Benjamin Franklin flies a kite during a thunderstorm and collects an ambient electrical charge in a Leyden jar, enabling him to demonstrate the connection between lightning and electricity. He discovered and showed that sparks produced from our clothes and lighting are essentially the same phenomena. Both lightning and sparks are caused by the accumulation of charges in the clouds and clothes respectively.

Hence, the correct option is (B).

88. A rainbow is a meteorological phenomenon that is caused by reflection, refraction, and dispersion of light in water droplets resulting in a spectrum of light appearing in the sky. It takes the form of a multicolored circular arc.

Hence, the correct option is (D).

89. The logical sequence of food chain is: producer → consumer → decomposer.

In the Carbon cycle, carbon is fixed in the biosphere through photosynthesis. A considerable amount of carbon returns to the atmosphere as CO_2 through the respiratory activities of the producers and consumers.

Decomposers also contribute substantially to CO_2 pool by their processing of waste materials and dead organic matter of land or oceans.

Hence, the correct option is (A).

90. Crop field is an artificial ecosystem.

Crops fields are known as artificial ecosystems because they are manmade where certain biotic and abiotic components are manipulated. A crop field is an ecosystem where the plants such as rice, wheat, vegetables etc. are grown. Farmers employ the relationship between the abiotic factors and producers. For example, when they add manure to their farm they increase the abiotic factors (nutrients) required for the growth of their plants.

Hence, the correct option is (B).

91. An ecosystem includes both living organisms and non-living objects.

An ecosystem is a functional unit comprising all the organisms in a particular place interacting with one another and with their physical environment. Thus, an ecosystem is an interacting system made up of all living and non-living objects in a specified volume of space. It is visualized as a functional unit of nature.

Hence, the correct option is (C).

92. Excessive exposure of humans to UV-ray s results in damage to immune system and skin cancer.

The UV-rays have extremely harmful effects on human beings, other animals as well as plants. It can cause skin cancer, damage the eyes by causing cataract, also damage immune system by lowering the body's resistance to diseases.

Hence, the correct option is (C).

93. Helium is a monoatomic gas.

By definition, the number of units in one mole of a substance is Avogadro's number.

1 mole $= 6.022 \times 10^{23}$ units

So for atoms, 1 mole $= 6.022 \times 10^{23}$ atoms.

Thus, 6.022×10^{23} atoms of Helium contain 1 mole.

Hence, the correct option is (A).

94. Five basic laws are required to govern the combination of elements to form compounds. They are:

- Law of Conservation of Mass
- Law of Definite Proportions
- Law of Multiple Proportions
- Gay Lussac's Law of Gaseous Volumes
- Avogadro's Law

अतः विकल्प (B) सही है।

95. $NaHCO_3$ is the chemical formula for Baking soda.

Its chemical name is Sodium bicarbonate and it is a chemical compound. It is a salt composed of sodium ions and bicarbonate ions.

Sodium bicarbonate is a white solid that is crystalline but often appears as a fine powder.

Hence, the correct option is (D).

96. The individual mass of carbon is 12 amu and the individual mass of oxygen is 16 amu. The formula for carbon dioxide is CO_2. Thus one carbon and two oxygens. 12(carbon Molecular weight) + 2 x 16 (oxygen Molecular weight) = 12 + 32 = 44. Therefore the molecular mass of carbon dioxide is 44.

Hence, the correct option is (C).

97. All objects experience buoyancy when they are immersed in a fluid. Buoyancy is an upward force.

When a body is either wholly or partially immersed in a fluid, a lift is generated due to the net vertical component of hydrostatic pressure forces experienced by the body. This lift is called the buoyant force and the phenomenon is called buoyancy. The Archimedes principle states that the buoyant force on a submerged body is equal to the weight of the liquid displaced by the body and acts vertically upward through the centroid of the displaced volume.

Hence, the correct option is (C).

98. The statement "The buoyant force on the object is equal to the weight of the object" is true.

Archimedes' Principle states that the buoyant force on a submerged body is equal to the weight of the liquid displaced by the body and acts vertically upward through the centroid of the displaced water.

- If the buoyant force is greater than the object's weight, the object will rise to the surface and float.
- If the buoyant force is less than the object's weight, the object will sink.
- If the buoyant force is equal to the object's weight, the object will be suspended at the depth.

Hence, the correct option is (A).

99. We know,

$$Pressure(P) = Force(F)/Area(A)$$

We have,

$$Force(F) = 1000N$$

$$Area(A) = 5m^2$$

Therefore,

$$P = 1000/5 = 200N/m^2 = 200Pa$$

So, the pressure is $2000Pa$

Hence, the correct option is (A).

100. Given:

Dimension of Body $= 1.5m \times 1.0m \times 2m, W_{\text{Apparent}} = 1962N, g = 9.81m/s^2$

Displaced Volume $(V_d) =$ Volume of Body $= 1.5 \times 1.0 \times 2 = 3m^3$

After putting all these values in equation (i), we have

$$1962 = W_{\text{Air}} - 1000 \times 9.81 \times 3$$

$$1962 = W_{\text{Air}} - 29430$$

$$W_{\text{Air}} = 1962 + 29430$$

$$W_{\text{Air}} = 31392N$$

Hence, the correct option is (A).

Mock Test 03

Q.1 What is quantization of photons?

A. Photons are massless.
B. Photons are discrete energy parcels
C. Photons are stable.
D. Photons carry energy

Q.2 Protons and alpha particles have the same de-Broglie wavelength. What is same for both of them?

A. Energy **B.** Time period
C. Frequency **D.** Momentum

Q.3 The process of change of state from solid to liquid is called:

A. Melting **B.** Freezing
C. Boiling **D.** Condensation

Q.4 During the melting of solid, its temperature ______.

A. May increase or decrease depending on the nature of solid
B. Decreases
C. Does not change
D. Increases

Q.5 Which one of the following gases produces a red light when electricity flows through it?

A. Helium **B.** Argon **C.** Nitrogen **D.** Neon

Q.6 The states of matter having no definite shape but definite volume ______.

A. Gas **B.** Liquid
C. Solid **D.** None of these

Q.7 Which of the following property of water can be used to explain the spherical shape of rain droplets?

A. Viscosity **B.** Surface tension
C. Critical phenomena **D.** Pressure

Q.8 The energy of a hydrogen atom in the ground state is $13.6eV$. The energy of He^+ ion in the first excited state will be:

A. $-13.6eV$ **B.** $-27.2eV$
C. $-54.4eV$ **D.** $-6.8eV$

Q.9 The number of electrons in an element X is 15 and the number of neutrons is 16 . The element can be represented as:

A. ${}^{31}_{15}X$ **B.** ${}^{31}_{16}X$ **C.** ${}^{16}_{15}X$ **D.** ${}^{15}_{16}X$

Q.10 Identify the false statement among the following.

A. Heisenberg's principle is contradictory to Bohr's theory.
B. Planck's quantum theory is taken as the basis for Bohr's theory.
C. Splitting up of spectral lines in presence of external magnetic field is due to the existence of sub shells.
D. None of these

Q.11 From which of the following tertiary butyl alcohol is obtained by the action of methyl magnesium bromide?

A. HCHO **B.** CH_3CHO
C. CH_3COCH_3 **D.** CO_2

Q.12 Benzene reacts with H_2 in presence of Ni at 200°C to give:

A. n-hexane **B.** Cyclohexane
C. Iso hexane **D.** n-hexene

Q.13 Benzene reacts with CO and HCl under pressure to form:

A. C_6H_5Cl **B.** C_6H_5CHO
C. $COCl_2$ **D.** C_6H_5COOH

Q.14 Aspirin is an acetylation product of:

A. p-dihydrobenzene
B. Salicylic acid
C. o-dihydroxybenzene
D. m-hydroxybenzoic acid

Q.15 Which one of the following is an example of efflorescent salts?

A. Sodium carbonate
B. Magnesium sulphate
C. Sodium sulfate decahydrate
D. All of the above

Q.16 Buffer solution of known pH can be prepared from which one of the following?

A. pK_a of the acid
B. pK_b of base
C. By controlling the ratio of the salt and acid or salt and base
D. All of the above

Q.17 Which of the following gases is produced during roasting?

A. H_2S **B.** CO_2 **C.** H_2 **D.** SO_2

Q.18 Which of the following contains some soluble salts such as sodium chloride, magnesium chloride, etc.,?

A. Distilled water **B.** Tap water
C. Sea water **D.** Lake water

Q.19 Which of the following gases is produced during calcination?

A. CO_2 **B.** CO **C.** SO_2 **D.** SO_3

Q.20 I.U.P.A.C. name of $CH_3COOC_2H_5$ is-

A. Ethyl ethanoic acid
B. Butanoate
C. Ethyl ethanoate
D. Ethyl methyl carboxylic acid

Q.21 What is the chemical formula of aldehyde?

A. ROH **B.** RCHO **C.** RCOX **D.** RCOOH

Q.22 How many single bonds are present in methane?

A. Six **B.** Four **C.** Seven **D.** Five

Q.23 Name of the hydrocarbon group having a double bond between carbon atoms.

A. Alkane B. Alkene
C. Alkyne D. Aldehyde

Q.24 Lampbrush chromosomes found in oocytes occur in:
A. Leptotene **B.** Zygotene
C. Pachytene **D.** Diplotene

Q.25 Phragmoplast is formed during
A. Prophase of meiosis
B. Cytokinesis of animal cells
C. Late cytokinesis
D. Metaphase of mitosis

Q.26 Which of the following cells consist of an organised and differentiated cellular structure having cytoplasm without any nucleus at maturity?
A. Phloem parenchyma
B. Xylem parenchyma
C. Tracheids
D. Sieve tubes

Q.27 One of the additional functions of the Smooth Endoplasmic Reticulum (SER) is:
A. protein synthesis
B. lipid synthesis
C. storage of biomolecules
D. detoxification of toxic substances

Q.28 Which one of the following is an organelle that is NOT found in prokaryotic cells?
A. Cell wall **B.** Mitochondria
C. Plasma membrane **D.** Ribosome

Q.29 Who among the following first discovered cells?
A. Robert Brown **B.** Robert Hooke
C. Leeuwenhoek **D.** Rudolf Virchow

Q.30 Which one of the following types of tissues will have contractile proteins?
A. Nervous tissue **B.** Muscle tissue
C. Bone tissue **D.** Blood tissue

Q.31 Vegetative reproduction of Agave occurs through:
A. Rhizome **B.** Stolon
C. Bulbils **D.** None of the above

Q.32 Which metabolic pathway is common to both fermentation, a type of anaerobic respiration, and aerobic respiration?
A. Glycolysis
B. Krebs cycle
C. Electron transport chain
D. Acetyl Co-A formed from pyruvate

Q.33 Which pigment prevents photo-oxidation and destruction of chlorophyll?
A. Carotene **B.** Phycocyanin
C. Phycoerythrin **D.** Phytocorythrin

Q.34 Neurons that carry information to an effector are called as ______neurons.
A. sensory neurons **B.** motor neurons
C. interneurons **D.** spinal neurons

Q.35 Name the hormone responsible for ripening of fruits.
A. Ethylene **B.** Abscisic acid
C. Auxin **D.** None of these

Q.36 What is the function of pituitary gland?
A. To develop sex organs in males
B. To stimulate growth in all organs
C. To regulate sugar and salt level in the body
D. To initiate metabolism in the body

Q.37 The movement of plant towards the stimulus is called as :
A. Tropic **B.** Nastic
C. Locomotion **D.** None of these

Q.38 What are the cysts containing sticky gel-like substances in an ovary called?
A. Endometriomas **B.** Cystadenomas
C. Dermoid **D.** Polycystic

Q.39 Shotgun technique is employed in
A. Stitching of genes
B. Isolation of genes
C. Splicing of DNA
D. Duplicating genomic DNA

Q.40 Which of the following structures temporarily stores sperms?
A. Vas deferens **B.** Epididymis
C. Vasa efferentia **D.** Urinary bladder

Q.41 Variations that result from factors such as climate, food supply and actions of other organisms are called as:
A. Both Genetic and somatic
B. Somatic
C. Genetic
D. None of these

Q.42 ______________ are those that contain the genes for masculinity and femininity in humans.
A. Somatic ctromosomes
B. Sex chromosomes
C. Autosomes
D. None of these

Q.43 Which very ancient animal is still alive in the places of today's heterogeneous environment?
A. Dinosaur **B.** Virus **C.** Bacteria **D.** Bird

Q.44 Which of these is not a living fossil?
A. Archaeopteryx
B. Lungfish
C. Frog
D. Duck-billed platypus

Q.45 Which of the following has more inertia?
A. A rubber ball
B. A stone of same size as of ball
C. Both will have same inertia
D. Cannot be determined

Q.46 Which of the following is an example of a non- uniform accelerated motion?

A. Freely falling body
B. Movement of a fan
C. A roller coaster
D. Motion of a ball rolling down an inclined plane

Q.47 A car starts moving from rest on a straight path and covers a distance of 100 m in 20 seconds with uniform acceleration. Find the velocity gained by the car in 30 seconds.

A. 60 m/sec **B.** 20 m/sec
C. 15 m/sec **D.** None of these

Q.48 In the case of Uniform Circular Motion, the work done by the centripetal force is:

A. Equal to the displacement of the body
B. Equal to the force applied on the body
C. Zero
D. Equal to the impulse created on the body

Q.49 Newton's first law of motion is also known as:

A. Law of movement
B. Law of displacement
C. Law of inertia
D. Law of momentum

Q.50 Galileo's law of ________ was Newton's starting point which he formulated as the 'First Law of motion'.

A. Inertia **B.** Momentum
C. Energy **D.** Equilibrium

Q.51 The value of acceleration due to gravity is:

A. Same at equator and poles
B. Increased from pole to equator
C. Least at equator
D. Least at poles

Q.52 Satellite going round the earth in a circular orbit loses some energy due to collision. Its speed is v and distance from the earth is d_____.

A. d will increase, v will increase.
B. d will increase, v will decrease.
C. d will decrease, v will decrease.
D. d will decrease, v will increase.

Q.53 If the horizontal velocity given to a satellite is greater than the critical velocity but less than the escape velocity, then the satellite will ________.

A. Revolve in a circular orbit
B. Will strike the earth along a parabolic path
C. Start revolving in an elliptical orbit
D. It will disappear in the outer space

Q.54 Law of gravitation gives the gravitational force between ________.

A. The Earth and a point mass only
B. The Earth and Sun only
C. Any two bodies having mass
D. Two charged bodies only

Q.55 Work energy theorem is the "Work done by ________ force acting on the particle is equal to change in kinetic energy".

A. Only Conservative
B. Only Non-conservative
C. Net
D. None of these

Q.56 Work is best defined as:

A. Work has only direction, no magnitude
B. Work has magnitude and direction
C. Work has no magnitude and no direction.
D. Work has only magnitude, no direction

Q.57 Water stored in a dam possesses _______.

A. Electrical energy
B. Potential energy
C. Gravitational energy
D. Kinetic energy

Q.58 Name the type of energy (kinetic energy K or potential energy U) possessed in a compressed spring:

A. Potential energy **B.** Kinetic energy
C. Both (A) and (B) **D.** None of the above

Q.59 At a particular temperature, sound propagates in _____ at the fastest speed.

A. water **B.** vacuum **C.** iron **D.** air

Q.60 What does the amplitude of sound wave determine ?

A. Loudness **B.** Pitch
C. Frequency **D.** Amplitude

Q.61 To hear a distinct echo each time interval between the original sound and the reflected sound must be:

A. 0.2 s **B.** 1s **C.** 2s **D.** 0.1 s

Q.62 The function of MCB Is close to the function of a:

A. Switch **B.** Fuse
C. Earth wire **D.** Transformer

Q.63 The objective of earthing in houses is ________.

A. to provide as low resistance as possible for conduction of current to the ground
B. to provide as high resistance as possible for conduction of current to the ground
C. to provide high voltage to the equipments
D. to provide high current to the equipments

Q.64 A galvanometer can be converted into a volt meter by connecting a:

A. High resistance in parallel
B. High resistance in series
C. Low resistance in parallel
D. Low resistance in series

Q.65 If the current flowing through a circuit is $0.6\ A$ for $6\ mins$, the amount of electric charge flowing through it is:

A. 360 C **B.** 216 C **C.** 60 C **D.** 36 C

Q.66 An electric motor ________.

A. Measures electric current

B. Converts electrical energy into mechanical energy
C. Provides a constant potential difference
D. Measures potential difference

Q.67 What will happen when a magnet is taken towards a circular coil?
A. No effect on the circular coil
B. No effect of magnetic field
C. Induced current will start flowing
D. No current will flow in the circuit

Q.68 Who said that current can cause magnetic field?
A. Oersted **B.** Fleming
C. Maxwell **D.** Michael Faraday

Q.69 An electron beam is moving vertically upwards if it passes through a magnetic field which is directed from south to north in a horizontal plane then in which direction will the beam be deflected?
A. Towards south **B.** Towards east
C. Towards west **D.** Towards north

Q.70 The waves produced on the earth's surface is called:
A. Seismic wave **B.** Longitudinal wave
C. Microwave **D.** Radio wave

Q.71 What are halos caused by?
A. Diffraction of light **B.** Refraction of light
C. Reflection of light **D.** Diffusion of light

Q.72 Which group of organisms are not constituents of a food chain?
A. Grass, lion, rabbit
B. Plankton, man, fish, grasshopper
C. Wolf, grass, snake, tiger
D. Frog, snake, eagle, grass, grasshopper

Q.73 If a grasshopper is eaten by a frog, then the energy transfer will be from:
A. Producer to decomposer
B. Producer to primary consumer
C. Primary consumer to secondary consumer
D. Secondary consumer to primary consumer

Q.74 Which of the following is an abiotic component of an ecosystem?
A. Humus **B.** Bacteria **C.** Plants **D.** Fungi

Q.75 Which of the following chemicals causes depletion of the ozone layer?
A. Carbon tetrachloride
B. Methane
C. Chlorofluorocarbon
D. Carbon monoxide

Q.76 The condition for the stable equilibrium of a floating body is :
A. the metacentre should lie above the centre of gravity
B. the centre of buoyance and the centre of gravity must lie on the same vertical line
C. a righting couple should be formed
D. All of the above

Q.77 An object floats in water with one–third of its volume underwater. The density of the object is n times the density of water where n is:
A. $\frac{1}{6}$ **B.** $\frac{1}{3}$ **C.** $\frac{1}{4}$ **D.** 2

Q.78 Isotopes of an element contain:
A. the same number of protons but different number of neutrons
B. The same number of neutrons but different number of protons
C. Equal number of protons and electrons
D. Equal number of nucleons

Q.79 Nuclides which have the same mass number are called:
A. Isotopes **B.** Isobars **C.** Isotones **D.** Isomers

Q.80 The difference between the mass of a nucleus and the combined mass of its nucleons is:
A. zero
B. positive
C. negative
D. zero, positive or negative

Q.81 Thrust is a weak function of ___________
A. throat area **B.** chamber pressure
C. mass flow rate **D.** thrust coefficient

Q.82 A two-to-one thrust decrease can be achieved using _______ in a liquid propellant rocket engine.
A. throttle valves
B. gas pressure feed system
C. spark ignitor
D. using BATES grain

Q.83 Rutherford's alpha-particle scattering experiment was responsible for the discovery of:
A. Atomic Nucleus **B.** Electron
C. Proton **D.** Neutron

Q.84 Avogadro's number is the number of molecules present in:
A. 1 g of molecule **B.** 1 atom of molecule
C. 1 mole **D.** 1 litre of molecule

Q.85 Bee sting causes, severe pain and burning sensation due to the presence of:
A. Acetic acid **B.** Sulfuric acid
C. Citric acid **D.** Methanoic acid

Q.86 Which chemical is used in the manufacturing of chloroform?
A. Plaster of Paris **B.** Sodium Carbonate
C. Sodium bicarbonate **D.** Bleaching powder

Q.87 Motion of a tight thread when stretched and left will be _______.
A. circular **B.** vibrational
C. rotational **D.** linear

Q.88 The female sex hormone is:
A. estrogen **B.** androgen

C. insulin
D. oxytocin

Q.89 Which of the following is not a cell?

A. Red Blood Corpuscle (RBC)
B. Bacterium
C. Spermatozoa
D. Virus

Q.90 Gold and copper happen to absorb _____ and violet light, leaving yellow light.

A. green
B. blue
C. red
D. orange

Q.91 What phenomenon is responsible for twinkling of stars?

A. Diffraction
B. Refraction
C. Dispersion
D. Scattering of Light

Q.92 Speed of sound wave in air:

A. Increases with pressure
B. Decreases with increase in humidity
C. Increases with increase in humidity
D. Is independent of temperature

Q.93 A free fall in true sense occurs only _____.

A. In the sea
B. In the atmosphere
C. In air
D. In vacuum

Q.94 Which of the following does the de-Broglie wavelength depend on?

1. The velocity of the particle
2. Mass of the particle
3. Nature of the particle

A. Only 3
B. 1, 2 and 3
C. Only 2
D. Only 1 and 2

Q.95 The plant undergoes wilting, when:

A. Xylem is blocked.
B. Cambium is blocked.
C. Phloem is blocked.
D. Some roots are reduced in number.

Q.96 Apis is economically important as it produces:

A. Honey
B. Wax
C. Both (A) and (B)
D. None of the above

Q.97 Which of the following secretes honey?

A. Honey bee
B. Housefly
C. Lac insects
D. Mosquito

Q.98 Cultivation of fishes, oysters, shrimps and crabs come under ______.

A. Sericulture
B. Aquaculture
C. Silviculture
D. Pisciculture

Q.99 Major fish production from inland water is carried out through culture called:

A. Aquaculture
B. Sericulture
C. Apiculture
D. None of the above

Q.100 In absence of the earth's atmosphere, the sky will appear:

A. black
B. red
C. green
D. blue

// Smart Answer Sheet //

Correct Percentage of students who answered correctly. **Skipped** Percentage of students who skipped.

Q.	Ans.	Correct	Skipped	Q.	Ans.	Correct	Skipped	Q.	Ans.	Correct	Skipped	Q.	Ans.	Correct	Skipped	Q.	Ans.	Correct	Skipped	Q.	Ans.	Correct	Skipped
1	B	66.1 %	1.4 %	18	C	69.16 %	1.79 %	35	A	42.18 %	1.02 %	52	D	52.35 %	1.7 %	69	C	13.11 %	3.44 %	86	D	53.07 %	1.53 %
2	D	41.64 %	1.76 %	19	A	58.56 %	1.5 %	36	B	43.56 %	1.07 %	53	C	76.52 %	0.0 %	70	A	52.51 %	2.0 %	87	B	52.75 %	1.55 %
3	A	84.91 %	0.0 %	20	C	63.79 %	1.8 %	37	A	88.67 %	0.0 %	54	C	87.36 %	0.0 %	71	A	61.57 %	1.31 %	88	A	68.19 %	1.23 %
4	C	84.86 %	0.0 %	21	B	61.31 %	1.0 %	38	B	84.08 %	0.0 %	55	C	44.94 %	1.62 %	72	C	30.49 %	3.36 %	89	D	43.27 %	1.32 %
5	D	23.47 %	4.07 %	22	B	61.74 %	1.94 %	39	D	54.71 %	1.87 %	56	D	81.68 %	0.0 %	73	C	77.2 %	0.0 %	90	B	47.45 %	1.79 %
6	B	49.92 %	1.76 %	23	B	55.7 %	1.78 %	40	B	87.35 %	0.0 %	57	B	47.33 %	1.06 %	74	A	55.69 %	1.2 %	91	B	63.12 %	1.58 %
7	B	48.56 %	1.17 %	24	D	43.07 %	1.64 %	41	B	16.68 %	3.19 %	58	A	60.92 %	1.32 %	75	C	87.69 %	0.0 %	92	C	53.24 %	1.07 %
8	A	64.29 %	1.12 %	25	C	67.58 %	1.76 %	42	B	62.6 %	1.86 %	59	C	59.69 %	1.92 %	76	D	65.02 %	1.21 %	93	D	48.82 %	1.74 %
9	A	54.98 %	1.33 %	26	D	68.97 %	1.54 %	43	C	65.75 %	1.03 %	60	A	66.94 %	1.7 %	77	B	49.9 %	1.64 %	94	D	53.03 %	1.9 %
10	C	19.43 %	4.4 %	27	D	46.95 %	1.51 %	44	A	77.7 %	0.0 %	61	D	59.6 %	1.01 %	78	A	47.19 %	1.41 %	95	A	65.96 %	1.16 %
11	C	27.55 %	4.42 %	28	B	46.62 %	1.58 %	45	B	43.37 %	1.98 %	62	B	42.83 %	1.54 %	79	D	66.12 %	1.02 %	96	C	41.86 %	1.9 %
12	B	46.07 %	1.08 %	29	B	85.39 %	0.0 %	46	C	64.24 %	1.22 %	63	A	50.48 %	1.88 %	80	C	42.79 %	1.39 %	97	A	63.04 %	1.51 %
13	B	53.82 %	1.6 %	30	B	54.26 %	1.3 %	47	C	88.96 %	0.0 %	64	B	67.3 %	1.75 %	81	D	48.42 %	1.82 %	98	B	69.91 %	1.23 %
14	B	16.84 %	4.13 %	31	C	55.69 %	1.45 %	48	C	26.4 %	4.99 %	65	B	42.97 %	1.58 %	82	A	44.81 %	1.91 %	99	A	40.73 %	1.18 %
15	D	50.96 %	1.54 %	32	A	58.51 %	1.75 %	49	C	83.12 %	0.0 %	66	B	89.03 %	0.0 %	83	A	54.6 %	1.06 %	100	A	44.12 %	1.24 %
16	D	86.88 %	0.0 %	33	A	48.58 %	1.35 %	50	A	45.67 %	1.12 %	67	C	84.58 %	0.0 %	84	C	42.47 %	1.08 %				
17	D	58.37 %	1.34 %	34	B	68.32 %	1.26 %	51	C	40.19 %	1.23 %	68	A	45.29 %	1.82 %	85	D	68.16 %	1.17 %				

//Hints and Solutions//

1. The quantization of the photons means that photons are discrete energy parcels.

- These parcels are massless particles of definite energy, a definite momentum, and definite spin.
- The quantization of the photons means that photons are discrete energy parcels.
- Quantization means they exist in discrete particles with each discrete particle has a different energy, different momentum, etc.

Hence, the correct option is (B).

2. According to wave-particle duality, the De Broglie wavelength is a wavelength manifested in all the objects in quantum mechanics which determines the probability density of finding the object at a given point of the configuration space. The de Broglie wavelength of a particle is inversely proportional to its momentum. Therefore momentum remain the same.

Hence, the correct option is (D).

3. The process of a solid becoming a liquid is called melting. Melting is a physical process that results in the phase transition of a substance from a solid to a liquid.

Hence, the correct option is (A).

4. When heat is given to any substance, its temperature increases and it expands. Its expansion depends on the increase in its temperature. During the melting of solid, all the heat given to the solid spend in the change of state from solid to liquid. That's why the temperature of the material does not change.

Hence, the correct option is (C).

5. Neon gas produces red light when electricity is passed through it.

Electric discharge in gases occurs when electric current flows through a gaseous medium due to the ionization of the gas.

Gas	Colour
Hydrogen	Blue-violet
Helium	Pink-orange
Neon	Red
Argon	Violet
Krypton	Lavender
Oxygen	Blue-violet
Mercury	Blue-violet
Xenon	Blue
Water	Vapour Pink

Hence, the correct option is (D).

6. The states of matter having no definite shape but definite volume is Liquid.

Gases do not have definite shape or volume, liquids have definite volume but no definite shape and solids have definite shape and volume. Water is a liquid hence it has definite volume but no definite shape.

Hence, the correct option is (B).

7. Surface tension is a property of water can be used to explain the spherical shape of rain droplets.

Surface tension depends mainly upon the forces of attraction between the particles within the given liquid and also upon the gas, solid, or liquid in contact with it. The molecules in a drop of water, for example, attract each other weakly. Water molecules well inside the drop may be thought of as being attracted equally in all directions by the surrounding molecules.

Hence, the correct option is (B).

8. Given,

The energy of a hydrogen atom in the ground state $= -13.6eV$

Atomic number of helium $Z = 2$

$n = 2$

The energy of He^+ ion in the first excited state is,

$$E_n = -13.6\left(\frac{Z^2}{n^2}\right)$$

$$= (-13.6)\left(\frac{4}{4}\right)$$

$$= -13.6eV$$

Hence, the correct option is (A).

9. ${}_Z^AX$, where A stands for the atomic mass number which is the sum of protons and neutrons in the atom of an element and Z stands for an atomic number of the element which is the number of electrons in an atom of an element.

Atomic mass $=$ Number of protons $+$ Number of neutrons

Atomic number $=$ Number of protons $=$ Number of electrons

Therefore, atomic mass $= 15 + 16 = 31$ and atomic number is $= 15$

Hence, the correct option is (A).

10. Option C is false. Bohr theory could not explain the Zeeman effect. In presence of magnetic field, each spectral line gets split up into fine lines, the phenomenon, is known as Zeeman effect.

Option A is true. Bohr gave the theory of fixed orbits, which was contradictory to Heisenberg's theory.

Option B is true. The electrons can only orbit stably, without radiating, in certain orbits (called by Bohr the "stationary orbits") at a certain discrete set of distances from the nucleus. These orbits are associated with definite energies and are also called energy shells or energy levels. In these orbits, the electron's acceleration does not result in radiation and energy loss as required by classical electromagnetics. The Bohr model of an atom was based upon Planck's quantum theory of radiation.

Hence, the correct option is (B).

11. Methyl magnesium bromide is CH_3MgX and falls in the category of Grignard Reagents.

The methyl group bears a partial negative charge and the metal bears a partial positive charge.

Ketones react with a Grignard reagent to give tertiary alcohols as addition products.

Aldehydes give secondary alcohol and formaldehyde gives primary alcohol.

The reaction is a step-up reaction as the number of carbon atoms increases in the product.

The reaction of acetone with methyl magnesium halide is given as follows:

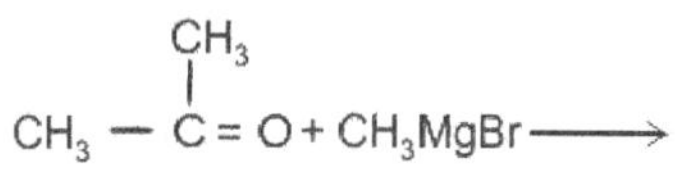

Acetone

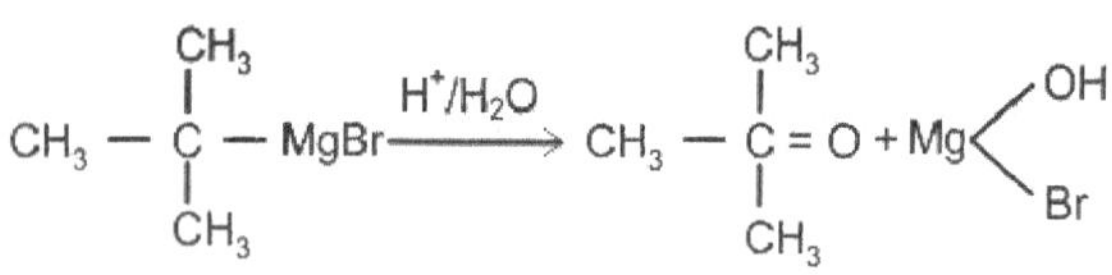

Addition product t-Butyl alcohol

The product of the reaction is tertiary butyl alcohol.

Hence, tertiary butyl alcohol is obtained by the action of methyl magnesium bromide on acetone CH_3COCH_3.

Hence, the correct option is (C).

12. Addition reaction:

Unsaturated hydrocarbons such as alkenes add Hydrogen in the presence of catalysts such as Ni to form saturated hydrocarbons. This is called an addition reaction.

The reaction is commonly used in the hydrogenation of vegetable oils using a Nickel catalyst.

The reaction is:

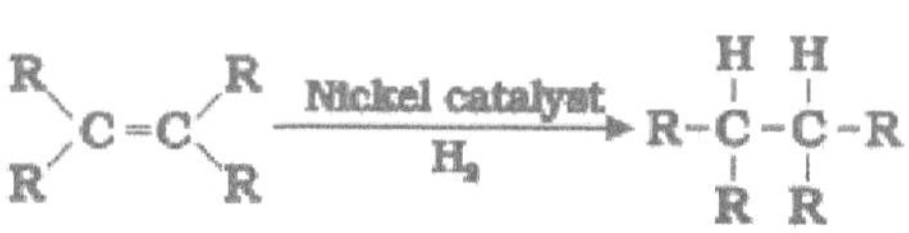

Benzene and Other aromatic hydrocarbons do not give most of the addition reactions as shown by aliphatic unsaturated hydrocarbons.

This is because of the extra stability of the benzene ring due to the presence of delocalized π electrons.

However, they have the tendency to give some of the reactions such as halogenation, hydrogenation, and addition of Ozone.

Benzene reacts with Hydrogen in the presence of a catalyst such as Rhodium, platinum, or Raney Nickel to form Cyclohexane.

In the reaction, 3 moles of hydrogen is added to the double bonds to yield saturation.

The reaction is:

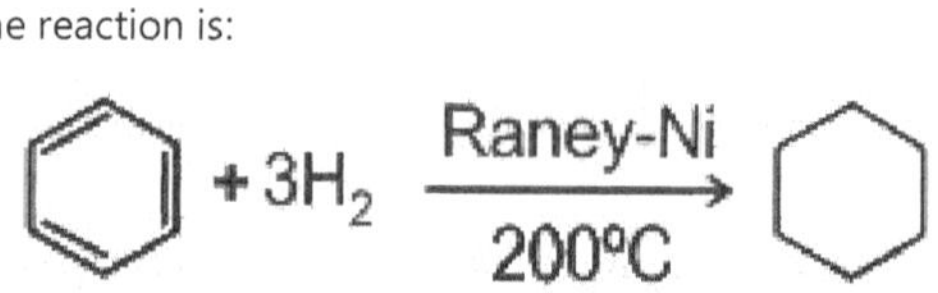

Benzene Cyclohexane

Thus, Benzene reacts with H_2 in presence of Ni at 200°C to give Cyclohexane.

Hence, the correct option is (B).

13. Benzene reacts with Carbon monoxide and HCl gas to undergo formylation of benzene.

The electrophile here is H-C(+)=O and the reaction is an electrophilic substitution reaction.

The reaction is called the Gatterman Koch reaction and the reaction proceeds as follows:

The first step is the generation of the electrophile.

The second step is the donation of the pi-electron density of benzene to the electrophile.

The aromatic ring is finally regenerated in the last step.

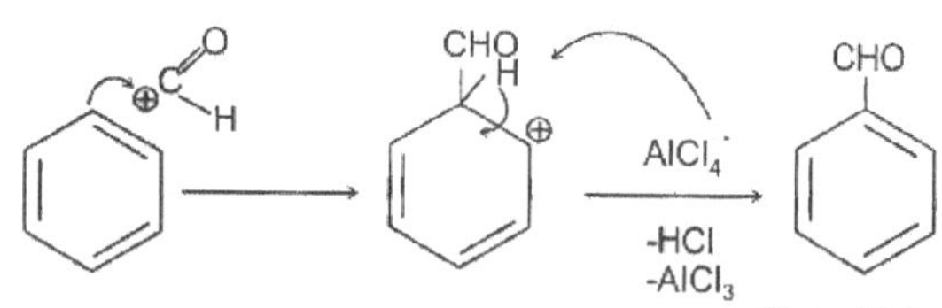

(Benzaldehyde)

The net reaction is the formation of benzaldehyde.

Thus, Benzene reacts with CO and HCl under pressure to form C_6H_5CHO.

Hence, the correct option is (B).

14. 2 - acetoxybenzoic acid is commonly known as aspirin.

It is prepared by the reaction of acetylation of salicylic acid which is o-hydroxybenzoic acid. It can be achieved by the reaction of salicylic acid with acetic acid in presence of catalyst acids.

However, the yield is low when acetic acid is used and it can be replaced by acetic anhydride which gives a comparatively much higher yield.

The acetylation of the phenol group of salicylic acid occurs giving the product Acetylsalicylic acid commonly known as aspirin.

The reaction is:

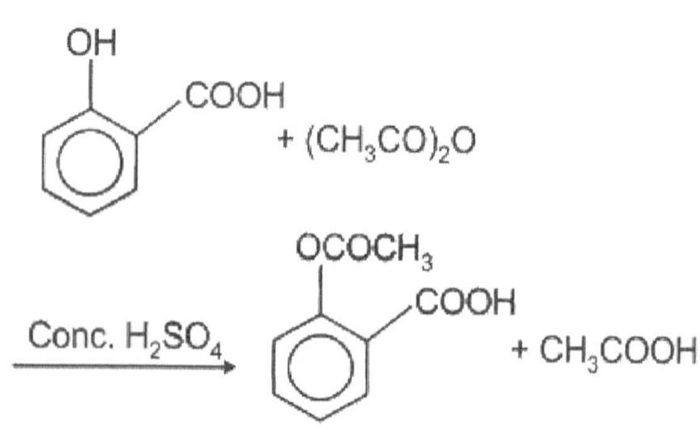

2-Acetoxy benzoic acid

Thus, Aspirin is an acetylation product of o-hydroxybenzoic acid or Salicylic acid.

Hence, the correct option is (B).

15. Certain hydrated salts when exposed to air at ordinary temperature lose their water of crystallisation either partially or completely, are called efflorescent salts. Efflorescence salts refers to the powdery white coat normally seen on brick and rocks surfaces. Magnesium sulphate, sodium sulfate decahydrate, calcium sulphate, sodium sulphate and carbonate all are the examples of efflorescent salts.

Hence, the correct option is (D).

16. The solutions which resist change in pH on dilution or with the addition of small amounts of acid or alkali are called buffer solutions. Buffer solutions of known pH can be prepared from the pK_a (strength of acid) of the acid or pK_b (strength of base) of base and by controlling the ratio of the salt and acid or salt and base. A mixture of acetic acid and sodium acetate acts as buffer solution around pH 4.75 and a mixture of ammonium chloride and ammonium hydroxide acts as a buffer around pH 9.25.

Hence, the correct option is (D).

17. Roasting: In roasting, the ore is heated in a regular supply of air in a furnace at a temperature below the melting point of the metal. Some of the reactions involving supplied ores are:

$$2ZnS + 3O_2 \rightarrow 2ZnO + 2SO_2$$

$$2PbS + 3O_2 \rightarrow 2PbO + 2SO_2$$

$$2Cu_2S + 3O_2 \rightarrow 2Cu_2O + 2SO_2$$

Hence, the correct option is (D).

18. Seawater is a complex mixture of 96.5 percent water, 2.5 percent salts(sodium chloride, magnesium chloride), and smaller amounts of other substances, including dissolved inorganic and organic materials, particulates, and a few atmospheric gases.

Hence, the correct option is (C).

19. CO_2 is produced during calcination. It involves heating when the volatile matter escapes leaving behind the metal oxide.

$$ZnCO_3(s) \xrightarrow{\Delta} ZnO(s) + CO_2(g)$$

$$CaCO_3 \cdot MgCO_3(s) \xrightarrow{\Delta} CaO(s) + MgO(s) + 2CO_2(g)$$

Hence, the correct option is (A).

20. I.U.P.A.C. name of $CH_3COOC_2H_5$ is Ethyl ethanoate. It is also known as Ethyl acetate.

Hence, the correct option is (C).

21. RCHO is the chemical formula of aldehyde. The organic compound obtained when a hydrogen atom is displaced by two hydrogen atoms attached to the final carbon in an alkane is called an aldehyde.

Hence, the correct option is (B).

22. Methane is a saturated hydrocarbon with single bonds between carbon and hydrogen atoms. There are four single bonds present in methane.

Hence, the correct option is (B).

23. Alkenes have a double bond between carbon atoms.

Alkanes have single bonds of carbon between atoms.

Alkynes have triple bonds of carbon between atoms.

Hence, the correct option is (B).

24. Lampbrush chromosome (immature eggs) of most animals, except mammals. Chromosomes transform into the lampbrush form during the diplotene stage of meiotic prophase I due to active transcription of many genes. They are highly extended meiotic half-bivalents, each consisting of 2 sister chromatids. Lampbrush chromosomes are also called diplotene chromosomes because they are formed during the diplotene stage of prophase1 of meiosis cell division due to the active transcription of many genes.
Hence, the correct option is (D).

25. The phragmoplast is a plant cell-specific structure that forms during late cytokinesis. It serves as a scaffold for cell plate assembly and subsequent formation of a new cell wall separating the two daughter cells.
Hence, the correct option is (C).

26. Sieve elements are specialized cells that are important for the function of phloem, which is a highly organized tissue that transports organic compounds made during photosynthesis. Sieve elements are the major conducting cells in phloem. Conducting cells aid in transport of molecules especially for long-distance signaling. In plant anatomy, there are two main types of sieve elements ts. Companion cells and sieve cells originate from meristems, which are tissues that actively divide throughout a plant's lifetime. They are similar to the development of xylem, a water conducting tissue in plants whose main function is also transportation in the plant vascular system.
Hence, the correct option is (D).

27. The smooth endoplasmic reticulum (smooth ER) is a membranous organelle found in most eukaryotic cells. Its functions include-

- Synthesis of Lipids, including cholesterol and phospholipids.
- Steroid Hormones.
- Storage and metabolism of calcium ions within the cell.
- One of the additional functions also includes detoxification of harmful metabolic byproducts/toxic substances.

Hence, the correct option is (D).

28. Prokaryotes are single-celled organisms that belong to the group of Bacteria and Archaea.

- They are smaller than Eukaryotic cells and have no nucleus, and lack major organelles. They also lack mitochondria.
- All prokaryotic cells are encased by a cell wall.
- They contain Plasma membrane, Ribosomes, Capsule, and Bacterial Flagellum for locomotion towards nutrients.

Hence, the correct option is (B).

29. Robert Hooke was the first to study and discover cells. He discovered it from a thin section of dead cork. The small honeycomb-like structures were named cells by him.

Robert Brown discovered the presence of a nucleus in a cell.

Leeuwenhoek was the first to observe cells under the microscope.

Rudolf Virchow proposed cells arising from pre-existing cells.

Hence, the correct option is (B).

30. Contractile proteins are found in muscle tissues. The contractile proteins are myosin and actin. They form thin and thick filaments that control skeletal muscle contraction and relaxation. Troponin and tropomyosin are regulatory proteins. Blood proteins are plasma proteins like albumin and globulin.

Hence, the correct option is (B).

31. Vegetative reproduction in Agave occurs through bulbils.

Bulbils are the specialised buds vegetative or floral that modify into a swollen structure. It seperates from the parent plant and on approach of favourable condition gives rise to new plant.

Hence, the correct option is (C).

32. Glycolysis is a part of cellular respiration and is common to both aerobic and anaerobic respiration. It occurs in the cytosol of the cells. It is an enzyme controlled 10 steps reaction by which glucose, fructose or sucrose is reduced to form 3 carbon compound pyruvate with the production of ATP and NADH.

Hence, the correct option is (A).

33. Carotene prevents photo-oxidation and destruction of chlorophyll.

Though chlorophyll is the major pigment responsible for trapping light, other thylakoid pigments like chlorophyll b, xanthophylls and carotenes (xanthophylls and carotenes are types of carotenoids), which are called accessory pigments, also absorb light and transfer the energy to chlorophyll a. Indeed, they not only enable a wider range of wavelength of incoming light to be utilized for photosynthesis but also protect chlorophyll a from photo-oxidation.

Hence, the correct option is (A).

34. There are two types of neurons, motor neurons and sensory neurons. Motor neurons carry signals from the brain to the peripheral body parts. Sensory neurons carry signals from the peripheral body parts to the brain. In the reflex action, there are two body parts involved effector and affector. The effector is the organ that responds once the motor neuron brings the interpreted response from the brain to the effector organ.

Hence, the correct option is (B).

35. Ethylene stimulates ripening of fruit such as tomatoes, lemons, oranges etc.

- It also increases the rate of respiration.
- It also regulate abscission and senescence.
- It is also responsible for breaking dormancy.

Hence, the correct option is (A).

36. The function of pituitary gland is to stimulate growth in all organs. The pituitary gland is an endocrine gland the size of a pea. The pituitary gland regulates hormone-secreting homeostasis, which includes tropic hormones that stimulate other endocrine glands. Functionally it is connected to the hypothalamus by a median bulge.

Hence, the correct option is (B).

37. Tropic moments can be defined as the growth moments in plants in which the direction of the external stimulus is a factor. For example, The growing movement towards the direction of the stimulus(light, heat, chemicals, etc) is known as positive tropism. The movement of the plant towards the stimulus is called Tropic.

Hence, the correct option is (A).

38. The cysts containing sticky gel-like substances in an ovary called Cystadenomas.

Cystadenomas can develop from cells on the outer surface of a woman's ovary. The cysts are many times filled with a thick and sticky gel or watery fluid. The cysts may become large, causing the woman pain.

Hence, the correct option is (B).

39. Shotgun cloning (also known as the shotgun method) is a method to duplicate genomic DNA. The DNA to be cloned is cut using a restriction enzyme or by randomly using a physical method to smash the DNA into small pieces. These fragments are then taken together and cloned into a vector.

Hence, the correct option is (D).

40. Sperm are produced in tightly coiled tubes inside of the testes called seminiferous tubules. The epididymis temporarily stores mature sperm cells. Each sperm cell has a flagellum for locomotion or movement. A tube called the vas deferens passes from each epididymis into the body.

Hence, the correct option is (B).

41. Variations that result from factors such as climate, food supply and actions of other organisms are called as somatic (phenotypic) variations. These variations are not due to differences in genes or chromosomes, and in general are not transmitted future generations. They do not have any significance in the process of evolution.

Hence, the correct option is (B).

42. Sex chromosomes are those that contain the genes for masculinity and femininity in humans.

In humans the sex chromosomes comprise one pair of the total of 23 pairs of chromosomes. The other 22 pairs of chromosomes are called autosomes.

Individuals having two X chromosomes (XX) are females; individuals having one X chromosome and one Y chromosome (XY) are males.

Hence, the correct option is (B).

43. The bacterium is still alive today in the places of today's heterogeneous environment. Bacteria are microscopic organisms that are usually unicellular. They are unicellular, cell walled, unicellular simple organisms and are found almost everywhere. Their size is only up to a few millimeters. The ancestors of modern bacteria were single-celled microorganisms, which originated 400 million years ago at the beginning of life on Earth. After this, for about 300 million years, there were only microorganisms in the name of life on earth. The main among them were bacteria and archaea.

Hence, the correct option is (C).

44. Archaeopteryx is an iconic fossil, often thought of as the 'missing-link' between dinosaurs and birds. It was first described in 1861 by the German paleontologist Hermann von Meyer (1801-1869). Since then Archaeopteryx has been the focus of controversy surrounding the origin of birds and their links with dinosaurs.

Hence, the correct option is (A).

45. A stone of same size as of ball has more inertia.

Inertia is defined as the natural tendency of an object to resist the change in its state of motion or rest. The mass of an object is a measure of its inertia.

The mass of the stone is more than the mass of the rubber ball. Therefore, stone of the same size as of ball have more inertia.

Hence, the correct option is (B).

46. A roller coaster is an example of a non- uniform accelerated motion.

Acceleration: The increase in the velocity of a moving body with time is called acceleration.

Now, there are two types of acceleration-

1) Uniform acceleration- The change in velocity is constant here. For example, if starting velocity is 5m/s , next will be 10m/s, then 15m/s and so on.

2) Non- uniform acceleration- The change in velocity is not constant as in uniform acceleration.

The velocity of a roller coaster changes randomly and this is a perfect example of non- uniform accelerated motion.

Hence, the correct option is (C).

47. Given:

$u = 0\ m/sec, s = 100\ m$ and $t = 20\text{sec}$

By the second equation of motion,

$$s = ut + \frac{1}{2}at^2$$

Where, $u =$ Initial velocity, $a =$ Acceleration, $t =$ time, and $s =$ Displacement covered

$$100 = (0 \times 20) + \frac{1}{2} \times a \times 20^2$$

$$\Rightarrow 100 = 200a$$

$$\Rightarrow a = 0.5\ m/sec^2$$

By the first equation of motion the velocity gained by the car in 30 seconds,

$$V = u + at$$

$$\Rightarrow V = 0 + (0.5 \times 30)$$

$$\Rightarrow V = 15\ m/sec$$

Hence, the correct option is (C).

48. In the case of Uniform Circular Motion, the work done by the centripetal force is zero.

Circular Motion: Circular motion is a movement of an object along the circumference of a circle or rotation along a circular path. The force acts continuously at right angles to the velocity of the particle.

Uniform circular motion: The circular motion in which the speed of the particle remains constant is called uniform circular motion. In a uniform circular motion, force supplies the centripetal acceleration.

If the Force F acts on a body and it gets displaced by a distance of S, the work done in that case is given by:

$$W = FS\cos\theta$$

In the case of uniform circular motion, $\cos 90° = 0$ and that is why $W = 0$ (The force and displacement are perpendicular to each other).

Hence, the correct option is (C).

49. Newton's first law of motion is also known as the Law of inertia.

Law of inertia: It states that an object at rest remains at rest, and an object in motion remains in motion at a constant speed and in a straight line unless acted on by an unbalanced force. This tendency to resist changes in a state of motion is inertia.

Hence, the correct option is (C).

50. Galileo's law of inertia: A body moving with a certain speed along a straight path will continue to move at the same speed along the same straight path in the absence of the external field.
Newton's First law:

Newton's First Law stated that a body continues to be in its state of rest or of uniform motion along a straight line unless it is acted upon by some external force to change the state.

If no net force acts on a body, then the velocity of the body cannot change i.e. the body cannot accelerate.

From above it is clear that, Galileo's law of inertia was Newton's starting point which he formulated as the 'First Law of motion'.

Hence, the correct option is (A).

51. Acceleration due to gravity (g):

- The force of attraction exerted by the earth on a body is called gravitational pull or gravity.
- We know that when a force acts on a body, it produces acceleration.
- Therefore, a body under the effect of gravitational pull must accelerate.
- Acceleration due to gravity at the surface of the earth is given by:

$$\Rightarrow g = \frac{GM}{R^2}$$

- As Earth is elliptical in shape i.e., it is flattened at the poles and bulged out at the equator, due to which the equatorial radius is about 21 km longer than the polar radius.

- As the polar radius is smaller than the equatorial radius, therefore the acceleration due to gravity is maximum at poles and **minimum at the equator.**

Hence, the correct option is (C).

52. Satellite going round the earth in a circular orbit loses some energy due to collision. Its speed is v and distance from the earth is d will decrease, v will increase.

Given that, the particle lost some energy due to a collision. So, it can no longer continue in that orbit as the earth's gravitational force is more than centripetal force. Due to this, the distance d decreases gradually and the particle moves towards earth at certain accelaration gaining speed. Thus distance d decreases and speed v increases.

Hence, the correct option is (D).

53. If the horizontal velocity given to a satellite iS greater than the critical velocity but less than the escape velocity, then the satellite will start revolving in an elliptical orbit.

If the velocity of the projection is less than the critical velocity then the satellite moves in elliptical orbit, but the point of projection is apogee and in the orbit the satellite comes closer to the earth with its perigee point lying at $180°$.

Hence, the correct option is (C).

54. The universal law of gravitation gives the gravitational force between any two bodies having some mass.

The gravitational force between any two bodies having some mass can be determined from Newton's law of gravitation.

The force of attraction between bodies is directly proportional to the product of their masses and inversely proportional to the square of the distance between them.

This force is applied in the direction of the line joining the two bodies.

$$F = G\frac{Mm}{r^2}$$

Here, G is called the universal gravitational constant.

Hence, the correct option is (C).

55. Work energy theorem: Work done by net force acting on the particle is equal to change in kinetic energy So,

Work done $= (KE)_{\text{final}} - (KE)_{\text{initial}} = \Delta KE$

From the above definition it is clear that work done by net force is the reason to change the kinetic energy of particle.

Hence, the correct option is (C).

56. The correct sentence is that work has only magnitude but no direction.

- Work is done when the body moves with the application of external force or the moving body stop after the external force applied.
- Work done is the dot product of force and displacement.
- W = F × d
  a. Where F = force applied
  b. d = displacement
- The dot product of vector quantities is always scalar which means work is having only magnitude but no direction.

Hence, the correct option is (D).

57. Water stored in a dam possesses Potential energy.

Potential energy is a form of energy that results from an object's position or arrangement of parts. It is stored energy that can become kinetic energy. The measurement of potential energy in an object is calculated based on the object's mass and its height or distance.

Hence, the correct option is (B).

58. When you compress a spring, it possess potential energy. The force of compression is proportional to the compression, according to Hooke's Law. Releasing the spring turns the potential energy into kinetic energy. The spring can be then used to propel some object.

Hence, the correct option is (A).

59. At a particular temperature, sound propagates in iron at the fastest speed.

The term "speed of sound" refers to the distance sound waves travels per unit of time as it propagates through a medium. So, sound, in order to travel always, needs a medium for its propagation. The speed of sound is thus determined by the properties of the medium in which the dissemination occurs.

Hence, the correct option is (C).

60. The amplitude of the sound wave determines its loudness.

A louder sound is represented by a larger amplitude. A softer sound indicates a smaller amplitude. Due to the larger amplitude, there is a more energetic vibration. The sensitivity of the ear also determines the loudness of a sound.

Hence, the correct option is (A).

61. To hear a distinct echo each time interval between the original sound and the reflected sound must be 0.1 Seconds of time. The human ear cannot distinguish between two sounds if they came at a time interval of fewer than 0.1 seconds. This is the Average time period as it varies from person to person.

Hence, the correct option is (D).

62. The function of MCB Is close to the function of a fuse. A fuse is a safety device that prevents damages to electrical circuits and possible fires. Fuse comprises Wires made from some special materials that melt quickly and break when large electric currents are passed through them.

The function of MCB is close to the function of a Fuse as both are the devices that provide protection to the electrical circuit when the current in the electrical circuit is more than the permissible limit.

Both the devices break the loop of the circuit whenever there is an extreme supply of current, this ensures the protection of the electric appliances.

Hence, the correct option is (B).

63. The objective of earthing in houses is to provide as low resistance as possible for conduction of current to the ground.

Earthing:

- Ground or earth is the reference point in an electrical circuit from which voltages are measured, it provides a common return path for electric current, thus Earthing is done by fitting an earth wire from the electronic tool to the ground.
- Earthing is used to connect specific parts of an electric power device with the ground, typically the Earth's conductive surface, for safety and operative purpose.
- An earth wire ensures a very low resistance path for the current to flow through it to the ground and therefore, it restricts the person from getting a shock.

Hence, the correct option is (A).

64. A galvanometer can be converted into a volt meter by connecting a high resistance in series.

Galvanometer:

- A galvanometer is an instrument used for detecting and indicating the presence of an electric current.
- A galvanometer is a sensitive device and can detect only a very small current of the order of $100mA$.
- Full-scale deflection of galvanometer refers to the maximum reading available on the meter. Anything beyond this scale cannot be measured by this instrument.
- In order to convert, Galvanometer into a voltmeter, a high resistance R is connected in series with it.
- The equivalent resistance of the combination $= G + R$, where $G =$ resistance of galvanometer.

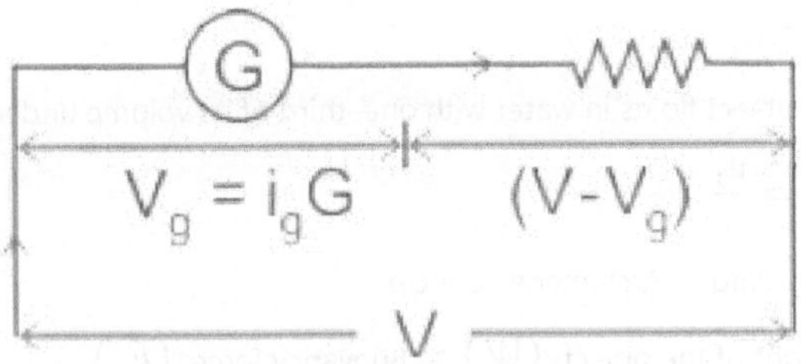

Hence, the correct option is (B).

65. Given that:

Current (I) = 0.6 A

Time (t) = 6 mins $= 6 \times 60$ sec

Electric charge = Current × Time

$Q = I \times t$

$Q = 0.6 \times 6 \times 60$ C

$Q = 216$ C

Hence, the correct option is (B).

66. An electric motor is an electrical machine that converts electrical energy into mechanical energy. The reverse of this is the conversion of mechanical energy into electrical energy and is done by an electric generator, which has much in common with a motor.

Hence, the correct option is (B).

67. According to Lenz's law, when a closed coil is linked with a varying magnetic flux, then some current is induced in the coil.

So, when a magnet is taken towards a circular coil, then a varying magnetic flux is linked with the coil so that current is induced in the coil. This phenomenon is said to be electromagnetic induction.

Hence, the correct option is (C).

68. Hans Christian Oersted was a Danish Physicist who discovered that electric current can create magnetic fields which was the first connection between electricity and magnetism. The wire will carry a current that creates a magnetic field around itself. Bringing the compass near the wire or in the loop will cause the compass needle to move. The current had produced a magnetic field strong enough to cause the compass needle to turn.

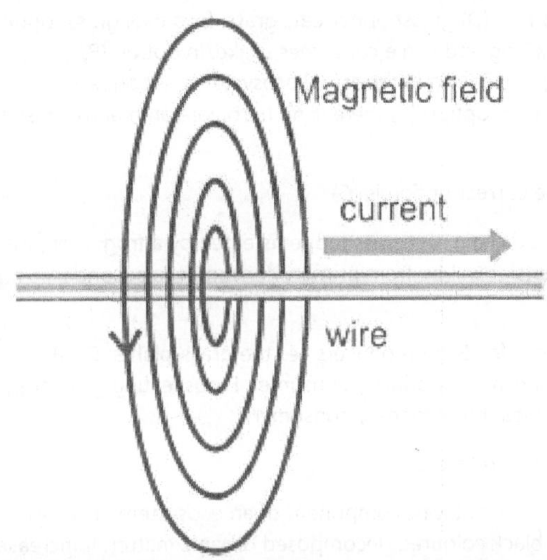

Hence, the correct option is (A).

69. When a current-carrying conductor is exposed to an external magnetic field, it is subjected to a force that is perpendicular to both the field and the current flow direction. John Ambrose Fleming was the one who came up with the idea. In this rule a left hand may be held in such a way that the thumb, forefinger, and middle finger serve three mutually orthogonal axes.

When the thumb, centre finger, and forefinger of the left hand are arranged at right angles to one another, the thumb points in the direction of magnetic power, the centre finger points in the direction of current, and the forefinger points in the direction of a magnetic field.

So, the magnetic field is from south to north, and electrons are travelling upwards, but we can consider the conventional direction, which is downwards, so we can deflate the beam to the west using the left hand thumb law.

Hence, the correct option is (C).

70. Seismic waves are waves of energy that travel through Earth's layers and are a result of earthquakes, volcanic eruptions, magma movement, large landslides and large man-made explosions that give out low-frequency acoustic energy. Many other natural and anthropogenic sources create low-amplitude waves commonly referred to as ambient vibrations. Seismic waves are studied by geophysicists called seismologists. Seismic wave fields are recorded by a seismometer, hydrophone (in water), or accelerometer.

Hence, the correct option is (A).

71. Halos are caused by the diffraction of light.

A halo is an optical phenomenon produced by light interacting with ice crystals suspended in the atmosphere. Halos can have many forms, ranging from colored or white rings to arcs and spots in the sky. Seeing halos around lights is a result of diffraction, an effect that occurs when the light bends while entering the eye. Diffraction can sometimes be caused by glasses and contact lenses, but it can also be a disease's side effect.

Hence, the correct option is (A).

72. The organisms in an ecosystem are related through food requirements. This relationship is called food chain. In option (A) grass is eaten by rabbit, rabbit is consumed by wolf and lion eats wolf. In option (D) grasshopper eats grass, frog eats grasshopper, snake eats frog and eagle consumes snake. In option (B) grasshopper is found in terrestrial ecosystems not aquatic ecosystems. In option (C) there is no herbivore animal to consume grass.

Hence, the correct option is (C).

73. In a food chain, if a grasshopper is eaten by a frog, then the energy transfer will be from primary consumer to secondary consumer.

Grasshopper feeds on producers i.e., the grass/plants. So, it occupies the lavel of primary consumer. Frogs, eating grasshopper thus becomes the secondary consumer.

Hence, the correct option is (C).

74. Humus is an abiotic component of an ecosystem. It is dark brown or black coloured decomposed organic matter. It increases the fertility of soil.

Biotic Components: It includes producers, consumers and decomposers. All the living things that have a direct or indirect influence on other organisms in an environment. Ex- Plants, Animals, Microorganism etc.

Abiotic components: All the in-organic components of the ecosystem, non-living physical and chemical composition of nature are abiotic components. Ex- stones, water, Humus (organic waste), air etc.

Hence, the correct option is (A).

75. Chlorofluorocarbon causes depletion of the ozone layer.

Chlorofluorocarbons (CFCs) are nontoxic, nonflammable chemicals containing atoms of carbon, chlorine, and fluorine. They are used in the manufacture of aerosol sprays, blowing agents for foams and packing materials, as solvents, and as refrigerants. CFCs have destructive effects on the ozone layer.

Hence, the correct option is (C).

76. Condition of stable equilibrium for a floating body in terms of metacentric height (GM) as follows:

- Stable equilibrium : GM > 0 (M is above G)
- Neutral equilibrium : GM = 0 (M coinciding with G)
- Unstable equilibrium : GM < 0 (M is below G)
- Stable condition.

- The equilibrium of a floating body is stable if there is a righting moment to restore it to its original position whenever it is given a small angular displacement.
- In such equilibrium, the metacenter lies above the center of gravity i.e. metacentric height is positive.
- The external couple is balanced by the couple developed by the internal forces.

Unstable condition.

- The equilibrium of a floating body is said to be unstable if any small tilting of the body is accompanied by the development of forces or moments which tend to further increase the displacement of the body. In unstable equilibrium, the metacenter (M) lies below the center of gravity (G) i.e. the metacentric height is negative.
- External applied couple and couple developed due to internal forces acting in the same direction, thereby increasing the displacement and making the equilibrium unstable.

Neutral condition.

- The equilibrium of a body is said to be neutral when on the small tilting of the body, the body takes a new position. In this equilibrium, the metacenter and center of gravity coincide.
- As neither a righting moment nor an overturning moment acts on the body, the body remains at rest a new position.

Hence, the correct option is (D).

77. Given that:

The object floats in water with one–third of its volume underwater:

$$V_f = \frac{V_0}{3}$$

According to Archimedes principle:

Weight of the object (W) = Buoyancy force (F_b)

So $\rho_0 V_o g = \rho_f V_f g$

$$\rho_0 V_o g = \rho_f \left(\frac{V_0}{3}\right) g$$

The density of the object $(\rho_0) = \frac{1}{3} \times$ Density of fluid (ρ_f)

Hence, the correct option is (B).

78. Isotopes of an element must have same atomic number (Z) but different mass number A.

Number of protons is equal to the atomic number.

So, isotopes of an element have same number of protons.

Mass number is equal to the sum of number of protons and neutrons i.e. A=p+n

As isotopes of an element have different mass number but same number of protons, thus they must have different number of neutrons.

Hence, the correct option is (A).

79. Nuclides which have the same number of proton are called isotopes. When nuclides have same mass number are called isobars. When nuclides have same number of neutron are called isotones. When the elements have same molecular formula but have different arrangements of atom in space are called isomers.

Hence, the correct option is (D).

80. We know that mass defect = combined mass of nucleons – mass of the nucleus.

Since mass defect is always positive quantity so the difference of nucleus and the combined mass of its nucleons will be negative. The combined mass is greater than the mass of nucleus.

Hence, the correct option is (C).

81. Thrust is a weak function of thrust coefficient

Thrust is a weak function of thrust coefficient CF. It is in turn dependent on specific heat ratio, pressure ratio, expansion ratio, and altitude.

Hence, the correct option is (D).

82. A two-to-one thrust decrease can be achieved using throttle valves in a liquid propellant rocket engine.

Throttle valve helps in controlling the mass flow rate thereby reducing the thrust. It usually consists of a flow controlling unit and an electro-mechanical-actuator.

Hence, the correct option is (A).

83. Rutherford's alpha-particle scattering experiment was responsible for the discovery of the atomic nucleus.

Rutherford's alpha-particle scattering experiment:

- Ernest Rutherford was interested in knowing how the electrons are arranged within an atom. Rutherford designed an experiment for this.
- In this experiment, fast-moving alpha (α)-particles were made to fall on a thin gold foil.
- He selected a gold foil because he wanted as thin a layer as possible. This gold foil was about 1000 atoms thick.
- α-particles are doubly charged helium ions. Since they have a mass of 4 u, the fast-moving α-particles have a considerable amount of energy.
- It was expected that α-particles would be deflected by the sub-atomic particles in the gold atoms. Since the α-particles were much heavier than the protons, he did not expect to see large deflections.

On the basis of his experiment, Rutherford put forward the nuclear model of an atom, which had the following features:

- There is a positively charged centre in an atom called the nucleus. Nearly all the mass of an atom resides in the nucleus.
- The electrons revolve around the nucleus in circular paths.
- The size of the nucleus is very small as compared to the size of the atom.

Hence, the correct option is (A).

84. Avogadro's number is the number of molecules present in 1 mole.

The Avogadro constant is defined as the number of constituent particles per mole of a given substance. It is equal to 6.022×10^{23}.

Hence, the correct option is (C).

85. Bee sting causes, severe pain and burning sensation due to the presence of Methanoic acid.

- Bee sting venom contains proteins that affect skin cells and the immune system, causing pain and swelling around the sting area.
- Histamine makes up 0.9% of the sting and causes itching and pain at the site of the sting.
- The acids present, which include formic, hydrochloric and orthophosphoric acids are also present in the sting.
- Formic acid is also known as Methanoic acid.
- If a person is allergic, the bee sting will cause the immune system to produce a type of antibody called immunoglobulin E (IgE).
- Usually, IgE protects the body from dangerous substances, such as viruses and parasites.
- However, in response to a sting, the body produces IgE that then causes inappropriate immune responses, such as hives, swelling, and respiratory problems the next time a person is stung.

Hence, the correct option is (D).

86. Bleaching powder chemical is used in the manufacturing of chloroform.

- Bleaching powder is calcium oxychloride.
- The chemical formulae of bleaching powder are $CaOCl_2$.
- It is also called chloride of lime.
- Bleaching powder is used for bleaching cotton and linen in the textile industry and for bleaching wood pulp in the paper industry.
- It is also used for bleaching washed clothes in the laundry.
- Bleaching powder is used for disinfecting the drinking water supply. That is, for making drinking water free from germs.
- A mixture of bleaching powder ($CaOCl_2$) is heated with ethanol or acetone to prepare chloroform in the laboratory.
- Bleaching powder acts as an oxidizing chlorinating and hydrolyzing agent.
- Bleaching powder is used for making wool unshrinkable.
- Bleaching powder is used as an oxidizing agent in many chemical industries.

Hence, the correct option is (D).

87. Motion of a tight thread when stretched and left will be vibrational.

- When a tight string is stretched, we can see the string is moving up and down at a very fast speed.
- It may be so fast, that we cannot predict the exact location of the string for a while.
- This type of phenomenon is called vibration and such motion is called vibrational motion.
- This can also be observed while playing the guitar.
- The guitar strings vibrate when pulled while playing it.

Hence, the correct option is (B).

88. The female sex hormone is estrogen.

Hormones are chemical messengers that the endocrine glands produce & release directly into the bloodstream.

- Hormones help regulate many bodily processes, such as hunger, sleep, and growth.

Sex hormones play an essential role in sexual development and reproduction.

- The main glands that produce sex hormones are the adrenal glands and the gonads.
- It includes the ovaries in females and testes in males.

Hence, the correct option is (A).

89. Virus is not a cell.

The virus is an acellular microscopic infection-causing agent. It has only a protein cover and a nucleic acid (either DNA or RNA). These are intracellular parasites that depend upon the host for nutrition.

Hence, the correct option is (D).

90. Gold and copper happen to absorb blue and violet light, leaving yellow light in the spectrum.

- So gold and copper are yellowish in colour.
- The only two non-silvery metals in the world are gold and copper.
- A metal is defined as an element that readily forms positive ions (cations) and has metallic bonds.
- These elements have electrons that are loosely held to the atoms, and will readily transfer them.
- Most metals' electrons reflect all colours equally which are in the visible spectrum of light.
- So those metals appear as white silver.

Hence, the correct option is (B).

91. Refraction phenomenon is responsible for twinkling of stars.

- The starlight, on entering the earth's atmosphere, undergoes refraction continuously before it reaches the earth's surface.
- The atmosphere bends starlight towards the normal, the apparent position of the star is slightly different from its actual position.
- The star appears slightly higher (above) than its actual position when viewed near the horizon.
- This apparent position of the star is not stationary but keeps on changing slightly since the physical conditions of the earth's atmosphere are not stationary.
- As the path of rays of light coming from the star goes on varying slightly, the apparent position of the star fluctuates and the amount of starlight entering the eye flickers – the star sometimes appears brighter and at some other time, fainter, which is the twinkling effect.

Hence, the correct option is (B).

92. Speed of sound wave in air Increases with increase in humidity.

Effect of humidity:

$$\Rightarrow v = \sqrt{\frac{\gamma P}{\rho}} \Rightarrow v \propto \frac{1}{\sqrt{\rho}}$$

- The density of air varies with the relative humidity. When the amount of moisture in the air increases the amount of oxygen and nitrogen per unit volume in the air decreases. Thus, the mass of air per unit volume decreases, and as a result the density of air decreases.
- As the humidity increases, the density of air decreases which increases the velocity of sound.
- Therefore, as humidity increases the speed of sound also increases.

Hence, the correct option is (C).

93. A free fall in true sense occurs only In vacuum.

- A fall is considered as a free fall if only force acting on it was gravity.
- As the vacuum contains no matter, there is no opposite force against the free fall due to gravity.
- In air and atmosphere, there is aerodynamic drag and in the sea, there is a buoyancy force of water to oppose the movement due to gravity.

Hence, the correct option is (D).

94. The de-Broglie wavelength (λ) is given by

$$\lambda = \frac{h}{mv}$$

Where m is the mass of the particle

v is the velocity of the particle

As can be seen from the relation,

The de-Broglie wavelength is inversely proportional to the mass of the particle and its velocity but is independent of the nature of the particle.

Hence, the correct option is (D).

95. The plant undergoes wilting, when Xylem is blocked.

- Xylem tracheids and vessels are the most important tissues involved in the transport of water in plants.
- In case xylem is blocked, then water transport will be hindered.
- This will lead to the reduction or lack of water supply to the different parts of the plant.

- As a result the turgor pressure gradually reduces. This will lead to the loss of rigidity of cells and ultimately wilting.
- So, the leaves will droop down or wilt, causing the entire plant to wilt and die.

Hence, the correct option is (A).

96. Apis is economically important as it produces honey, wax.

Apis mellifera and A. cerena are the species of honey bee and are economically very important as they have the high yielding capacity. They are used for the production of both honey and wax. Honey is the complex substance made when the nectar and sweet deposits from plants and trees are gathered, modified, and stored in the honeycomb by honey bees as a food source for the colony.

Hence, the correct option is (C).

97. Honey bee secretes honey.

Honey is a sweet food made by honeybees using nectar from flowers. The other main product of honey bees is beeswax.

Hence, the correct option is (A).

98. The cultivation of fishes, oysters, shrimps, and crabs comes under aquaculture.

- Sericulture is the culture and rearing of silkworms.
- Silviculture is the practice of controlling the growth, composition/structure, and quality of forests to meet values and needs, specifically timber production.
- Pisciculture is the culture of only fishes for commercial production.

Hence, the correct option is (B).

99. Major fish production from inland water is carried out through culture called aquaculture.

Aquaculture (less commonly spelled aquiculture), also known as aquafarming, is the controlled cultivation ("farming") of aquatic organisms such as fish, crustaceans, mollusks, algae and other organisms of value such as aquatic plants (e.g. lotus).

Hence, the correct option is (A).

100. In absence of the earth's atmosphere, the sky will appear black.

- If earth were deprived of atmosphere, the absence of atmosphere and molecules of air would lead to no scattering of sunlight.
- The sky would look pitch dark/black with bright stars and sun. Sun would appear white and brighter in the dark background.

Hence, the correct option is (A).

Mock Test 04

Q.1 Which of these choices will not change the state of matter?

A. Temperature **B.** Heat

C. Pressure **D.** Crushing a crystal

Q.2 The scale of temperature in which the temperature is only positive is:

A. Farenheit **B.** Celcius

C. Kelvin **D.** All of the above

Q.3 Out of the following, an example of matter which can be termed as fluid is _______.

A. Carbon **B.** Sulphur

C. Oxygen **D.** Phosphorus

Q.4 The common characteristics of solid and liquid states are _______.

A. Both have fixed shape

B. Both have fixed volume

C. Both are rigid

D. Both have maximum force of attraction

Q.5 Calculate (a) wavenumber and (b) frequency of yellow radiation having wavelength $5800Å$.

A. $1.724 \times 10^2\ cm^{-1}$, 5.172×10^{10} Hz

B. $2.724 \times 10^4\ cm^{-1}$, 5.172×10^{14} Hz

C. $5.724 \times 10^4\ cm^{-1}$, 5.172×10^{14} Hz

D. $1.724 \times 10^4\ cm^{-1}$, 5.172×10^{14} Hz

Q.6 A 100 watt bulb emits monochromatic light of wavelength $400\ nm$. Calculate the number of photons emitted per second by the bulb.

A. $3 \times 10^{20}\ s^{-1}$ **B.** $2.012 \times 10^{20}\ s^{-1}$

C. $5 \times 10^{20}\ s^{-1}$ **D.** $2.012 \times 10^{19}\ s^{-1}$

Q.7 In the lowest energy level of hydrogen atom, electron has an angular momentum equal to:

A. $\frac{\pi}{h}$ **B.** $\frac{h}{\pi}$ **C.** $\frac{h}{2\pi}$ **D.** $\frac{2\pi}{h}$

Q.8 The atomic numbers of elements X, Y and Z are 19, 21 and 25 respectively. The order of number of electrons present in the M shells of these elements _____.

A. $Z > X > Y$ **B.** $X > Y > Z$

C. $Z > Y > X$ **D.** $Y > Z > X$

Q.9 Notice the equation $PbO + HCl \rightarrow PbCl_2 + H_2O$

The balance of the above equation requires__________ moles of HCl.

A. 1 **B.** 4 **C.** 2 **D.** 3

Q.10 Manganese is extracted by heating manganese dioxide with aluminum powder. Which one of the following statements with regard to the reaction is correct?

A. The reaction is exothermic.

B. The reaction is endothermic.

C. Manganese is produced as a solid.

D. Manganese is more reactive than aluminium.

Q.11 Iron nails become _____ after being dipped in copper sulphate solution.

A. greenish **B.** brownish

C. greyish **D.** bluish

Q.12 When Sulphur Dioxide is dissolved in Water __________ is formed.

A. Sulphur Trioxide **B.** Sulphur Pentaoxide

C. Hydrochloric acid **D.** Sulfurous Acid

Q.13 Why is calamine solution rubbed over an area of ant bite?

A. Because calamine solution is antiseptic.

B. Because calamine solution is anti-allergic.

C. Because calamine solution is antacid.

D. Because calamine solution is antibiotic.

Q.14 Sodium carbonate is a basic salt because it is a salt of:

A. Strong acid and strong base

B. Strong acid and weak base

C. Weak acid and strong base

D. Weak acid and weak base

Q.15 Sodium hydrogen carbonate when added to acetic acid evolves a gas. Which of the following statements are true about the gas evolved?

(1) It turns lime water milky.

(2) It extinguishes a burnings splinter.

(3) It dissolves in a solution of sodium hydroxide.

(4) It has a pungent odour.

A. (1) and (2) **B.** (1), (2) and (3)

C. (2), (3) and (4) **D.** (1) and (4)

Q.16 Which of the following indicators are used in non-aqueous titrations?

A. Crystal Violet indicator

B. Thymol Blue indicator

C. Both (A) and (B)

D. Quinaldine blue

Q.17 Which non-metal is stored under water at room temperature due to its high reactivity?

A. Chlorine **B.** Phosphorus

C. Carbon **D.** Sulphur

Q.18 All of the following compounds are non-ionic, except:

A. Calcium chloride **B.** Sodium chloride

C. Potassium chloride **D.** Water

Q.19 Bronze is made by mixing ______ and ______ to manufacture coins, turbines, blades, etc.

A. 82% copper, 18% tin

B. 88% copper, 12% tin

C. 88% copper, 12% iron

D. 82% copper, 18% iron

Q.20 What happens when copper chloride is electrolysed?

A. Copper chloride is broken down to form copper.

B. Chlorine gas is formed.

C. It turns black in colour.

D. Both (A) and (B)

Q.21 In graphite, each carbon atom is bonded to three other carbon atoms:

[Officers Training Academy (OTA), 2019], [Indian Military Academy (IMA), 2019]

A. Forming a three-dimensional structure

B. In the same plane giving a hexagonal array

C. In the same plane giving a square array

D. In the same plane giving a pentagonal array

Q.22 Priya is writing some statements, choose the incorrect statement and help her:

A. The unsaturated hydrocarbons (having double bonds or triple bonds between the carbon atoms) are less reactive than saturated hydrocarbons.

B. The ethane molecule (C_2H_6) is made up of 2 carbon atoms and 6 hydrogen atoms.

C. The simplest alkyne is ethyne having the molecular formula C_2H_2.

D. An unsaturated hydrocarbon in which the two carbon atoms are connected by a triple bond is called an alkyne.

Q.23 Name of the hydrocarbon group having double bond between carbon atoms is ______.

A. Alkane **B.** Alkene

C. Alkyne **D.** Aldehyde

Q.24 The double bond between the two carbon atoms in the C_2H_4 molecule indicates:

A. Two pairs of of lone electrons

B. Two pairs of unpaired electrons

C. Two pairs of mobile electrons

D. Two pairs of shared electrons

Q.25 Which of the following characteristics is correct for epithelial tissues?

A. The cells are compactly packed with the fluid intercellular matrix.

B. The cells are loosely packed with the abundant intercellular matrix.

C. The cells are compactly packed with little or no intercellular matrix.

D. The cells are loosely packed with little intercellular matrix.

Q.26 Which statement is incorrect for the post-mitotic gap phase of interphase?

A. In this phase, the cell is metabolically active and grows continuously.

B. It involves the replication of RNA, DNA, and proteins.

C. Cell organelles increase in number.

D. The cell has an option to stop the cell cycle and undergo differentiation.

Q.27 Select the correct pairing:

A. Amyloplast - Photosynthesis

B. Centrosome - Enzymes of digestion

C. Lysosomes - Synthesis of amino acids

D. Endoplasmic Reticulum - Formation of the new nuclear membrane

Q.28 Which of the following is correct about phases of the cell cycle?

A. In G_1 -phase, DNA content is double the amount of DNA present in the original cell.

B. DNA replication takes place in S-phase.

C. A short interphase is followed by a long mitotic phase.

D. G_2 -phase follows mitotic phase.

Q.29 The cell wall of any fungus is different from plants in having:

A. Cellulose **B.** Chitin

C. Cholesterol **D.** Glycogen

Q.30 Growth rings are formed due to the activity of:

A. Intrastelar cambium

B. Intercalary cambium

C. Extrastelar cambium

D. Primary cambium

Q.31 Velamen, the spongy tissue, is present in:

A. Breathing roots **B.** Parasitic roots

C. Tuberous roots **D.** Epiphytic roots

Q.32 The husk of the coconut is made of _____ tissues.

A. collenchyma **B.** xylem and phloem

C. sclereids **D.** sclerenchyma

Q.33 The organelles in which aerobic respiration occurs in a cell are:

A. Ribosomes **B.** Chloroplasts

C. Dictyosomes **D.** Mitochondria

Q.34 Which of the following is the site of photolysis of water?

A. Stroma of chloroplast

B. Cristae of chloroplast

C. Ribosome of chloroplast

D. Lumen of thylakoid sacs

Q.35 Which of the following statements is/are false?

a. In eukaryotes, aerobic respiration takes place within the cytoplasm.

b. In many prokaryotes, fermentation takes place under anaerobic conditions.

c. The metabolic pathway through which the electron passes from one carrier to another is called the electron transport system.

A. Only a **B.** Only a and b

C. Only b **D.** Only b and c

Q.36 Which of the following assumptions is/are made to make calculations of the net gain of ATP for every glucose molecule oxidised?

A. Only glucose is being respired.

B. No other intermediate in the pathway is utilised to synthesise any other compound.

C. The NADH synthesised in glycolysis is transferred into the

mitochondria.
D. All of the above.

Q.37 The brain is responsible for ________.
A. Thinking
B. Regulating the heartbeat
C. Balancing the body
D. All of the above

Q.38 Which of the following statements are true?
(i) Sudden action in response to something in the environment is called reflex action.
(ii) Sensory neurons carry signals from spinal cord to muscles.
(iii) Motor neurons carry signals from receptors to spinal cord.
(iv) The path through which signals are transmitted from a receptor to a muscle or a gland is called reflex arc.
A. (i) and (ii)
B. (i) and (iii)
C. (i) and (iv)
D. (i), (ii) and (iii)

Q.39 Which of the following statements are true about the brain?
(i) The main thinking part of the brain is the hindbrain.
(ii) Centers of hearing, smell, memory, sight, etc., are located in the forebrain.
(iii) Salivation, vomiting, and blood pressure is controlled by the medulla in the hindbrain.
(iv) The cerebellum does not control the posture and balance of the body.
A. (i) and (ii)
B. (ii) and (iii)
C. (i), (ii) and (iii)
D. (iii) and (iv)

Q.40 In a synapse chemical signal is transmitted from ________.
A. dendrite of one neuron to axonal end of other neuron
B. axon to cell body of same neuron
C. axon to cell body to axonal end of same neuron
D. axonal end of one neuron to dendrite of another neuron

Q.41 Which one of the following statement is incorrect about menstruation?
A. The menstrual fluid can easily clot.
B. The beginning of the cycle of menstruation is called menarche.
C. During normal menstruation, about 40 ml of blood is lost.
D. At menopause in females, there is an especially abrupt increase in gonadotropic hormones.

Q.42 During the follicular phase, the dominant follicle arises as a result of secretion of:
A. LH
B. Androgen
C. FSH
D. Matrix-degrading proteases

Q.43 A tadpole develops into an adult frog by the process of:
A. Metamorphosis
B. Fertilization
C. Budding
D. Cloning

Q.44 A plant that reproduces vegetatively by leaves is:
A. Ginger
B. Potato
C. Bryophyllum
D. Onion

Q.45 The component of a chromosome that controls heredity is:
A. Histones
B. RNA
C. DNA
D. Proteins

Q.46 Alternative forms of a gene are called ________.
A. multiples
B. loci
C. chromosomes
D. alleles

Q.47 A Mendialian experiment consisted of breeding of tall pea plants bearing violet flowers with short pea plants bearing white flowers. The progeny all bore violet flowers but almost half of it were short. This suggests that the genetic make up of tall parent can be depicted as:
A. TTWW
B. TTww
C. TtWW
D. TtWw

Q.48 The process in which the pollens are transferred from anther of a flower to stigma of same flower is:
A. Double fertilization
B. Self pollination
C. Cross pollination
D. No fertilization

Q.49 The inertia of an object tends to cause the object:
A. to increase its speed
B. to decrease its speed
C. to resist any change in its state of motion
D. to decelerate due to friction

Q.50 When a particle moves along a straight path, then the particle has:
A. Tangential acceleration only
B. Centripetal acceleration only
C. Both tangential and centripetal acceleration
D. None of the above

Q.51 Momentum of a system of particles is conserved if:
A. The particles are charged and moving
B. There is no external force acting on the system
C. There is a force provided to the system externally
D. All of the above

Q.52 The angular velocity (in rad/s) of a body rotating at N revolutions per minute is:
A. $\pi \frac{N}{60}$ rad/s
B. $2\pi \frac{N}{60}$ rad/s
C. $\pi \frac{N}{120}$ rad/s
D. $\pi \frac{N}{180}$ rad/s

Q.53 When a particle moves with a uniform velocity along a circular path, then the particle has:
A. Tangential acceleration only
B. Centripetal acceleration only
C. Both tangential and centripetal acceleration
D. None of the above

Q.54 What causes the motion of a body which is initially in the state of rest?
A. Force
B. Displacement
C. Speed
D. Velocity

Q.55 People sitting in a moving bus experience a jerk when the bus stops. This is due to _____
A. Inertia of motion

B. Inertia of rest
C. Inertia of turning
D. Inertia of acceleration

Q.56 Which of the following is an example of the linear motion?
A. A ball is thrown straight up and falling back straight down
B. A top
C. A Turning Wheel
D. A spinning skater

Q.57 What is the value acceleration due to gravity of a black hole?
A. $g = \frac{GM}{R^2}$ **B.** $g = \infty$
C. $g = 0$ **D.** $g = \sqrt{\frac{GM}{R^2}}$

Q.58 If there were a reduction in gravitational effect, which of the following forces do you think would change in some respect?
A. Magnetic force **B.** Electrostatic force
C. Viscous force **D.** Archimede's uplift

Q.59 What is the intensity of gravitational field of the centre of a spherical shell?
A. Variable **B.** Minimum
C. Maximum **D.** Zero

Q.60 A particle falls from infinity to the earth. Its velocity on reaching earth of radius R, is _______.
A. $2Rg$ **B.** Rg **C.** $\sqrt{Rg}$ **D.** $\sqrt{2Rg}$

Q.61 For one dimensional motion, the force F(x) and the potential energy U(x) are related as:
A. $F(x) = \frac{-dU(x)}{dx}$ **B.** $F(x) = \frac{dU(x)}{dx}$
C. $U(x) = \frac{dF(x)}{dx}$ **D.** $U(x) = \frac{-dF(x)}{dx}$

Q.62 A body is moved along a straight line by a machine delivering a constant power. The distance moved by the body in time t is proportional to:
A. $t^{\frac{3}{4}}$ **B.** $t^{\frac{3}{2}}$ **C.** $t^{\frac{1}{4}}$ **D.** $t^{\frac{1}{2}}$

Q.63 Find the energy possessed by a stationary object at a height of 6 m and with a mass of 50 kg. $(g = 10\ m/s^2)$
A. 3000 J **B.** 3×10^4 J **C.** 300 J **D.** 30 J

Q.64 The potential energy (P.E.) of a body at a certain height is 200 J. The kinetic energy possessed by it when it just touches the surface of the earth is: (neglect air resistance)
A. Zero **B.** = P.E. **C.** <P.E. **D.** >P.E.

Q.65 The large amplitude of sound vibrations will produce:
A. Feeble sound **B.** Shrill sound
C. Loud sound **D.** Gruff sound

Q.66 Which of the following characteristic(s) of a sound wave determine the loudness of the sound?
(i) Frequency
(ii) Amplitude
(iii) Timbre
A. Only (i) and (ii) **B.** Only (iii)
C. Only (ii) **D.** Only (i) and (iii)

Q.67 If the frequency of a sound is below 20Hz it is known as __________ sound.
A. Audible **B.** Infrasonic
C. Ultrasonic **D.** None of the above

Q.68 What is the frequency of a human heart that is found to beat 75 times in a minute on an average?
A. 75 Hz **B.** 0.8 Hz
C. 1.25 Hz **D.** 0.013 Hz

Q.69 Which direction does the thumb point to in Fleming's left-hand rule?
A. Stream's **B.** Magnetic field
C. Force **D.** None of the above

Q.70 The fuse wire should have __________.
A. Low resistance, Low melting point
B. High resistance, Low melting point
C. High resistance, High melting point
D. Low resistance, High melting point

Q.71 Transformer works on the principle of ________.
A. Electricity
B. Electric field
C. Electro magnetic Induction
D. Magnetic field

Q.72 For a current in a long straight solenoid N-pole and S-pole are created at the two ends. Among the following statements, the incorrect statement is:
A. The field lines inside the solenoid are in the form of straight lines which indicates that the magnetic field is the same at all points inside the solenoid.
B. The strong magnetic field produced inside the solenoid can be used to magnetise a piece of magnetic material like soft iron, when placed inside the coil.
C. The pattern of the magnetic field associated with the solenoid is different from the pattern of the magnetic field around a bar magnet.
D. The N-pole and S-pole exchange position when the direction of current through the solenoid is reversed.

Q.73 Choose the incorrectly matched pair from the following:
A. Sonalika - Wheat
B. Parbhani Kranti - Bhindi
C. Pusa Komal - Cauliflower
D. Pusa Swarnim - Brassica

Q.74 Direction: Read the following statements and choose the correct answer/s:
Statement I: Fertilizers that are incorporated into the soil prior to planting to increase the soil's biological fertility are known as top dressing.
Statement II: Phosphorus is most commonly used as top dressing fertilizers.
A. Statement I is true but statement II is false.
B. Statement I is false but statement II is true.
C. Both statements I and II are true.

D. Both statements I and II are false.

Q.75 Choose the incorrect pair from the following.

A. Vermicompost → Earthworms
B. Farm compost → Farm waste
C. Farmyard manure → Cattle dung, urine and litter
D. Green manures → Chemical compound

Q.76 Urea is a __________ fertilizer.

A. nitrogenous **B.** phosphorus
C. potassic **D.** None of these

Q.77 Tsunami means:

A. earthquake
B. floods
C. an earthquake under the sea
D. eruption of the volcano in a sea

Q.78 During lightning actually __________ takes place.

A. Electric discharge
B. Electric charging
C. Electric charge accumulation
D. All of the above

Q.79 The intensity of an earthquake is expressed in terms of magnitude on a scale called:

A. Richter Scale **B.** Quake scale
C. Earth Scale **D.** None of these

Q.80 Which of the following properties of light can be used to explain the phenomenon of shadow formation?

A. Light travels in a straight line.
B. Light travels at a high speed.
C. Light is composed of seven colours.
D. Light does not pass through opaque objects.

[CTET Paper-II (Science & Mathematics), 2021]

A. C and D **B.** D and A **C.** A and B **D.** B and C

Q.81 Edaphic factors include:

A. Abiotic components **B.** Biotic components
C. Producers **D.** Consumers

Q.82 Green plants utilize ________ percent of sun's energy to prepare their food by the process of photosynthesis.

A. 1 percent **B.** 10 percent
C. 20 percent **D.** 99 percent

Q.83 The process of accumulation of harmful chemical substances like pesticides, in the body of living organisms at each trophic level of a food chain is known as:

A. Biological magnification
B. Biological accumulation
C. Chemical magnification
D. Chemical accumulation

Q.84 In food chain, flow of energy is:

A. Non directional **B.** Bidirectional
C. Unidirectional **D.** None of the above

Q.85 What is the number of electrons that constitutes a current of one Ampere?

A. 2.25×10^{18} **B.** 2.25×10^{-18}
C. 6.25×10^{18} **D.** 6.25×10^{-18}

Q.86 The core of an electromagnet is made of soft iron because soft iron has _______.

A. large density and large retentivity
B. small density and large retentivity
C. large susceptibility and small retentivity
D. small susceptibility and small retentivity

Q.87 What will be the effect on the force between two straight currents carrying wire, when the radius of 1st wire is increased keeping the distance same between two straight currents carrying wire?

A. It will increase
B. It will decrease
C. It will remain the same
D. It will increase and then decrease

Q.88 The process of electroplating, using the phenomenon of electrolysis, is primarily based on

A. Electromagnetic induction
B. Chemical effect of electric current
C. Heating effect of electric current
D. Magnetic effect of electric current

Q.89 Which of the following is not a pure substance?

A. Copper **B.** Gold
C. Sugar solution **D.** Water

Q.90 A mixture that consists of different components is called__________.

A. Homogeneous mixture
B. Heterogeneous mixture
C. Dilute solution
D. None of the above

Q.91 Water is a/an ______.

A. Element **B.** Compound
C. Pure substance **D.** Mixture

Q.92 What is Dry Ice?

A. Ice having no water of crystallization
B. Ice that does not melt
C. Solid carbon dioxide
D. None of these

Q.93 How many moles are present in 40 g of He?

A. 5 moles **B.** 20 moles **C.** 6 moles **D.** 10 moles

Q.94 Who proposed Law of Conservation of Mass?

A. Antoine Lavoisier **B.** Joseph Proust
C. Lorenzo Romano **D.** Joseph Louis

Q.95 The chloride of the element X has the molecular formula XCl. Which of the following will be present in the same group as X?

A. Mg **B.** Al **C.** Zn **D.** Na

Q.96 What is the mass of hydrogen in terms of amu?

A. 1.0020 amu **B.** 1.0180 amu
C. 1.0070 amu **D.** 1.0080 amu

Q.97 Why does an object float or sink when placed on the surface of water?

A. Due to the gravitational force in the downward direction
B. Due to upthrust of the water on the object
C. Both (A) and (B)
D. None of these

Q.98 A wood of density $0.45\ g/cm^3$ and volume of $80\ cm^3$ floats in liquid of density $0.8\ g/cm^3$. What is the fraction of the wood above the water line?

A. $\frac{7}{16}$ **B.** $\frac{2}{16}$ **C.** $\frac{3}{16}$ **D.** $\frac{4}{16}$

Q.99 If two pieces of metal when immersed in a liquid have equal upthrust on them, then:

A. Both pieces must have equal weights
B. Both pieces must have equal densities
C. Both pieces must have equal volumes
D. Both are floating in the same depth

Q.100 A metal block is thrown into deep lake. As it sinks deeper in water, the buoyant force acting on it:

A. increases
B. remains the same
C. decreases
D. first increases and then decreases

// Smart Answer Sheet //

Correct — Percentage of students who answered correctly. Skipped — Percentage of students who skipped.

Q.	Ans.	Correct	Skipped	Q.	Ans.	Correct	Skipped	Q.	Ans.	Correct	Skipped	Q.	Ans.	Correct	Skipped	Q.	Ans.	Correct	Skipped	Q.	Ans.	Correct	Skipped
1	D	46.71 %	1.79 %	18	D	86.76 %	0.0 %	35	A	57.96 %	1.53 %	52	B	62.69 %	1.81 %	69	C	51.62 %	1.71 %	86	C	51.69 %	1.43 %
2	C	79.98 %	0.0 %	19	B	83.56 %	0.0 %	36	D	55.73 %	1.8 %	53	B	55.79 %	1.18 %	70	B	86.9 %	0.0 %	87	C	49.81 %	1.1 %
3	C	64.81 %	1.29 %	20	D	54.87 %	1.45 %	37	D	82.29 %	0.0 %	54	A	63.41 %	1.12 %	71	C	81.92 %	0.0 %	88	B	78.22 %	0.0 %
4	B	87.69 %	0.0 %	21	B	57.17 %	1.46 %	38	C	32.72 %	3.5 %	55	A	65.26 %	1.14 %	72	C	67.32 %	1.48 %	89	C	82.34 %	0.0 %
5	D	64.71 %	1.34 %	22	A	56.05 %	1.65 %	39	B	19.57 %	3.84 %	56	A	51.52 %	1.46 %	73	C	86.92 %	0.0 %	90	B	89.09 %	0.0 %
6	B	14.25 %	3.6 %	23	B	44.67 %	1.06 %	40	D	24.42 %	4.91 %	57	B	40.55 %	1.62 %	74	D	42.94 %	1.82 %	91	B	60.98 %	1.72 %
7	C	67.82 %	1.67 %	24	D	56.89 %	1.48 %	41	A	84.99 %	0.0 %	58	D	86.98 %	0.0 %	75	D	48.2 %	1.21 %	92	C	50.43 %	1.95 %
8	C	18.45 %	3.26 %	25	C	60.35 %	1.62 %	42	C	24.32 %	4.9 %	59	D	84.99 %	0.0 %	76	A	84.71 %	0.0 %	93	D	57.38 %	1.92 %
9	C	84.18 %	0.0 %	26	B	68.91 %	1.04 %	43	A	11.25 %	4.61 %	60	D	28.76 %	3.81 %	77	C	49.35 %	1.15 %	94	A	88.08 %	0.0 %
10	A	16.27 %	4.74 %	27	D	60.9 %	1.74 %	44	C	44.03 %	1.82 %	61	A	88.57 %	0.0 %	78	A	66.39 %	1.19 %	95	D	44.47 %	1.59 %
11	B	55.9 %	1.97 %	28	B	48.22 %	1.06 %	45	C	69.81 %	1.98 %	62	B	62.25 %	1.52 %	79	A	54.55 %	1.73 %	96	D	56.71 %	1.72 %
12	D	86.02 %	0.0 %	29	A	58.32 %	1.88 %	46	D	83.03 %	0.0 %	63	A	62.04 %	1.75 %	80	B	67.63 %	1.69 %	97	C	54.11 %	1.6 %
13	C	54.99 %	1.3 %	30	A	47.29 %	1.09 %	47	C	15.87 %	3.18 %	64	B	79.17 %	0.0 %	81	A	78.11 %	0.0 %	98	A	60.3 %	1.62 %
14	C	14.28 %	4.57 %	31	D	45.06 %	1.66 %	48	B	45.28 %	1.14 %	65	C	68.87 %	1.55 %	82	A	42.16 %	1.75 %	99	C	51.97 %	1.3 %
15	B	58.39 %	1.7 %	32	D	11.45 %	3.36 %	49	C	57.09 %	1.78 %	66	C	44.84 %	1.49 %	83	A	49.6 %	1.36 %	100	B	42.03 %	1.32 %
16	C	77.15 %	0.0 %	33	D	40.64 %	1.2 %	50	A	76.62 %	0.0 %	67	B	46.31 %	1.19 %	84	C	87.37 %	0.0 %				
17	B	48.4 %	1.0 %	34	D	12.26 %	4.76 %	51	B	89.21 %	0.0 %	68	C	63.94 %	1.57 %	85	C	48.91 %	1.38 %				

//Hints and Solutions//

1. Crushing a crystal will not change the state of matter.

Change in state of matter means a change in the physical state of a substance that is, from solid to liquid or liquid to vapour state.

When we crush a solid then it will break down into small particles but it will remain solid. This means there will occur no change in the state of the matter.

Hence, the correct option is (D).

2. Temperature: It is the measure of degree of hotness and coldness of the body. The SI unit of temperature is Kelvin (K). Since the freezing point on the Kelvin scale is at (273 K) and the vapor point at (373 K). The absolute zero temperature is 0 Kelvin. Below this temperature, we cannot measure in Kelvin scale. Therefore, the Kelvin scale of temperature is only positive.

Hence, the correct option is (C).

3. Oxygen can be considered to be a fluid because oxygen is a gas and its particles are completely free to move. So, they have the ability to flow.

Fluid is a substance that has no fixed shape and yields easily to external pressure. For example: a gas or (especially) a liquid.

Hence, the correct option is (C).

4. The common characteristics of solid and liquid states are both have fixed volume.

Solids have a fixed shape and occupy a fixed volume. Fluid, a substance that has no shape but has volume, can flow freely through space. That is, the shape of the vessel in which it is kept, it takes the form of that shape. Example: milk, water, mercury, blood, alcohol, mineral oil etc.

Hence, the correct option is (B).

5. Given,

Wavelength $= 5800\text{Å} = 5800 \times 10^{-10}\ m$

As we know,

The speed of light,

$c = 3 \times 10^8\ m/s$

(a) Wavenumber is given as,

$\bar{\nu} = \frac{1}{\lambda}$

$= \frac{1}{5800\times10^{-10}}$

$= 1.724 \times 10^6\ m^{-1}$

$= 1.724 \times 10^4\ cm^{-1}$

(b) The frequency is given as,

$\nu = \frac{c}{\lambda}$

$= \frac{3\times10^8}{5800\times10^{-10}}$

$= 5.172 \times 10^{14}$ Hz

Hence, the correct option is (D).

6. Given,

Power of the bulb $= 100 watt = 100\ J\ s^{-1}$

Wavelength, $\lambda = 400 \times 10^{-9} m$

Planck's constant, $h = 6.626 \times 10^{-34} Js$

The speed of light, $= 3 \times 10^8\ m\ s^{-1}$

Energy of one photon, $E = h\nu$

$= \frac{hc}{\lambda}$

$= \frac{6.626\times10^{-34}\times3\times10^8}{400\times10^{-9}}$

$= 4.969 \times 10^{-19}\ J$

Number of photons emitted $= \frac{\text{Power of the bulb}}{\text{Energy of one photon}}$

$= \frac{100}{4.969\times10^{-19}}$

$= 2.012 \times 10^{20}\ s^{-1}$

Hence, the correct option is (B).

7. As we know,

The angular momentum is given as,

$L = mvr$

The angular momentum is on integer multiple of $\frac{h}{2\pi}$.

Then we can write,

$mvr = \frac{nh}{2\pi}$

For, $n = 1$

$mvr = \frac{h}{2\pi}$

Hence, the correct option is (C).

8. $X - 19: 1\ s^2, 2\ s^2 2p^6, 3\ s^2 3p^6 4\ s^1$, here M shell is 3 rd energy level which contain 8 electrons $3s^2 3p^6$

$Y - 21: 1s^2, 2s^2 2p^6, 3s^2 3p^6 4s^2 3d^2$, here M shell indicates 3 rd enegy level which contain 9 electrons $3s^2 3p^6 3d^1$

$Z - 25: 1\ s^2, 2\ s^2 2p^6, 3\ s^2 3p^6 4\ s^2 3\ d^5$, here M shell indicates 3 rd energy level which contain 13 electrons $3\ s^2 3p^6 3\ d^5$

So, here Z contains more electrons in M shell than Y and than X. So the order is $Z > Y > X$.

Hence, the correct option is (C).

9. To balance a chemical reaction:

Check the number of atoms before and after the reaction.

Balance the elements one at a time by adding coefficients before them.

Change the coefficients as required.

Never change the subscripts.

$PbO + 2HCl \rightarrow PbCl_2 + H_2O$ is the balanced equation.

- The balance of the above equation requires $\underline{2}$ moles of HCl.

Hence, the correct option is (C).

10. The reaction is exothermic is correct.

A more reactive metal like aluminium can also be used as a reducing agent in the extraction of metals from their oxides. Aluminium is used as a reducing agent where the metal oxide is of a comparatively more reactive metal than zinc, etc. The oxides of manganese and chromium metals are not satisfactorily reduced by carbon. So, manganese and chromium metals are extracted by the reduction of their oxides with aluminium powder. The aluminium powder reduces the metal oxide to metal and is itself oxidised to aluminium oxide. Manganese metal is extracted by the reduction of its oxide with aluminium powder as the reducing agent. When manganese dioxide is heated with aluminium powder, then manganese metal is produced, and the reaction is:

$$3MnO_2 + 4Al \rightarrow 3Mn + 2Al_2O_3 + \text{Heat}$$

From the above reaction, it is clear that the reduction of manganese dioxide with aluminium is a highly exothermic reaction. A lot of heat is evolved during the reduction of manganese dioxide with aluminium powder because of which the manganese metal produced is in the molten state (or liquid state).

Hence, the correct option is (A).

11. Iron nails become brownish after being dipped in copper sulphate solution.

Displacement reaction:

- It is a reaction wherein the atom or a set of atoms is displaced by another atom in a molecule.
- The reaction shows that iron is more reactive than copper because it displaces copper from the copper sulphate solution.

Therefore, Iron nails become brown whereas the solution turns green.

$$CuSO4(aq) + Fe(s) \rightarrow FeSO4(aq) + Cu(s)$$

In this reaction following two processes take place:

- $Cu^{2+} + 2e = Cu^0$ (reduction process, Cu^{2+} is the oxidizing agent)
- $Fe^\circ - 2e = Fe^{2+}$ (oxidation process, Fe^0 is the reducing agent) The reaction can be double displacement reaction as well as redox reaction (oxidation and reduction both take place simultaneously).

Hence, the correct option is (B).

12. When Sulphur Dioxide is dissolved in Water Sulfurous Acid is formed.

$$SO_2 + H_2O \rightarrow H_2SO_3$$

Sulfurous acid:

- Sulfurous acid is a good reducing agent.
- Sulfurous acid is a colourless liquid.
- Sulfurous acid is unstable and has never been isolated in its pure state. It decomposes readily into water and sulfur dioxide.
- Sulfurous acid being powerful reducing agents, it is used as a disinfecting agent.
- It is also used as a mild bleaching agent for applications having chlorine-sensitive elements.

Hence, the correct option is (D).

13. The calamine solution rubbed over an area of ant bite because calamine solution is antacid.

The sting of an ant contains formic acid. Therefore, when an ant bites, it injects formic acid into our skin and due to which we feel a burning sensation. Calamine is basic in nature. When an acid reacts with base, neutralisation reaction takes place. The reaction which takes place during this process is:

$$2HCOOH + ZnCO_3 \rightarrow Zn(HCOO)_2 + H_2CO_3$$

H_2CO_3 formed further undergoes a chemical reaction to form water and carbon dioxide.

$$H_2CO_3 \rightarrow H_2O + CO_2$$

And hence, calamite solution is applied on the skin when an ant bites so that aid-base neutralisation reaction takes place.

Hence, the correct option is (C).

14. Sodium carbonate is a basic salt because it is a salt of weak acid and strong base.

Sodium carbonate, Na_2CO_3 dissociates in water to form sodium ions, $Na^+$and carbonate ions, CO_3^{2-}. Carbonate ion is a nucleophile so it would easily react with protons to form carbonic acid, H_2CO_3. Therefore, the acid-base reaction taking place to form sodium carbonate is given as,

$$H_2CO_3 + 2NaOH \rightarrow Na_2CO_3 + 2H_2O$$

We know that sodium hydroxide is a strong base and carbonic acid is a weak acid. Therefore, sodium carbonate is a basic salt because it is a salt derived from a weak acid and strong base.

Hence, the correct option is (C).

15. Sodium hydrogen carbonate when added to acetic acid evolves a gas. The gas that evolved is carbon dioxide, which has the property of turning lime water milky. It can extinguish the burning candle or splinter and it gets dissolved in sodium hydroxide solution to form sodium carbonate but this gas is odourless in nature. So, statement (1), (2) and (3) are correct and statement (4) is wrong.

Hence, the correct option is (B).

16. Non-aqueous titration is the titration of weakly acidic or basic analytes in a solvent medium that lacks water. The resonant, ionised and unionised forms of indicators are used for non-aqueous titration; however, the colour change at the endpoint of reaction varies among titrations depending on the titrant nature.

- Crystal violet indicator: It is widely used and employed in glacial acetic acid titration as a 0.5% w/v solution.
- Thymol Blue: It is frequently used as a pH indicator in various titrations. It is utilised as a 0.2% w/v solution in methanol, with a yellow to blue colour change.
- Methyl red indicator: It is made in a 0.2% w/v dioxin solution and its endpoint indicates a change in colour from yellow to red.

Hence, the correct option is (C).

17. Phosphorus is the non-metal, which is stored underwater at room temperature.

Phosphorus is a very reactive non-metal. It catches fire if exposed to air. To prevent the contact of phosphorus with atmospheric oxygen, it is stored in water.

Hence, the correct option is (B).

18. Water is a covalent compound. A single water molecule consists of an oxygen atom attached to two hydrogen atoms. Each of the hydrogen atoms is bound to the oxygen atom through a covalent bond.

Water has a covalent bond because of the nature of oxygen and hydrogen, they share electrons to attain stability, and their electronegativities are close enough for their bond to be considered covalent.

Covalent bond: The bond form between two atoms by mutual sharing of their electrons is known as a covalent bond and the compound is known as a covalent compound.

Hence, the correct option is (D).

19. Bronze consists of $85 - 88\%$ copper, $12 - 12.5\%$ tin, and with the addition of some other metals like aluminium, manganese, zinc or nickel in small proportions. This mixture is made to improve the properties of copper.

Hence, the correct option is (B).

20. The electrolysis of copper chloride is a way of splitting up (decomposition) of the compound (copper chloride) using electrical energy. The electrical energy comes from a d.c. (direct current) battery or power pack supply. A conducting liquid, containing ions, called the electrolyte (aqueous or molten sodium chloride), must contain the compound (copper chloride) that is being broken down. The electricity must flow through electrodes dipped into the electrolyte to complete the electrical circuit with the battery.

The electrolyte copper (II) chloride, provides a high concentration of copper (II) ions Cu^{2+} and chloride ions Cl^{-} to carry the current during the electrolysis process.

Hence, the correct option is (D).

21. Graphite has a giant covalent structure in which each carbon atom is joined to three other carbon atoms by covalent bonds the carbon atoms form layers with a hexagonal arrangement of atoms the layers have weak forces between them each carbon atom has one non-bonded outer electron, which becomes delocalized.

Hence, the correct option is (B).

22. The unsaturated hydrocarbons (having double bonds or triple bonds between the carbon atoms) are more reactive than saturated hydrocarbons. In other words, alkenes and alkynes are chemically more reactive than alkanes.

Hence, the correct option is (A).

23. The name of the hydrocarbon and their characteristic is given below:

Hydrocarbon	Characteristic
Alkane	Carbon-Carbon single bond
Alkene	Carbon-Carbon double bond
Alkyne	Carbon-Carbon triple bond
Alcohol	-OH functional group
Aldehyde	-CHO functional group
Ketone	-CO- Functional group

Hence, the correct option is (B).

24. The double bond existing between C_2H_4 is a coordinate covalent bond that is shared electrons. Lone electrons will not form a bond, similarly unpaired and mobile electrons will not form a bond.

Hence, the correct option is (D).

25. Epithelial tissues are the major tissue in glands and form the outer covering or layer of all body surfaces and organs. It consists of closely aggregated cells that adhere firmly to each other and forming either single or multiple layers. Due to the cells being tightly packed there is the very little intercellular matrix. The intercellular matrix consists of protein and is on the cell membrane of epithelial cells.

Hence, the correct option is (C).

26. Interphase is the first growth stage after cell division. Three stages occur during interphase i.e. G_1, S, and G_2 stage wherein G_1 stage cells mature by making more cytoplasm and cell organelles. S phase is called the post-mitotic gap phase and during that phase, the cell synthesizes enzyme and energy needed for DNA duplication. It occurs between the G_1 and G_2 phases of the interphase. In the G_2 phase, all cell structures needed for cell division are made. Example: centriole.

Hence, the correct option is (B).

27. Amyloplast is the site of the storage of carbohydrates. The centrosome is responsible for the organization, and nucleation of microtubules while the lysosome contains a digestive enzyme that is used to destroy invading viruses and bacteria.

The function of the endoplasmic reticulum is to form the structure of the cell. There are two types of endoplasmic reticulum (ER) rough endoplasmic reticulum (RER) and smooth endoplasmic reticulum (SER). Rough endoplasmic reticulum contains ribosomes on which proteins are synthesized. Smooth endoplasmic reticulum forms fat or lipid. Some proteins and fats help build cell membranes. The endoplasmic reticulum also serves as the cytoplasmic framework for certain biochemical activities of the cell. Endoplasmic reticulum viruses are not found in bacteria, blue-green algae and red blood cells of mammals.

Hence, the correct option is (D).

28. S Phase or Synthesis phase: It is synthetic phase. It occurs between G_1 phase and G_2 phase. Replication of DNA takes place during this S Phase and the DNA content doubles.

Cell Cycle: The sequence of events in which the cell doubles its genome and synthesizes other components and then divides to form two new daughter cells is called the cell cycle.

Hence, the correct option is (B).

29. The main difference between fungi and the plant cell wall is instead of cellulose which is present in plant cell walls, fungi have chitin as a major component of their cell wall. Both chitin and cellulose are composed of polysaccharide chains. Further, while fungi don't have chlorophyll, it is present in plants. This is because instead of performing photosynthesis, fungi extract nutrients from the soil.

Hence, the correct option is (A).

30. Each year in the growing season, the tree forms new cells arranged in concentric circles which are called growth rings or annual rings, or annual. These annual rings show the amount of wood produced during one growing season. These annual rings furnish valuable information regarding the age of the wood, the rapidity, and the uniformity of its growth.

- A cambium that is present between the xylem and phloem is called intrafascicular cambium. This is a type of primary meristem.
- Firstly, some cells of medullary rays become meristematic to form interfascicular cambium which is a secondary meristem.
- Intrafascicular and interfascicular cambium are collectively known as vascular cambium.
- Vascular cambium is formed in form of a complete ring.
- Thus, the growth ring is derived from vascular cambium which is present between the xylem and phloem i.e., also called intrastelar cambium.

Thereby Growth rings are formed due to the activity of the Intrastelar cambium.

Hence, the correct option is (A).

31. Epiphytes are small plants that grow on other plants in the tropical rainforest.

Examples of epiphytes are orchids and hanging mosses. Velamen is spongy, multiple epidermises that cover the roots of some epiphytic or semi epiphytic plants, such as orchid and Clivia species. The function of Velamen is the Absorption of water. The velamen of an orchid is the white or gray covering of aerial roots. It is many cell layers thick and capable of absorbing atmospheric moisture and nutrients. Often, the roots of orchids are associated with symbiotic fungi or bacteria. The latter may fix nutrients from the air. This functionality allows the orchid to exist in locations that provide a reproductive or vegetative advantage such as improved exposure or reduced competition from other plant species.

Hence, the correct option is (D).

32. The husk of the coconut is made of *sclerenchyma* tissues.

Sclerenchyma tissue is one of the Simple Permanent tissue. It is the tissue that makes the plant hard and stiff like a husk of a coconut. The cells of this tissue are dead. They are long and narrow as the walls are thickened due to lignin. Often these walls are so thick that there is no internal pace inside the cell. This tissue is present in stems, around vascular bundles, in the veins of leaves, and in the hard covering of seeds and nuts. It provides strength to the plant parts.

Hence, the correct option is (D).

33. In the process of cellular respiration, mitochondria function as the main organelle. Mitochondria are known as the powerhouse of the cell. They are rod-shaped organelles which convert nutrients into ATP. ATP is the energy currency of the cell which is produced by mitochondria. Aerobic respiration takes place in the powerhouse of the cell, i.e mitochondria. Ribosomes are involved in protein synthesis. Chloroplasts are concerned with the photosynthesis. Dictyosomes perform the packaging and modification of the biomolecules.

Hence, the correct option is (D).

34. The photolysis of water occurs during light reaction. The site for occurrence of photolysis is thylakoid lumen. The photolysis of water releases protons, which accumulate in the lumen and contribute to the electrochemical gradient of protons. The electrons released are used up to fill the electron hole in the reaction centre of PSII and oxygen molecule is released as by product of photosynthesis.

So, the correct answer is 'Lumen of thylakoid sacs'.

Hence, the correct option is (D).

35. Most aerobic respiration (with oxygen) takes place in the cell's mitochondria, and anaerobic respiration (without oxygen) takes place within the cell's cytoplasm. Therefore statement (a) is incorrect.

Fermentation takes place under anaerobic conditions in many prokaryotes, unicellular eukaryotes and ger- minating seeds. Therefore statement (b) is correct.

The metabolic pathway through which the electron passes from one carrier to another is called the electron transport system (ETS). Therefore statement (c) is correct.

Hence, the correct option is (A).

36. For theoretical calculation of ATP molecules, various assumptions are made, which are as follows :

- It is assumed that various parts of aerobic respiration such as glycolysis, TCA cycle, and ETS occur in a sequential and orderly pathway.
- NADH produced during the process of glycolysis enters into mitochondria to undergo oxidative phosphorylation.
- A glucose molecule is assumed to be the only substrate while it is assumed that no other molecule enters the pathway at intermediate stages.
- The intermediates produced during respiration are not utilized in any other process.

Hence, the correct option is (D).

37. The fore-brain is responsible for thinking and interpreting sensory information. The hind-brain is responsible for maintaining the posture and balance of the body. Since all the above functions are controlled by the brain.

Hence, the correct option is (D).

38. Reflex action is a sudden and involuntary response to stimuli. It helps organisms to quickly adapt to an adverse circumstance that could have the potential to cause bodily harm or even death. Pulling our hands away immediately after touching a hot or cold object is a classic example of a reflex action.

The reflex arc is the nerve pathway that is followed by reflex action. The path through which signals are transmitted from a receptor to a muscle or a gland is called reflex arc. An example of the reflex arc is it happens when we accidentally touch something hot.

Hence, the correct option is (C).

39. The forebrain comprises the majority of the brain in humans. It is the main thinking part of the brain. It controls most bodily functions and behavior. The forebrain includes the cerebrum, thalamus, hypothalamus and limbic system. Visual perception, language, smell, memory, hearing, sight, etc., are the functions of the forebrain. Involuntary actions like salivation, vomiting, blood pressure are controlled by the medulla in the hindbrain. Cerebellum maintains balance and posture of the body.

Hence, the correct option is (B).

40. In a synapse, the electrical signal is 'translated' into the neurotransmitter by the presynaptic neuron the chemical diffuses (swims) across the synaptic cleft until it reaches the other neuron. The signal thus travels from axonal end of one neuron to dendritic end of the next neuron.

Hence, the correct option is (D).

41. Menstrual blood is loaded with anticoagulants that break down the thick blood clots and prevents blood from clotting. This helps in maintaining a free flow consistency. In menstrual blood, plasminogen activators are also present which causes fibrinolysis, which dissolves the clot. Thus, the correct option is 'The menstrual fluid can easily clot'.

Hence, the correct option is (A).

42. Theca cells are stimulated by the Luteinizing hormone (LH) to synthesize androgens, which diffuse into the granulosa cells as estrogen precursors. The antral or "dominant" follicles secrete estrogen and inhibin, which exert negative feedback on Follicle-stimulating hormone (FSH), thus "turning off" their neighboring antral follicles.

The increase in FSH also stimulates the secretion of Inhibin B by the granulosa cells. Inhibin B will eventually blunt the secretion of FSH toward the end of the follicular phase. Inhibin B levels will be highest during the LH surge before ovulation, and will quickly taper off after.

One follicle in one ovary continues to mature. This dominant follicle suppresses all of the other follicles in the group.

Hence, the correct option is (C).

43. The correct answer is Metamorphosis.

Metamorphosis:

- It is a biological process through which an animal physically develops after birth or hatching.
- It involves a conspicuous and relatively abrupt change in the animal's body structure through cell growth and differentiation.
- The metamorphosis is a Greek word that means transformation or transforming.

Fertilization:

- It is also known as insemination, pollination, syngamy, and impregnation.
- It is the fusion of gametes to initiate the development of a new individual or offspring.

Budding:

- It is a type of asexual reproduction.
- In this, a new organism develops from an outgrowth due to cell division at one particular site.
- Bud is the small bulb-like projection coming out from the yeast cell.
- Reproduction is asexual, therefore the newly formed organism is a clone and excepting mutations is genetically identical to the parent organism.

Cloning:

- It is the process of producing individuals with identical or virtually identical DNA, either artificially or naturally.
- It is coined by Herbert J. Webber.
- Its application in Biotechnology is very prevalant.

Hence, the correct option is (A).

44. A plant that reproduces vegetatively by leaves is Bryophyllum.

Bryophyllum (sprout leaf plant) has buds in the margins of leaves. If a leaf of this plant falls on moist soil, each bud can give rise to a new plant. The roots of some plants can also give rise to new plants. Sweet potato and dahlia are examples.

Hence, the correct option is (C).

45. Heredity is the passing on of traits from parents to their offspring, either through asexual reproduction or sexual reproduction the offspring cells or organisms acquire the genetic information of their parents.

Heritable traits are known to be passed from one generation to the next via DNA, a molecule that encodes genetic information.

Hence, the correct option is (C).

46. An alternative form of a gene is known as an alleles. Alleles vary in their sequence which may or may not result in a variant phenotype of a particular trait. Alleles represent variations of a gene that is responsible for a particular trait.

Hence, the correct option is (D).

47. The plant in question is homozygous for violet flower because in the progeny all the flowers are of violet colour and heterozygous for tallness because in the progeny half of the plants are short. As the other parent is double recessive, and will not be expressed at any of the two loci. We can easily visualize the result in terms of gametes that will be produced by first plant, i.e., "Tw" which when mixes with "tw" will produce a tall violet plant and "tw" which when mixes with "tw" will produce a dwarf white plant.

Hence, the correct option is (C).

48. The process in which the pollens are transferred from anther of a flower to stigma of same flower is self pollination. It is also known as autogamy and is seen in bisexual flowers (that contain both stamens and pistil) like Hibiscus.

Hence, the correct option is (B).

49. The inertia of a object tends to cause the object to resist any change in its state of motion.

Newton's first law of motion: It is also called the law of inertia. Inertia is the ability of a body by virtue of which it opposes a change. According to Newton's first law of motion, an object will remain at rest or in uniform motion in a straight line unless acted upon by an external force.

Hence, the correct option is (C).

50. When a particle moves along a straight path, then the particle has tangential acceleration only

The acceleration of a particle at any instant moving along a circular path in a direction tangential to that instant, is known as tangential component of acceleration or tangential acceleration.

Hence, the correct option is (A).

51. According to the law of conservation of momentum, the total momentum of a system is conserved for an isolated system.

An isolated system means that there is no external interaction on the system.

Thus, the momentum of a system of particles is conserved if there is no external force acting on the system.

Hence, the correct option is (B).

52. The angular velocity (in rad/s) of a body rotating at N revolutions per minute is $2\pi \frac{N}{60}$ rad/s.

Angular velocity is defined as the rate of change of angular displacement with respect to time. It is usually expressed by a Greek letter ω (omega).

Mathematically,

Angular velocity $\omega = \frac{d\theta}{dt}$

If a body is rotating at the rate of N revolutions per minute then its angular velocity $\omega = 2\pi \frac{N}{60}$ rad/s

Hence, the correct option is (B).

53. When a particle moves along a circular path with uniform velocity, the particle has only centripetal acceleration.

The acceleration of a particle at any instant moving along a circular path in a direction normal to the tangent at that instant and directed towards the center of the circular path is known as normal component of the acceleration or normal acceleration. It is also called radial or centripetal acceleration.

Hence, the correct option is (B).

54. The first law of motion states that a body remains in the state of uniform motion or in the state of rest until and unless an external force is applied on it. This is also known as the law of inertia.

Hence, the correct option is (A).

55. When the bus stops, the people sitting in it experience a jerk. This is because, while the bus was moving, the people were moving with it. Hence, they were having an inertia of motion. When the bus stops, the inertia of the bus changes from that of motion to that of rest. But the inertia of the people still remains that of motion. So, they experience a jerk.

Hence, the correct option is (A).

56. A ball thrown straight up and falling back straight down is an example of linear motion.

Linear motion involves an object moving from one point to another in a straight line.

Hence, the correct option is (A).

57. Blackhole is a very dense body where the gravitational field is so strong that it absorbs all the radiation flowing from near it.

Blackhole is just like any other star but because of its high density and small radius it exerts huge force due to gravity hence acceleration due to gravity on its surface will be very large.

This was proved experimentally, that the value acceleration due to gravity of a black hole is infinity i.e., $g = \infty$

Hence, the correct option is (B).

58. If there were a reduction in gravitational effect, Archimede's uplift would change in some respect.

Archimedes' principle states that the buoyant force acting on a body is equal to the weight of the fluid displaced by it. Since the weight of a body is a gravitational effect, the Archimedes' uplift decreases with reduction in gravitational effect.

Hence, the correct option is (D).

59. Zero is the intensity of the gravitational field at the center of a spherical shell.

It's because the pull from every direction is exactly the same. This is obvious from the center, but as you move to one side, you're closer to that side, which increases its pull, but this is exactly offset by the fact that there's now more mass on the other side.

Hence, the correct option is (D).

60. $P.E$ at infinity is zero and $K.E$ is also zero as the particle starts from rest at infinity.

Using conservation of mechanical energy at the surface of earth and at infinty,

$$K \cdot E_R + P \cdot E_R = 0$$

$$\frac{1}{2}mv^2 + \left(-\frac{GMm}{R}\right) = 0$$

$$\left(\frac{1}{2}\right)mv^2 = \left(\frac{GMm}{R}\right)$$

$$v^2 = \left(\frac{2GM}{R}\right)$$

$$v^2 = 2gR \quad \left(\text{since } g = \frac{GM}{R^2}\right)$$

$$\Rightarrow v = \sqrt{2gR}$$

Hence, the correct option is (D).

61. The potential energy is equal to negative work done in shifting an object from some reference point to a given position for conservative force.

In mathematical form, it is given as,

$$dU(x) = -F(x)dx$$

$$\therefore F(x) = \frac{-dU(x)}{dx}$$

where F is the force in newton and $\frac{dU}{dx}$ is change in potential energy per unit length.

Hence, the correct option is (A).

62. Let's consider a body is moved along a straight line by a machine delivering a constant power P. The distance moved by the body is S.

Power, $P = F.v. \ldots..(1)$

Force, $F = ma....(2)$

Where, $v = \frac{S}{t}$

Acceleration, $a = \frac{S}{t^2}$

m= mass

From equation (1) and equation (2), we get

$$P = \frac{mS}{t^2} \times \frac{S}{t}$$

$$S^2 = \frac{Pt^3}{m}$$

From the above equation, we get

$$S^2 \propto t^3$$

$$S \propto t^{\frac{3}{2}}$$

$\therefore$ The distance moved by the body in time t is proportional to $t^{\frac{3}{2}}$.

Hence, the correct option is (B).

63. Given that:

Mass (m) = 50 Kg

Height (h) = 6 m

We know that,

Potential Energy = Mass × height × Gravitational constant

Potential Energy = 50 × 10 × 6

Potential Energy = 3000 J

Hence, the correct option is (A).

64. According to the energy conservation principle, the sum of the kinetic energy and potential energy of the body always remains constant.

- As the body comes down the height of the body decreases and hence the potential energy decreases. If the potential energy decreases the kinetic energy will increase.
- As soon as the body touches the ground, all the initial potential energy of the particle gets converted into kinetic energy.
- The potential energy (P.E) of a body at a certain height is 200 J. The kinetic energy possessed by it when it just touches the surface of the earth is the same as the Potential Energy (= P.E.).

Hence, the correct option is (B).

65. The large amplitude of sound vibrations will produce a loud sound.

Sound travels as a longitudinal wave. A sound wave traveling through air is indeed a longitudinal wave with compressions and rarefactions. The study of sound is called acoustics.

The large amplitude of sound vibrations will produce a loud sound.

- The intensity of sound is identified by loudness.
- The loudness of sound is proportional to the square of the amplitude of the vibration producing the sound.

The audible range of an average human is 20 Hz — 20 kHz. Speed of sound in air = 343 m/s. Hertz(Hz) is the unit of the frequency of sound. Decibels(dB) is the unit of Intensity of sound.

Hence, the correct option is (C).

66. Amplitude is the characteristic of a sound wave that determines the loudness of the sound.

Sound:

- Sound is longitudinal mechanical waves.
- Sound is produced due to vibration.
- Characteristics of sound waves are Intensity or loudness, Pitch, Quality (Timbre).
- The intensity of sound at any point in space is defined as the amount of energy passed normally per unit area held around that point per unit time.
- The unit of intensity of sound - Decibel (db)
- Pitch of a sound that distinguishes a sharp sound from a grave sound. Pitch depends on frequency.
- Quality (Timbre) enables us to distinguish between sounds produced by two sources having the same intensity and pitch.

- When sound enters from one medium to another medium, its speed and wavelength change but the frequency remains unchanged.

Hence, the correct option is (C).

67. If the frequency of a sound is below 20Hz it is known as Infrasonic sound.

Sound waves are of three types:

- Infrasonic waves: The sound waves of frequency between 0 Hz to 20 Hz are called infrasonic waves. The sound produced by thunders, volcanoes, etc. Animals like elephants and whales can hear infrasonic sounds.
- Audible waves: The sound waves of frequency between 20 Hz to 20,000 Hz are called Audible waves. The human ear can able to listen to these frequencies
- Ultrasonic waves: The sound waves of frequency above 20,000 Hz are called Ultrasonic waves. Many animals like bats, cats, dogs, mice, etc.

Hence, the correct option is (B).

68. To calculate the frequency in hertz, we have to measure the time in seconds.

That is, $t = 1$ minute $= 60$ seconds.

The number of times it beats $= 75$ times per minute.

Frequency is given as:

Number of times it beats/Total time taken in seconds $= \frac{75}{60} =$ 1.25 Hz.

So, the frequency of a human heart is 1.25 times per second.

Hence, the correct option is (C).

69. In Fleming's left-hand rule, the thumb indicates the direction of the force.

According to this rule, if we extend the middle, forefinger and thumb of our left hand three fingers perpendicular to each other and if the forefinger shows the direction of the magnetic field and the middle finger shows the direction of the current, then the thumb shows the direction of the force on the current carrying conductor.

Hence, the correct option is (C).

70. Fuse wire should have high resistance and low melting point. So that it prevents current higher than the prescribed value to pass . Low melting point will let it to break when high current passes through it because of the heat generated.

Hence, the correct option is (B).

71. Transformer works on the principle of electro magnetic Induction.

The transformer does this by linking together two or more electrical circuits using a common oscillating magnetic circuit which is produced by the transformer itself. A transformer operates on the principals of "electromagnetic induction", in the form of Mutual Induction.

Mutual induction is the process by which a coil of wire magnetically induces a voltage into another coil located in close proximity to it. Then we can say that transformers work in the "magnetic domain", and transformers get their name from the fact that they "transform" one voltage or current level into another.

Hence, the correct option is (C).

72. A solenoid behaves like a bar magnet. So the pattern of the magnetic field associated with the solenoid is exactly same as the pattern of the magnetic field around a bar magnet. It also has two poles on the two extreme end and the field lines are also looks same.

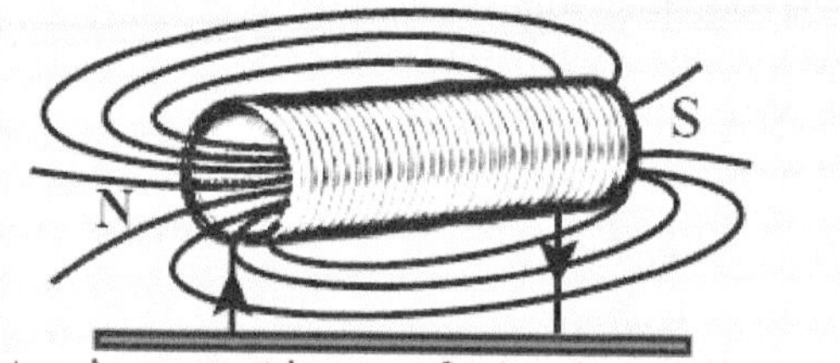

Hence, the correct option is (C).

73. 'Sonalika' is a high-yielding and disease-resistant variety of wheat. It was introduced in India in 1963 along with another wheat variety called 'Kalyan Sona'. So this is correctly matched.

'Parbhani Kranti' is a variety of bhindi or Abelmoschus esculentus. It was created by mutation breeding technique. The resistance gene for yellow mosaic virus was transferred from a wild species into a high-yielding species. So this is correctly matched.

'Pusa Komal' is a resistant variety of cowpea. It has resistance against bacterial blight. The resistant varieties of cauliflower are 'Pusa Shubhra' and 'Pusa Snowball K-1'. The cauliflower varieties are resistant against black rot and curl blight black rot. So this is incorrectly matched.

'Pusa Swarnim' is a variety of Brassica that is resistant against white rust. So this is correctly matched.

Hence, the correct option is (C).

74. Basal dose: Fertilizers that are incorporated into the soil prior to planting; to increase the soil's biological fertility is known as the basal dose of fertilizer application.

Topdressing: Addition of fertilizer to crops during the growing period in order to improve plant nutrition and boost yields. So, statements I is false.

Nitrogen fertilizer is most commonly used as top dressing fertilizers. Ammonium nitrate is a very widely used fertilizer for top dressing. Mineral fertilizers that are quickly water-soluble in water are most often used for topdressing. So, statements II is false.

Hence, the correct option is (D).

75. 'Green manures → Chemical compound' is incorrectly pair.

Green manure crop is raised and turned into the soil for decomposition. Green manures improve the physical structure of the soil, as well as, soil fertility. Crops, like dhaincha and sunn hemp, are used as green manure.

Hence, the correct option is (D).

76. Urea is a nitrogenous fertilizer.

Urea is the most important nitrogenous fertilizer in the country because of its high nitrogen content (46% N). In addition to its use in crops, it is used as a supplement to animal feed to replace a portion of protein requirements. It has many industrial uses, particularly for the production of plastics. Although urea often provides farmers with the most nitrogen on the market at the lowest cost, special steps must be taken when applying urea to the soil to prevent nitrogen loss through chemical reaction.

Hence, the correct option is (A).

77. A tsunami is a series of extremely long waves caused by a large and sudden displacement of the ocean, usually the result of an earthquake below or near the ocean floor. This force creates waves that radiate outward in all directions away from their source, sometimes crossing entire ocean basins. Unlike wind-driven waves, which only travel through the topmost layer of the ocean, tsunamis move through the entire water column, from the ocean floor to the ocean surface.

Hence, the correct option is (C).

78. During lightning actually *electric discharge* takes place.

Lightning is one of the most powerful natural forces on the planet. It is a natural discharge of the static electricity built up in storm clouds. Most lightning is formed as a part of thunderstorms. We know from observation of static electricity that static electrical discharges such as lightning are caused by the separation of charges into positive and negative ions. Over time more of one charge builds until its natural attraction to the opposite charge causes it to migrate in an electrical discharge.

Hence, the correct option is (A).

79. The intensity of an earthquake is expressed in terms of magnitude on a scale called the Richter Scale.

The Richter scale also called the Richter magnitude scale, is an instrument for measuring the intensity of earthquakes, developed by Charles Francis Richter and presented in his landmark 1935 paper, where he called it the "magnitude scale".

Hence, the correct option is (A).

80. For the shadow formation, source of light, screen and opaque object all are required.

So, these properties of light can be used to explain the phenomenon of shadow formation:

A. Light travels in a straight line.

D. Light does not pass through opaque objects.

Hence, the correct option is (B).

81. Edaphic factors include abiotic components.

Edaphic factor is an abiotic factor relating to the physical or chemical composition of the soil found in a particular area. The edaphic factors are the abiotic factors with respect to the soil. These factors include; soil texture, soil air, the temperature of the soil, soil water etc.

Hence, the correct option is (A).

82. Green plants utilize 1 percent of sun's energy to prepare their food by the process of photosynthesis.

The autotrophs in a terrestrial environment catch around 1% of the energy that falls on their leaves and transform it into feed, according to a study of energy exchange between ecosystems.

Hence, the correct option is (A).

83. The process of accumulation of harmful chemical substances like pesticides, in the body of living organisms at each trophic level of a food chain is known as biological magnification.

Biomagnification refers to the accumulation of toxic substances in the food chain. The toxic chemicals that are released into the environment are absorbed by the lower organisms such as plants, earthworms, etc. These chemicals are then transferred to different trophic levels when lower organisms are eaten by other organisms.

Hence, the correct option is (A).

84. The flow of energy in food chain in unidirectional because the sun is the only source of energy for all ecosystems on earth. Then the energy is captured by the autotrophs does not revert back to the sun. Therefore, in the food chain, the energy moves progressively through various trophic levels. The energy is no longer available to the previous trophic levels.

Hence, the correct option is (C).

85. Number of electrons, $n = \frac{\text{Current } (I) \times time(t)}{\text{Charge of 1 electron } (e)}$

$= \frac{(1 \times 1)}{1.6 \times 10^{-19}}$

$= 6.25 \times 10^{18}$

Hence, the correct option is (C).

86. The core of an electromagnet is made of soft iron because soft iron has large susceptibility and small retentivity.

Electromagnets are the magnets which looses all its magnetism as soon as the current through it vanishes, so it must have negligible retentivity. Since soft iron has large susceptibility and small retentivity, so soft iron is used to make the core of electromagnet.

The magnetic susceptibility is a measure of how much a material will become magnetized in an applied magnetic field. It is the ratio of magnetization M (magnetic moment per unit volume) to the applied magnetizing field intensity H.

Hence, the correct option is (C).

87. The effect on the force between two straight currents carrying wire, when the radius of 1st wire is increased keeping the distance same between two straight currents carrying wire is that it will remain the same.

The magnetic force per unit length between two parallel wires is given by;

$\frac{F}{l} = \frac{\mu_o}{4\pi} \frac{2I_1 I_2}{d}$

From the above, it is clear that the force between the two parallel wires depends on the medium in which two-wire is placed, the distance between two-wire and the current in wire 1 and wire 2.

The force between the two parallel wires is independent of the radius of wire, so there will be no impact on the force between the two parallel wires.

Hence, the correct option is (C).

88. The process of electroplating, using the phenomenon of electrolysis, is primarily based on chemical effect of electric current. any metals can be plated on to work-pieces electrically, and this process is called electroplating. Whenever a current is flowing in the resistance then heat is produced in it. The phenomenon of producing heat by the electric current is called the heating effect of electric current.

Due to the heating effect of the current, the filament of the bulb gets heated to a high temp and it starts glowing.

Similarly, the metals are melted and coated on another material to prevent corrosion. It is a chemical effect of electric current.

Hence, the correct option is (B).

89. Copper, gold, and water are pure but sugar solution is a homogeneous mixture. Copper, gold, and water are made of the same elements but sugar solution contains sugar as solute and water as a solvent.

Hence, the correct option is (C).

90. A mixture that consists of different components is called heterogeneous mixture.

Heterogeneous mixture: A heterogeneous mixture is a mixture with a non-uniform composition that contains components in different phases. The composition varies from one region to another with at least two phases that remain separate from each other, with clearly identifiable properties. Heterogeneous mixtures contain particles that retain their chemical properties when they are mixed and can be distinguished after they are mixed. The components of heterogeneous mixtures can be separated by the filtration of chemical procedures. The two types of heterogeneous mixtures are suspensions and colloids.

Example:

- Concrete is a heterogeneous mixture of an aggregate: cement and water.
- Sugar and sand form a heterogeneous mixture. If you look closely, you can identify tiny sugar crystals and particles of sand.
- Ice cubes in cola form a heterogeneous mixture.

Hence, the correct option is (B).

91. Water molecule consists of 2 Hydrogen and 1 Oxygen atoms. When two or more atoms of different elements combine with each other in a fixed ratio, the molecule of a compound is obtained.

Hence, the correct option is (B).

92. Dry ice is the common name for the solid form of carbon dioxide.

- It's called dry ice because it doesn't melt into a wet liquid.
- Dry ice sublimates, which means it goes from its solid form directly to its gaseous form.

Hence, the correct option is (C).

93. As we know,

1 mole of He = 4 gm

So, 40 gm of He = 10 moles

Hence, the correct option is (D).

94. Antoine Lavoisier conducted many experiments regarding combustion and noticed various physical and chemical changes and there is no change in overall mass. Hence he came to a conclusion that mass can neither be created nor destroyed i.e. Law of Conservation of Mass.

Hence, the correct option is (A).

95. The chloride ion exists as Cl^{-1} showing a charge of -1. A chemical formula of a compound is overall neutral. This causes metal to exhibit +1 oxidation state. Such oxidation state(charge) is shown by Alkali metals. The only alkali metal present here is Na (Sodium).

Hence, the correct option is (D).

96. The mass of a hydrogen atom is 1.6736×10^{-24} g.

When converted in terms of amu,

1.6736×10^{-24} g should be divided by 1.66056×10^{-24} g.

$\frac{1.6736\times10^{-24}}{1.66056\times10^{-24}} = 1.0078$ amu

$= 1.008$ amu

Hence, the correct option is (D).

97. When an object is placed on the surface of water, two forces act on the object.

- The gravitational force in the downward direction and
- Upthrust of the water on the object.

When the gravitational force acting on the object is greater than the upthrust of the water, then the object sinks in water. On the other hand, if the upthrust of water on the object is greater than the gravitational force, then the object floats.

Hence, the correct option is (C).

98. Mass of wood $=$ Volume $\times$ density of the wood

$= 80cm^3 \times 0.45\ g/cm^3$

$= 36\ g$

If wood floats, it will displace 36 grams of the liquid it is floating in.

$36\ g =$ volume of wood, submerged $\times$ density of liquid.

Volume of wood, submerged $= 36\ g \times 1cm^3/0.8\ g$

$= 45cm^3$

The fraction of the wood above the water line $= \frac{\text{(Total volume of wood - volume of the wood submerged)}}{\text{total volume of wood}}$

$$= \frac{(80cm^3 - 45cm^3)}{80cm^3}$$

$$= \frac{35}{80}cm^3$$

$$= \frac{7}{16}$$

Hence, the correct option is (A).

99. If two pieces of metal when immersed in a liquid have equal upthrust on them, then both pieces must have equal volumes.

Hence, the correct option is (C).

100. Buoyant force equals the weight of water which has been displaced by an object. Since, irrespective of the metal block position, the volume displaced by metal is same, hence, buoyant force remains the same.

Hence, the correct option is (B).

Mock Test 05

Q.1 Which of the following has the lowest density?

A. Liquid **B.** Sodium **C.** Gas **D.** Mercury

Q.2 Which has lowest kinetic energy?

A. Plasmas **B.** Gases **C.** Liquids **D.** Solids

Q.3 Helium gas is used in gas balloons instead of hydrogen gas because it is _______.

[Territorial Army Officer, 2019]

A. Lighter than hydrogen
B. More abundant than hydrogen
C. Non-combustible
D. More stable

Q.4 Which of the following relations between Kinetic energy and Potential energy is true about solids?

A. Kinetic energy $=$ Potential energy
B. Kinetic energy $>$ Potential energy
C. Kinetic energy $<$ Potential energy
D. None of these

Q.5 The valency of phosphorus is _______.

[Indian Military Academy (IMA), 2020], [Officers Training Academy (OTA), 2020]

A. 2, 3 **B.** 3, 4 **C.** 4, 5 **D.** 3, 5

Q.6 The main defect of Bohr's atom model is:

A. Mixing of classical and quantum theories
B. Exclusion of nuclear motion
C. Failed to explain the fine structure of spectral lines
D. Failed to explain larger atoms

Q.7 Multiplication of equivalent weight and valency of an element is equal to:

A. Density
B. Relative temperature
C. Atomic weight
D. Atomicity

Q.8 The valency of sulphur in sulphur dioxide is:

A. 3 **B.** 4 **C.** 2 **D.** 1

Q.9 The following is an example of which type of reaction.

NH_3 (g) + HCl (g) $\rightarrow$ NH_4Cl (s)

A. Addition **B.** Displacement
C. Decomposition **D.** Neutralisation

Q.10 Complete the following reaction.

Al_2O_3 + 6HCl $\rightarrow$ 2 $AlCl_3$ + ______

A. H_2O **B.** $2H_2O$ **C.** $4H_2O$ **D.** $3H_2O$

Q.11 Which of the following alcohol is most reactive with Lucas Reagent?

A. Ethanol **B.** Methanol
C. Isopropyl alcohol **D.** ter. Butyl alcohol

Q.12 The reaction $Na_2SO_4(aq) + BaCl_2 \rightarrow BaSO_4(s) + 2NaCl(aq)$ is the example of:

A. Reduction reaction
B. Addition reaction
C. Decomposition reaction
D. Double displacement reaction

Q.13 One of the constituents of baking powder is sodium hydrogen carbonate, the other constituent is:

A. Hydrochloric acid **B.** Acetic acid
C. Tartaric acid **D.** Sulphuric acid

Q.14 Which of the following phenomena occur, when a small amount of acid is added to water?

1. Ionization
2. Neutralization
3. Dilution
4. Salt formation

A. (1) and (3) **B.** (1) and (2)
C. (2) and (3) **D.** (2) and (4)

Q.15 When $K_2Cr_2O_7$ is mixed with H_2SO_4 and thoroughly shaken with H_2O_2 in presence of ether, then a floated blue coloured complex X is formed. The change in oxidation state and the percentage of Cr in the complex X is:

A. 6,49.8 **B.** 0,39.4 **C.** 2,76.9 **D.** 3,59.4

Q.16 Which of the following indicators is an olfactory indicator?

A. Litmus **B.** Turmeric
C. Vanilla **D.** Phenolphthalein

Q.17 Which of the following is a metal?

A. Sulphur **B.** Iodine **C.** Iron **D.** Carbon

Q.18 What are the constituents of bronze?

A. Al + Cu + Mn + Mg **B.** Cu + Zn
C. Cu + Sn **D.** Pb + Sn

Q.19 Which of the following lies in between magnesium and lead in the reactivity series?

A. Sodium **B.** Gold **C.** Calcium **D.** Zinc

Q.20 Which of the following is necessary for rusting to take place?

A. Only O_2 **B.** O_2 and H_2O
C. O_2, H_2O and CO_2 **D.** Only H_2O

Q.21 Which among the following is an example of a saturated carbon compound?

A. Ethane **B.** Ethene
C. Ethyne **D.** All of the above

Q.22 Which allotrope of carbon is a good conductor of electricity?

A. Diamond **B.** Graphite

C. Fullerene D. Coke

Q.23 Which of the following belongs to a homologous series of alkynes?

$C_6H_6, C_2H_6, C_2H_4, C_3H_4$

A. C_6H_6 **B.** C_2H_6 **C.** C_2H_4 **D.** C_3H_4

Q.24 Which of the following statements are correct for carbon compounds?

A. Most carbon compounds are good conductors of electricity.
B. Most carbon compounds are poor conductors of electricity.
C. Force of attraction between molecules of carbon compounds is not very strong.
D. Both (B) and (C)

Q.25 Which is the important site of formation of glycoproteins and glycolipids in eukaryotic cells?
[NEET UG, 2020], [MPPEB Sub Engineer (Mechanical), 2020]

A. Endoplasmic reticulum
B. Peroxisomes
C. Golgi bodies
D. Polysomes

Q.26 Water-soluble pigments found in plant cell vacuoles are:

A. Xanthophylls **B.** Chlorophylls
C. Carotenoids **D.** Anthocyanins

Q.27 The organsims which lack a nuclear membrane are called:

A. Eukaryotes
B. Prokaryotes
C. Unicellular organism
D. Multicellular organism

Q.28 Which of the following Cell organelle is responsible for Aerobic respiration?

A. Mitochondria **B.** Ribosomes
C. Nucleus **D.** Golgi apparatus

Q.29 Herbivores require a longer small intestine to digest ______.

A. Proteins **B.** Fats
C. Cellulose **D.** Vitamins

Q.30 The columnar cells that are specialized for secretion are called ______.

A. Cuboidal epithelium
B. Columnar epithelium
C. Ciliated epithelium
D. Glandular epithelium

Q.31 Chondrocytes are found in ______.

A. Blood **B.** Epithelial tissue
C. Nervous tissue **D.** Cartilage

Q.32 What is the connecting link between animal and plant called?

A. Amoeba **B.** Euglena
C. Plasmodium **D.** Paramecium

Q.33 Which of the following is not a characteristic property of aerobic respiration?

A. In aerobic respiration, there is a complete oxidation of pyruvate.
B. In aerobic respiration, two molecules of NADH are produced from the metabolism of two molecules of pyruvic acid.
C. NADH is oxidised to NAD^+ very slowly in aerobic respiration.
D. Glucose is completely degraded to CO_2 and H_2O in aerobic respiration.

Q.34 In the carbon cycle, the source of carbon to plants is:

A. Fossil fuels
B. Carbonate rocks
C. Atmospheric carbon dioxide
D. None of these

Q.35 Which are the end products of Aerobic respiration?

A. $CO_2 + H_2O +$ energy
B. CO_2 + energy
C. Sugar + energy $+H^2O$
D. $O_2 + CO_2 + H_2O$

Q.36 In which type of reaction related to plant photosynthesis, peroxisomes are involved?

A. Glycolate cycle
B. Calvin cycle
C. Bacterial photosynthesis
D. Glyoxylate cycle

Q.37 In a neuron, conversion of electric signal to chemical reaction occurs at ______.

A. cell body **B.** dendritic end
C. axonal end **D.** axon

Q.38 Electrical impulse travels in a neuron from:

A. Dendrite → axon → axonal end → cell body
B. Cell body → dendrite → axon → axonal
C. Dendrite → cell body → axon → axonal end
D. Axonal end → axon → cell body → dendrite

Q.39 The substance that triggers the fall of mature leaves and fruits from plants is ______.

A. Auxin **B.** Gibberellin
C. Abscisic acid **D.** Cytokinin

Q.40 The movement of shoot towards light is:

A. Geotropism **B.** Hydrotropism
C. Chemotropism **D.** Phototropism

Q.41 Which of the following hormones does NOT belong to the reproductive system?

A. Progesterone hormone
B. Adrenaline hormone
C. Estrogen hormone
D. Testosterone hormone

Q.42 Name the organ where the embryo develops:

A. Ureter **B.** Fallopian tube
C. Uterus **D.** Cervix

Q.43 Which of the following creatures is oviparous?

A. Frog **B.** Mouse **C.** Squirrel **D.** Rabbit

Q.44 Which hormone is released from the testes?

A. Thyroxin **B.** Adrenaline
C. Insulin **D.** Testosterone

Q.45 The number of pair of sex chromosomes in the zygote of humans is:

A. One **B.** Two **C.** Three **D.** Four

Q.46 Which of the following is totally impossible outcome of Mendel's Experiment (cross breeding pure bred tall and short pea plants)?

A. 3 tall 1 short plant
B. 24 tall and 8 short plants
C. 8 tall and o short plants
D. 4 tall plants and 1 medium-height plant

Q.47 Which of the following is not a direct conclusion that can be drawn from Mendel's Experiment?

A. Only one parental trait is expressed in F_1 generation.
B. Two copies of each trait is inherited in sexually reproducing orgainsm.
C. For recessive trait to be expressed, both copies should be identical.
D. Natural selection can alter frequency of an inherited trait.

Q.48 With whom you can associate theory of evolution?

A. Charles Darwin **B.** Mendel
C. Stanley miller **D.** Harold urey

Q.49 An object moves at a constant velocity v, for some distance x. How long it in motion?

A. $\frac{v}{x}$ **B.** $\frac{x}{v}$ **C.** $\frac{vx}{2}$ **D.** $\frac{v}{2x}$

Q.50 A picture hanging $1.5m$ above the ground falls off the wall and hits the ground. How long must it have been in the air before hitting the ground?

$g = -9.8\frac{m}{s^2}$

A. 0.55 s **B.** 4.9 s **C.** 0.15 s **D.** 0.39 s

Q.51 A man stands on a tall ladder of height h. He leans over a little too far and falls off the ladder. What would be the best way to describe his fall?

A. Parabolic motion
B. We would need to know his mass in order to determine the type of motion
C. Circular motion
D. One-dimensional motion

Q.52 What is the relationship between force, mass and acceleration?

A. Force = mass / acceleration
B. Force = mass × acceleration
C. Force = mass + acceleration
D. Force = mass - acceleration

Q.53 Which force moves an aircraft through the air?

A. Lift Force **B.** Drag Force
C. Thrust Force **D.** Gravity Force

Q.54 A bullet of mass 10 gm is fired with a velocity of 40 m/s from a gun of mass 8 kg. Find the recoil velocity (in m/s) of the gun.

A. 2 **B.** 0.1 **C.** 4 **D.** 0.05

Q.55 A heavy iron block is placed on the ground, a person tries to push the block with the force of 200 N and the block does not move. This means:

A. Friction force = Applied force
B. Friction force > Applied force
C. Friction force ≥ Applied force
D. None of the above

Q.56 Which type of force causes the change in position of a body?

A. Unbalanced Force **B.** Balanced Force
C. Mass **D.** Gravity

Q.57 The force that binds the atmosphere around the Earth is the:

A. Nuclear force
B. Force of gravity
C. Atmospheric pressure
D. None of the above

Q.58 How many times a two stage rocket should be fired to launch a satellite in its proper orbit?

A. One **B.** Two **C.** Three **D.** Four

Q.59 A missile is launched with a velocity less than the escape velocity. The sum of its kinetic and potential energy is ________.

A. Positive
B. Negative
C. Zero
D. May be positive or negative depending upon its initial velocity

Q.60 The velocity with which a projectile must be fired so that it escapes earth's gravitation does not depend on _______.

A. Mass of the earth
B. Mass of the projectile
C. Radius of the projectile's orbit
D. Gravitational constant

Q.61 The velocity of a body is increased by 4 times. Then its kinetic energy is increased by_________.

A. 16 times **B.** 4 times **C.** $\frac{1}{16}$ times **D.** $\frac{1}{4}$ times

Q.62 How much time is needed to perform 260 J of work at the rate of 10 W?

A. 24 s **B.** 52 s **C.** 26 s **D.** 32 s

Q.63 How much time is needed to perform 300 J of work at the rate of 15 W?

A. 24 s **B.** 52 s **C.** 20 s **D.** 32 s

Q.64 What would be the expenditure in 30 days at the rate of 75 paise per unit, if a bulb of 100 W is used five hours per day?

A. Rs. 10 **B.** Rs. 7.5

C. Rs. 15 D. Rs. 11.25

Q.65 Decibel is:

[UPTET Science and Maths, 2019]

A. The wavelength of noise
B. A measure of sound level
C. A musical note
D. A musical instrument

Q.66 Which of the following do not allow the sound wave to pass through it?

A. Liquid and solid B. Gas and liquid
C. Solid and gas D. Vacuum

Q.67 Sound wave in air are:

A. Transverse B. Longitudinal
C. Electromagnetic D. polarised

Q.68 1 hertz is equal to :

A. 1 vibration per minute
B. 10 vibrations per minute
C. 60 vibrations per minute
D. 600 vibrations per minute

Q.69 Which of these is a correct definition of electronic current?

A. Current that flows from lower potential to higher potential
B. The current which remains static
C. Current constituted by the flow of ions
D. Current that flows from higher potential to lower potential

Q.70 Choose the incorrect statements from the following regarding magnetic lines of field.

A. the direction of magnetic field at a point is taken to be the direction in which the north pole of a magnetic compass needle points
B. magnetic field lines are closed curves
C. if magnetic field lines are parallel and equidistant, they represent zero field strength
D. relative strength of magnetic field is shown by the degree of closeness of the field lines.

Q.71 Heating effect produced by current is due to the _______.

A. Collision of electrons
B. Movement of electrons
C. Resistance in electrons
D. Loss of energy

Q.72 On giving $220\ V$ to a resistor the power dissipated is 40 watt, then the value of resistance is:

A. 1210Ω B. 2000Ω
C. 1000Ω D. None of these

Q.73 A bar of diamagnetic material placed in an external magnetic field will ___________ field.

A. pull in the field lines and move from high to low
B. repel out the field lines and move from low to high
C. pull in the field lines and move from low to high
D. repel out the field lines and move from high to low

Q.74 Which among the following is correct regarding diamagnetic materials?

A. They have a small and positive magnetic susceptibility
B. They have a large and negative magnetic susceptibility
C. They are feebly attracted by magnets
D. They are feebly repelled by magnets

Q.75 A plotting compass is placed near the south pole of a bar magnet. The pointer of plotting compass will:

A. Point away from the south pole
B. Point parallel to the south pole
C. Point at right angles to the south pole
D. Point at right angles to the south pole

Q.76 When a hole is cut at the center of the bar magnet, then the pole strength of the bar magnet will_________.

A. Increase B. Decrease
C. Remain unchanged D. None of these

Q.77 A farming system in which crop production is combined with livestock production is:

A. Mixed farming system
B. Diversified farming system
C. Extensive farming system
D. Intercropping farming system

Q.78 The nutrients that are required by plants in smaller quantities are considered as:

A. Micronutrients B. Macronutrients
C. Mega nutrients D. Chemical nutrients

Q.79 Rice fields are preferred for pisciculture because ___________________.

A. rice is used as feed by fishes
B. it makes pisciculture more economic
C. rice grows in water beds
D. fields provide a conducive atmosphere to fishes for laying eggs

Q.80 The quality of honey largely depends upon ___________.

A. type of honeybee
B. the availability of flowers
C. climate of the area
D. conditions of the apiary

Q.81 Problem of solid waste disposal can be reduced through ________.

A. Recycling B. Lesser pollution
C. More timber D. Population control

Q.82 If Ravi is consuming curd/yogurt for lunch, which trophic level in a food chain should he be considered as occupying ?

A. First trophic level
B. Second trophic level
C. Third trophic level
D. Fourth trophic level

Q.83 The mussel can be described as:

A. Producer
B. Primary consumer
C. Secondary consumer
D. None of the above

Q.84 Which trophic level is incorrectly defined?

A. Carnivores - secondary or tertiary consumers
B. Decomposers - microbial heterotrophs
C. Herbivores - primary consumers
D. Omnivores - molds, yeast and mushrooms

Q.85 A substance has a definite shape as well as definite volume. This substance is:

[UPSESSB TGT Science, 2016]

A. Gas B. Liquid
C. Soild D. Any of these

Q.86 What is the melting point of ice?

A. - 273 C B. 273 K C. 273 C D. - 273 K

Q.87 The compound that does not form a clear solution with water is?

A. Baking powder B. Sand
C. Sugar D. Caustic soda

Q.88 In an earthen pitcher, the water remains cold due to the process of:

A. Condensation B. Evaporation
C. Sublimation D. None of these

Q.89 Which of the following is not made by quarks?

A. Neutron B. Positron
C. Proton D. π-meson

Q.90 According to Rutherford the radius of the nucleus is about _______ than the radius of the atom.

A. 10^5 times greater B. 10^5 times lesser
C. 10^9 times greater D. 10^7 times greater

Q.91 After a chemical reaction ________.

A. number of molecules remain same as before
B. number of compounds is same
C. number of atoms of each element is same
D. Both (A) and (B)

Q.92 What is the molecular formula of Propane?

A. C_4H_4 B. CH_4 C. C_2H_6 D. C_3H_8

Q.93 Upthrust on a body immersed in a fluid depends upon:

A. Depth below the surface of liquid
B. Density of body
C. Density of fluid
D. None of these

Q.94 Metacentric height is the distance between:

A. Water surface and center of pressure
B. Metacentre and center of gravity
C. Metacentre and center of buoyancy
D. Metacentre and water surface

Q.95 When on object sinks deeper in water, the force of buoyancy acting on it:

A. Decreases
B. Increases
C. Remains constant
D. First decreases, then increases

Q.96 Submarines works on which of the following principle?

A. Bernoulli's law B. Pascal's law
C. Darcy's law D. Archimedes law

Q.97 Rainbow is formed due to:

A. Only reflection
B. Dispersion and total internal reflection
C. Diffraction
D. Scattering

Q.98 Why red light is used in a danger signals?

A. Red light scattered less
B. Red light scattered more
C. Red light more deviate when passing through prism
D. None of these

Q.99 One cannot see through fog because:

A. Fog absorbs light
B. Light is scattered by the droplets in fog
C. Light suffers total reflection at the droplets in fog
D. The refractive index of fog is infinity

Q.100 The scattering of light by the colloidal particle is called:

A. Rayleigh scattering B. Tyndal scattering
C. Zeeman effect D. Compton effect

// Smart Answer Sheet //

Correct — Percentage of students who answered correctly. Skipped — Percentage of students who skipped.

Q.	Ans.	Correct / Skipped	Q.	Ans.	Correct / Skipped	Q.	Ans.	Correct / Skipped	Q.	Ans.	Correct / Skipped	Q.	Ans.	Correct / Skipped	Q.	Ans.	Correct / Skipped
1	C	89.33 % / 0.0 %	18	C	80.6 % / 0.0 %	35	A	87.1 % / 0.0 %	52	B	86.81 % / 0.0 %	69	A	68.21 % / 1.62 %	86	B	51.54 % / 1.62 %
2	D	64.09 % / 1.66 %	19	D	84.07 % / 0.0 %	36	A	13.17 % / 3.98 %	53	C	64.72 % / 1.34 %	70	C	45.08 % / 1.18 %	87	B	42.9 % / 1.33 %
3	C	48.45 % / 1.76 %	20	B	81.92 % / 0.0 %	37	C	46.0 % / 1.03 %	54	D	82.57 % / 0.0 %	71	A	41.72 % / 1.92 %	88	B	42.01 % / 1.27 %
4	C	11.53 % / 3.5 %	21	A	40.87 % / 1.19 %	38	C	62.23 % / 1.73 %	55	C	48.53 % / 1.82 %	72	A	66.82 % / 1.79 %	89	B	41.68 % / 1.5 %
5	D	67.89 % / 1.65 %	22	B	80.06 % / 0.0 %	39	C	46.65 % / 1.73 %	56	A	69.75 % / 1.6 %	73	D	60.1 % / 1.84 %	90	B	87.6 % / 0.0 %
6	D	61.41 % / 1.05 %	23	D	49.45 % / 1.09 %	40	D	52.62 % / 1.62 %	57	B	81.28 % / 0.0 %	74	D	45.56 % / 1.57 %	91	C	59.77 % / 1.94 %
7	C	86.47 % / 0.0 %	24	D	27.89 % / 4.72 %	41	B	50.08 % / 1.35 %	58	B	76.37 % / 0.0 %	75	C	26.07 % / 4.55 %	92	D	68.33 % / 1.1 %
8	B	42.97 % / 1.38 %	25	C	45.95 % / 1.87 %	42	C	63.78 % / 1.74 %	59	B	81.14 % / 0.0 %	76	C	50.67 % / 1.62 %	93	C	50.23 % / 1.86 %
9	D	18.78 % / 3.49 %	26	D	59.58 % / 1.38 %	43	A	31.7 % / 4.03 %	60	B	45.58 % / 1.39 %	77	A	42.45 % / 1.35 %	94	B	86.63 % / 0.0 %
10	D	67.53 % / 1.5 %	27	B	79.49 % / 0.0 %	44	D	53.14 % / 1.82 %	61	A	41.17 % / 1.01 %	78	A	47.56 % / 1.66 %	95	C	47.66 % / 1.18 %
11	D	22.95 % / 4.02 %	28	A	66.79 % / 1.2 %	45	A	67.34 % / 1.72 %	62	C	50.61 % / 1.67 %	79	C	52.25 % / 1.93 %	96	D	61.6 % / 1.06 %
12	D	46.3 % / 1.39 %	29	C	43.95 % / 1.24 %	46	D	52.49 % / 1.18 %	63	C	62.92 % / 1.19 %	80	B	40.89 % / 1.18 %	97	B	45.46 % / 1.76 %
13	C	40.96 % / 1.92 %	30	D	50.31 % / 1.68 %	47	D	19.04 % / 3.02 %	64	D	14.99 % / 3.44 %	81	A	77.7 % / 0.0 %	98	A	89.41 % / 0.0 %
14	A	27.24 % / 3.87 %	31	D	43.6 % / 1.1 %	48	A	53.9 % / 1.15 %	65	B	77.81 % / 0.0 %	82	C	47.21 % / 1.56 %	99	B	61.24 % / 1.5 %
15	B	67.25 % / 1.24 %	32	B	55.98 % / 1.61 %	49	B	84.92 % / 0.0 %	66	D	54.22 % / 1.6 %	83	C	55.61 % / 1.95 %	100	B	62.1 % / 1.61 %
16	C	65.26 % / 1.69 %	33	C	31.34 % / 3.86 %	50	A	22.65 % / 4.87 %	67	B	88.28 % / 0.0 %	84	D	78.69 % / 0.0 %			
17	C	67.62 % / 1.19 %	34	C	78.58 % / 0.0 %	51	A	58.63 % / 1.68 %	68	C	60.64 % / 1.92 %	85	C	49.58 % / 1.53 %			

//Hints and Solutions//

1. Gases usually have low densities mainly because the intermolecular force of attraction is better, the gas molecules are much smaller.

As a result, they move all over the space which further leads to the generation of larger intermolecular spaces. Furthermore, in comparison to solids and liquids, gases have a very small number of molecules per unit volume.

Hence, the correct option is (C).

2. Solids have the lowest kinetic energy since they cannot move and can only fluctuate about their mean position. While liquids have greater kinetic energy than solids, their molecules undergo convection and so have kinetic energy. Gas molecules have the most kinetic energy because they have random motion and travel at very high speeds.

Hence, the correct option is (D).

3. Helium gas is used in gas balloons instead of hydrogen gas because it is non-combustible.

Hydrogen and helium are the most commonly used lift gases. Although helium is twice as heavy as (diatomic) hydrogen, they are both so much lighter than air that this difference is inconsequential.

Today helium is used instead of hydrogen since it is non-combustible which makes things a lot safer. Hydrogen can ignite very easily when mixed with the oxygen of the surrounding air.

Hence, the correct option is (C).

4. Kinetic energy $<$ Potential energy: is true about solids.

In a solid the bonds are very strong already so not much potential to improve them there. A liquid has higher potential as the bonds can still increase quite a bit. When an object changes state its bonds break which increases potential energy.

Hence, the correct option is (C).

5. The atomic number of phosphorus is 15.

- The number of electronic configuration are 2,8,5.
- When the atom gains 3 electrons the orbit is filled. or otherwise the atoms should lose 5 electrons. the valency is the combining capacity of the atom. therefore the valency of phosphorus is 3 and 5.

Hence, the correct option is (D).

6. Bohr's model can only clearly explain hydrogen or hydrogen-like atoms, it fails when applied to larger and heavier atoms like iron, gold, mercury, etc.

In the Bohr model of the atom, electrons travel in defined circular orbits around the nucleus. The orbits are labeled by an integer, the quantum number n. Electrons can jump from one orbit to another by emitting or absorbing energy.

Hence, the correct option is (D).

7. Multiplication of equivalent weight and valency of an element is equal to Atomic weight.

In simple language, Equivalent weight is the mass of a compound which can combine with 1g of hydrogen or 8g of oxygen.

Atomic weight ÷ Valency = Equivalent weight

Atomic weight = Equivalent weight × Valency

Example:

Atomic weight of Calcium = 40 g and

Valency of Calcium = 2, then,

Equivalent weight of Calcium = Atomic weight of Calcium ÷ Valency of Calicium = 40 ÷ 2 = 20 g.

Hence, the correct option is (C).

8. The valency of sulphur in sulphur dioxide is 4.

- The number of electrons present in the valence shell of the atom is called the valency of an atom.
- The atomic wide variety of Sulphur is sixteen and the variety of electrons in its valence shell is 6.
- Thus each oxygen forms two bonds with the Sulphur atom making its valency 4.

Hence, the correct option is (B).

9. Neutralization reaction:

- The reaction of an acid with a base to give salt and water is called a neutralization reaction.
- Example is: NaOH (strong base) + HCl (strong acid) → NaCl + H_2O

Compounds capable of donating a pair of electrons are called Lewis Bases, and Compounds Capable of accepting a Lone pair of electrons is called a Lewis acid, this is Lewis's concept of acid and base.

- As per this concept, we see that Ammonia, NH_3, has a lone pair of electrons on its head and is capable of donating it, so it is a Lewis Base.
- On the other hand, HCl, which can donate a proton in solution, is a Bronsted Lowry Acid.
- In the given reaction, Ammonia which is a Lewis base is reacting with acid HCl, to give us a salt NH_4Cl of strong acid and weak base.

NH_3 (g) + HCl (g) → NH_4Cl (s)

- In the reaction, thus, an acid and a base is reacting to give a salt, and so, it can be categorized as a neutralization reaction.

So, the reaction NH_3 (g) + HCl (g) → NH_4Cl (s) is a Neutralisation reaction.

Hence, the correct option is (D).

10. Aluminum oxide on reaction with hydrogen chloride produces aluminum chloride and water.

- There are 2 Al atoms on both sides, so Al (Aluminium) is balanced.
- On the left side of the equation, there are 6 H atoms, so on the right side of the equation should be balanced with 6 H atoms i.e 3H2.

- There are 3 Oxygen atoms on the left side of the equation and therefore need to be balanced with 3 oxygen atoms on the right side of the equation i.e 3O.
- So, balanced equation is: $Al_2O_3 + 6HCl$ -----> $2AlCl_3 + 3H_2O$

Hence, the correct option is (D).

11. Ethanol is a primary alcohol and does not give instant turbidity with Lucas Reagent.

Methanol is also primary alcohol that does not give turbidity with Lucas Reagent.

Isopropyl alcohol is secondary alcohol that gives turbidity with Lucas Reagent after 5 to 10 minutes.

Tertiary butyl alcohol is tertiary alcohol that gives turbidity instantaneously on reaction with Lucas Reagent.

The reaction can be given as follows:

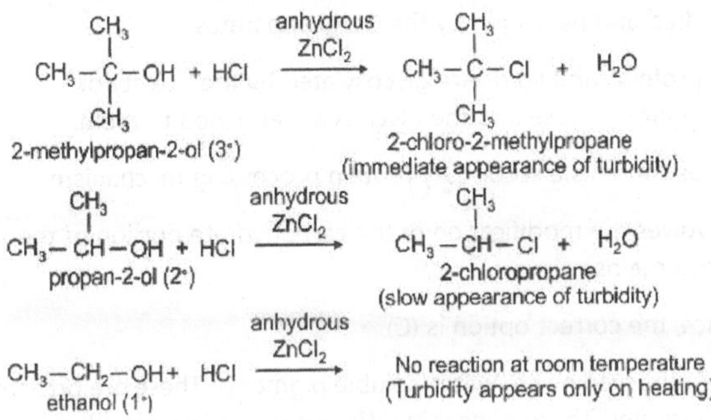

Thus, tertiary butyl alcohol is most reactive with Lucas Reagent.

Hence, the correct option is (D).

12. The reaction $Na_2SO_4(aq) + BaCl_2 \rightarrow BaSO_4(s) + 2NaCl(aq)$ is the example of double displacement reaction.

- The reaction between $Na_2SO_4 + BaCl_2$ is an endothermic reaction.
- When barium chloride $(BaCl_2)$ and sodium sulfate (Na_2SO_4), which leads to the formation of sodium chloride and barium sulphate.
- As a result of the above-given reaction, a white colour precipitate is formed due to the formation of barium sulphate.
- $\mathrm{Na_2SO_4(aq) + BaCl_2 \rightarrow BaSO_4(s) + 2NaCl(aq) + 2NaCl(aq)}$
- As the white precipitate formed is cool, the given reaction is inferred to be an endothermic reaction.
- This reaction is also an example of a double displacement reaction as two elements in the reactants are displacing each other.

Hence, the correct option is (D).

13. One of the constituents of baking powder is sodium hydrogen carbonate, the other constituent is tartaric acid.

Baking powder contains a base which is generally bicarbonate, a dry buffer and an acid salt. The acid salt is a weak acid which is responsible for reacting with the base and thus producing carbon dioxide, providing leavening to the mixture. Tartaric acid used in baking powder where it serves as the source of acid that reacts with baking soda. This reaction produces carbon dioxide gas and lets products rise using active yeast cultures as a source of carbon dioxide gas.

Hence, the correct option is (C).

14. Both the phenomenon of ionisation and dilution occurs when a small amount of acid is added to water.

When an acid is diluted with water, the concentration of H+ ions decreases. The dilution of acid is an exothermic process and releases heat. For diluting any acids, it is better to add acid to the water rather than adding water to the acid.

Ionization of acid is its dissociation into ions. Weak acids are only partially ionized in their solutions. The ionisation of weak acid is an equilibrium reaction and never reaches completion and hence a weak acid is never completely dissociated.

Hence, the correct option is (A).

15. When $K_2Cr_2O_7$, reacts with H_2O_2, a blue colored compound is formed which is CrO_5.

The oxidation number of Cr in CrO_5 is $+6$, because four of oxygen atoms are involved in peroxide linkage.

So, change in oxidation state from $K_2Cr_2O_7$, to CrO_5 is 0.

The percentage of chromium in the complex is $\frac{52}{132} \times 100 = 39.4\%$.

The structure of CrO_5 is shown below:

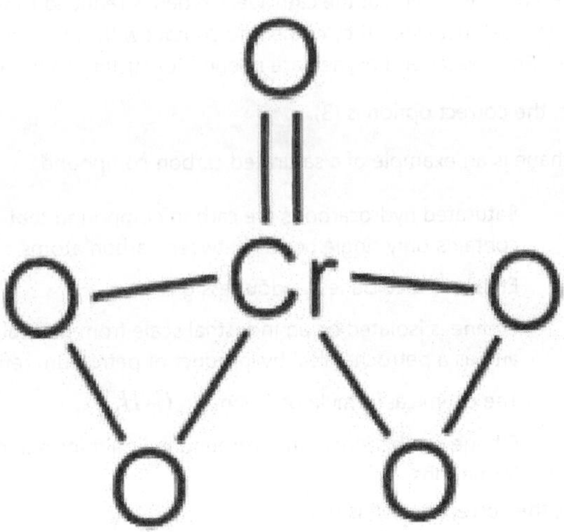

Hence, the correct option is (B).

16. Vanilla is an olfactory indicator.

An olfactory indicator is a substance whose smell varies depending on whether it is mixed with an acidic or basic solution. Moreover, these indicators can be used in the laboratory to test whether a solution is a base or an acid. Some of the examples of these types of indicators are vanilla extract, onion and clove oil. The vanilla extract has a characteristic pleasant smell. However, an acidic solution does not destroy the smell of vanilla extract whereas a basic solution does.

Hence, the correct option is (C).

17. Iron is a metal.

- Metals have a metallic bond and forms positive ion (cation).
- Metals have opaque, lustrous, ductile sonorous properties.
- Metal is a good conductor of heat and electricity.

Examples of metal are: Iron, copper, zinc, etc.

Hence, the correct option is (C).

18. An alloy is a homogenous mixture of two or more metals, or a metal and a non-metal.

Cu + Sn alloy called Bronze, are not good conductors of electricity whereas copper is used for making electrical circuits.

Hence, the correct option is (C).

19. Zinc lies between magnesium and lead in the reactivity series.

Reactivity series of metals and nonmetals are the lists, in which we arrange them in the decreasing order of their chemical activity. It is also known as the activity series. The reactivity series helps us to predict the capability of a metal to displace another metal during a displacement reaction.

Hence, the correct option is (D).

20. The rusting of iron (iron in contact with water forms the anode and in contact with air forms the cathode). At the anode, iron is oxidized to Fe^{2+} and at the cathode, oxygen is reduced to water. Iron and steel rust when they come into contact with water and oxygen. Both water and oxygen are needed for rusting to occur.

Hence, the correct option is (B).

21. Ethane is an example of a saturated carbon compound.

- Saturated hydrocarbons are carbon compound that contains only single bonds between carbon atoms.
- Ethane is a colourless, odourless gas.
- Ethane is isolated on an industrial scale from natural gas and as a petrochemical by-product of petroleum refining.
- The chemical formula of Ethane is C_2H_6.
- Ethane can be found underground in liquid form in rock formations.

Hence, the correct option is (A).

22. Graphite is a good conductor of electricity.

Graphite is an allotrope of carbon which conducts electricity due to de-localisation of the electrons above and below the planes of the carbon atoms.

Graphite is a good conductor of heat and electricity. This is because, like metals, graphite contains delocalised (free) electrons. These electrons are free to move through the structure of the graphite.

Hence, the correct option is (B).

23. Homologous series is a series of compounds with similar chemical properties and some functional groups differing from the successive member by CH_2. Carbon chains of varying lengths have been observed in organic compounds having the same general formula. C_3H_4 belongs to a homologous series of alkynes.

Hence, the correct option is (D).

24. Carbon compounds form covalent bonds, and they do not give rise to free electrons because all electrons are used to create the covalent bond. Also carbon compound does not dissociate itself into ions, so carbon compounds are poor electrical conductors. They do not have strong force of attraction between molecules of carbon compounds because covalent bond is weaker than ionic bond.

Hence, the correct option is (D).

25. The contents synthesized by the endoplasmic reticulum are modified and packaged by the Golgi apparatus.

The proteins and lipids are glycosylated by the activity of glycosyltransferase and the glycans are attached to them.

Glycosylation is a secondary protein processing mechanism.

It involves the modification of the carbohydrate portion of the glycoproteins.

Hence, the correct option is (C).

26. Anthocyanins are water-soluble pigments. These are present In the vacuoles. These appear in different colors like red, blue, or purple depending on the pH.

Xanthophylls are the typical yellow pigments of leaves.

Chlorophyll is a term used for several closely related green pigments found in cyanobacteria and the chloroplasts of algae and plants.

Carotenoids are plant pigments responsible for bright red, yellow, and orange hues in many fruits and vegetables. These pigments play an important role in plant's health.

Hence, the correct option is (D).

27. The organsims which lack a nuclear membrane are called prokaryotes.

- In some organisms like bacteria, the nuclear region of the cell may be poorly defined due to the absence of a nuclear membrane.
- Such an undefined nuclear region containing only nucleic acids is called a nucleoid.
- Such organisms, whose cells lack a nuclear membrane, are called prokaryotes (Pro = primitive or primary; karyote » karyon = nucleus).
- Organisms with cells having a nuclear membrane are called eukaryotes.
- Prokaryotic cells also lack most of the other cytoplasmic organelles present in eukaryotic cells.
- Many of the functions of such organelles are also performed by poorly organised parts of the cytoplasm.

Hence, the correct option is (B).

28. Mitochondria Cell organelle is responsible for Aerobic respiration.

Mitochondria are called the powerhouse of the cell because it produces ATP, which is the energy-giving molecule. The ATP is released in the process of aerobic respiration within the mitochondria, in the presence of oxygen.

Hence, the correct option is (A).

29. Herbivores require a longer small intestine to digest cellulose as it eats grass/green leafy vegetables, made up of cellulose and fiber which are hard to digest. Therefore, herbivores need a longer small intestine to allow the complete digestion of cellulose. Carnivores eat smaller amounts of food compared to herbivores and so are easy to digest and hence they have a shorter intestine.

Hence, the correct option is (C).

30. The columnar cells that are specialized for secretion are called Glandular epithelium.

- Some of the columnar or cuboidal cells get specialized for secretion and are called the glandular epithelium.
- They are mainly of two types: unicellular, consisting of isolated glandular cells (goblet cells of the alimentary canal), and multicellular, consisting of a cluster of cells (salivary gland).
- The Unicellular glandular columnar epithelium cells are present in the stomach, colon & rectum.

Hence, the correct option is (D).

31. Chondrocytes are found in Cartilage. Cartilage is a specialized type of skeletal connective tissue. It provides support to the body. Mature cells of cartilage are called "chondrocytes". They are found in matrix cavities called lacunae. Each lacuna has 1-4 chondrocytes.

Hence, the correct option is (D).

32. Euglena, a genus of more than 1,000 species of single-celled flagellated microorganisms that feature both plant and animal characteristics. Euglena lives in fresh and brackish water rich in organic matter and can also be found in moist soils.

Hence, the correct option is (B).

33. NADH is oxidised to NAD^+ very slowly is not a characteristic property of aerobic respiration.

Characteristic property of aerobic respiration:

- Glucose is completely degraded to CO_2 and H_2O in aerobic respiration.
- In aerobic respiration, two molecules of NADH are produced from the metabolism of two molecules of pyruvic acid.
- In aerobic respiration, there is a complete oxidation of pyruvate.
- Gases are exchanged in this form of respiration.
- It can be found in the cytoplasm and the mitochondria.
- Glucose breaks down into carbon dioxide and water.
- All higher organisms such as mammals have this type of respiration.

Hence, the correct option is (C).

34. In the carbon cycle, the source of carbon to plants is atmospheric carbon dioxide.

Plants take the atmospheric carbon dioxide in presence of Sunlight and do photosynthesis and produce glucose and oxygen as a byproduct. The plants are not able to take carbon directly from carbonate rocks and fossil fuels. In order to use the carbon by plants, it is necessary that carbon is taken as atmospheric carbon dioxide.

Hence, the correct option is (C).

35. Aerobic respiration is where oxygen is used for the breakdown of carbohydrates to release energy.

The overall process of aerobic respiration can be represented as:

$$C_6H_{12}O_6 + 6O_2 \rightarrow 6CO_2 + 6H_2O + \text{energy (as ATP)}$$

Hence, the correct option is (A).

36. Glycolate cycle is also known as photorespiration that takes place in C_3 plants and occurs in chloroplasts, mitochondria and peroxisomes of plant cells. This pathway is involved in the formation of amino acids glycine and serine from nonphosphorylated intermediates of carbon reduction cycle of photosynthesis. Glycolate is the chief metabolite of photorespiration. Photorespiration is an oxidative process where oxidation of glycolate occurs with subsequent release of CO_2.

Hence, the correct option is (A).

37. Signals are transferred from one neuron to another. The electrical signals are very fast as compared to that of chemical signals. Myelinated sheath present on the surface of neurons helps in better conduction of signals. At the end of the axon (axonal end), the electrical signal is converted into a chemical signal, and the axon releases chemical messengers called neurotransmitters (acetylcholine) which are received by their receptors on the dendrites of the subsequent neuron. This region is called synapse. So, the correct answer is 'Axonal end'.

Hence, the correct option is (C).

38. Electrical impulse travels in a neuron from Dendrite → cell body → axon → axonal end.

- Nerve or electrical impulses are the electrochemical processes that occur due to the difference in the action potential across the plasma membrane of the neurons.
- Dendrites receive impulses and transmit these toward the cell body.
- The axon transmits electrical impulses away from the cell body to a synapse or to a neuromuscular junction.
- The synaptic knobs are present in the axonal end and they contain neurotransmitters. These help to transmit impulses to another neuron.
- A nerve impulse leaves a neuron through the axonal ends.

Hence, the correct option is (C).

39. Abscistic acid is a plant hormone which promotes senescence of leaves and causes abscission of flowers and fruits. Abscisic acid is one example of a hormone which inhibits growth. Its effects include wilting of leaves.

Hence, the correct option is (C).

40. The movement of shoot towards light is phototropism.

- Phototropism is the growth movements of curvature in response to unidirectional light.
- The stimulus of sunlight allows movement of the plant by the bending of the shoots towards the incoming sunlight.
- The tip of the shoot is the perceptive region for the sensation of phototropism.
- It is of two types positive and negative phototropism.

Hence, the correct option is (D).

41. Adrenaline hormone does not belong to the reproductive system.

Adrenaline:

This hormone is secreted by the adrenal glands in the centre of the medulla. The main function of adrenaline is to produce contraction of the spleen so as to store the blood, increase heartbeat and sweating, reduce the blood clotting period, and pupillary dilation.

Progesterone hormone:

Progesterone is an endogenous steroid and progestogen sex hormone involved in the menstrual cycle, pregnancy, and embryogenesis of humans and other species. It belongs to a group of steroid hormones called progestogens and is the major progestogen in the body.

Estrogen hormone:

Estrogen, or oestrogen, is a category of sex hormones responsible for the development and regulation of the female reproductive system and secondary sex characteristics.

Testosterone hormone:

Testosterone is the primary sex hormone and an anabolic steroid in males. In male humans, testosterone plays a key role in the development of male reproductive tissues such as the testes and prostate, as well as promoting secondary sexual characteristics such as increased muscle and bone mass, and the growth of body hair.

Hence, the correct option is (B).

42. The embryo develops in Uterus.

Organ	Function
Ureter	The ureter is a tube in the human body that carries urine to the urinary bladder.
Fallopian Tube	Zygote is formed in Fallopian tube.
Uterus	It is also called as womb. Zygote travels to uterus to form Embryo/ foetus.
Cervix	It narrow tube that connects vagina to Uterus.

Hence, the correct option is (C).

43. Oviparous animals are those which lay eggs. Examples of Oviparous animals include birds, reptiles, amphibians, fish, etc. Viviparous animals give birth to completely developed living young animals. examples- cattle, human, etc.

Hence, the correct option is (A).

44. The hormone released from testes is Testosterone. Testosterone is the male sex hormone. It plays a key role in the development of male reproductive tissues such as the testis and prostate. It also increases the growth of body hair.

Hormone	Function	Gland
Thyroxin	It helps in maintaining the body's metabolism.	Thyroid
Insulin	It helps in regulating sugar levels in the body.	Pancreas
Adrenaline	It increases the heart rate, blood pressure etc during emergency situations.	Adrenal Gland

Hence, the correct option is (D).

45. The number of pairs of both the autosomes as well as sex chromosome remains the same in the human zygote, as in adult human. An adult human has twenty-three pairs of chromosomes out of which twenty-two pairs are autosomes and one pair is sex chromosome. The Same chromosomal constitution is expected in the human zygote because the adult human is derived from human zygote.

So, the human zygote has twenty-two pairs of autosomes and one pair of sex chromosome. In a zygote, which will develop into male the sex chromosome pair will comprise of one X and one Y chromosome. In a zygote, which will develop into female the sex chromosome pair will comprise of two X chromosomes.

Hence, the correct option is (A).

46. Mendelian phenotypic ratio of a Monohybrid cross is 3:1, where three represent the dominant trait while 1 represents the recessive trait. There is no blending inheritance present in Mendelian crosses so, a tall plant crossed with a dwarf plant will either give tall or dwarf plant but not a medium-height plant.

So, the wrong option is '4 tall plants and 1 medium-height plant.'

Hence, the correct option is (D).

47. The conclusions drawn by Mendel based on his experiments on Pea plants resulted in the laws of inheritance, those laws were,

Option (D). Natural selection is a concept put forth by Charles Darwin, where nature selects certain traits that are better adapted for survival over others, be it recessive or dominant. Therefore, can alter the frequency of an inherited trait. So, the correct answer is 'Natural selection can alter the frequency of an inherited trait.'

Option (A). Law of dominance: A cross between contrasting alleles of the same trait will result in progeny (F_1) expressing only one trait, that is, dominant.

Option (B). Law of purity of gamete: Every sexually reproducing organism produces gametes which are true for the traits they carry, that is, carry one copy of every trait. The fusion of male and female gametes results in two copies in the progeny.

Option (C). A recessive trait is always expressed in homozygous condition - example, tt, rr, etc.

Hence, the correct option is (D).

48. Charles Darwin gave the theory of evolution. Darwinism is a theory of biological evolution developed by the English naturalist Charles Darwin (1809–1882) and others, stating that all species of organisms arise and develop through the natural selection of small, inherited variations that increase the individual's ability to compete, survive, and reproduce.

Hence, the correct option is (A).

49. An object moves at a constant velocity v, for some distance x. Then it is in motion $\frac{x}{v}$

The relationship between velocity, distance and time is:

$$v = \frac{\Delta x}{\Delta t}$$

$$\Rightarrow \Delta t = \frac{\Delta x}{v}$$

The quotient of distance and velocity will give us the time that the object was in motion.

Hence, the correct option is (B).

50. Given:

$$g = -9.8\frac{m}{s^2}$$

Distance traveled $\Delta y = 1.5m$

The initial velocity of the figure is zero, because it starts from rest.

We can use the appropriate motion equation to solve for the final velocity:

$$\Delta y = v_i t + \frac{1}{2}at^2$$

The displacement will be negative because the ball is traveling in a downward direction.

$$-1.5 = 0t + \frac{1}{2}(-9.8)t^2$$

$$-1.5 = -4.9t^2$$

$$1.5 = 4.9t^2$$

$$\frac{1.5}{4.9} = t^2$$

$$0.306 = t^2$$

$$\sqrt{0.306} = \sqrt{t^2}$$

$$t = 0.55s$$

Hence, the correct option is (A).

51. The man's fall will be parabolic as there will be both horizontal and vertical components. His vertical component of the fall will be standard free-fall caused by his acceleration due to gravity. His horizontal component of the fall will come from him "leaning too far" in one direction. Even a small horizontal velocity will create a horizontal trajectory.

This is why when people lean and fall off of ladders they either try to grab onto the ladder (try to negate their horizontal velocity) or fall a small distance away from the base of the ladder.

Hence, the correct option is (A).

52. Newton's second law is often stated as F = ma, which means the force (F) acting on an object is equal to the mass (m) of object times its acceleration (a). This means the more mass an object has, the more force you need to accelerate it, and the greater the force, the greater the object's acceleration.

- Force(F) = Mass(m) × Acceleration(a).
- Unit of Force = SI unit of Force is in Newtons (N).
- 1 Newton is equal to 1 kg*m*s^{-2}.
- Acceleration of an object is directly related to the net force and inversely related to its mass.
- Acceleration of an object depends on two things, force and mass.
- Mass is a measure of the amount of matter in an object.
- Mass is usually measured in grams (g) or kilograms (kg).
- An object's mass is constant in all circumstances, contrast this with its weight, a force that depends on gravity.

Hence, the correct option is (B).

53. Thrust is the force that moves an aircraft through the air.

Thrust is a mechanical force. It is generated most often through the reaction of accelerating a mass of gas. The engine does work on the gas and as the gas is accelerated to the rear, the engine is accelerated in the opposite direction. The acceleration of the engine mass produces a force on the aircraft.

Hence, the correct option is (C).

54. Given:

Mass of bullet $= 10$ gm $= 0.01$ kg, Mass of Gun $= 8$ kg and Velocity of Bullet $= 40$ m/s

As we know,

$\Rightarrow$ Momentum $=$ Mass $\times$ Velocity

According to the Law of conservation of linear momentum,

$\Rightarrow$ Momentum of Bullet $(M_B) =$ Momentum of Gun (M_G)

$\Rightarrow$ Mass of Bullet $\times$ Velocity $=$ Mass of Gun $\times$ Velocity (V_G)

$\Rightarrow 0.01$ kg $\times 40$ m/s $= 8$ kg $\times V_G$

$\Rightarrow V_G = \left(\frac{1}{20}\right)$ m/s

$\Rightarrow V_G = 0.05$ m/s

Hence, the correct option is (D).

55. A heavy iron block is placed on the ground, a person tries to push the block with the force of 200 N and the block does not move. This means friction force ≥ applied force.

It is a kind of resisting force that acts between two contact bodies to avoid relative motion between them.

Since the block does not move so frictional force (fs) ≥ Applied force

This means frictional force (fs) ≥ 200 N

Hence, the correct option is (C).

56. Unbalanced Force causes the change in position of a body.

Unbalanced forces are not equal forces, and they cause the motion of an object to change the speed and/or direction that it is moving. When two unbalanced forces are exerted in opposite directions, Their combined force is equal to the difference between the two forces.

Hence, the correct option is (A).

57. The force that binds the atmosphere around the Earth is the Force of gravity.

Force of gravity acts between two bodies in which one of the body is always the Earth. It also provide the necessary centripetal force to the celestial bodies around the Earth including the moon to revolve around itself.

Thus, the force of gravity binds the atmosphere around the Earth.

Hence, the correct option is (B).

58. Two times a two stage rocket should be fired to launch a satellite in its proper orbit. The two forces acting on the rocket immediately after leaving the launching pad are gravitational force and frictional force. The gravitational force acts downwards towards the earth and frictional force acts due to surrounding air.

Hence, the correct option is (B).

59. A missile is launched with a velocity less than the escape velocity. The sum of its kinetic and potential energy is negative.

The sum of kinetic energy and potential energy is negative. This is because for the velocity less than escape velocity the missile is bounded due to gravitational field of the earth. so, its total energy is negative.

Hence, the correct option is (B).

60. The velocity with which a projectile must be fired so that it escapes earth's gravitation does not depend on mass of the projectile.

Escape velocity formula is given by:

$$v_e = \sqrt{\frac{2GM}{R}}$$

In this expression we can see mass of earth (M), Radius of Earth (R), Gravitational constant (G). Mass of projectile does not matter.

Hence, the correct option is (B).

61. Given that:

Velocity of a body is increased by 4 times.

So $v' = 4v$ i.e changed velocity

Kinetic Energy $= \frac{1}{2}(m \times v^2)$

Kinetic Energy $E' = \frac{1}{2}(m \times v'^2) = \frac{1}{2}(m \times (4v)^2)$

$E' = 16E$

Hence, the correct option is (A).

62. Given,

Work done $=$ W $= 260$ J

Power $=$ P $= 10$ W

Power is the rate of doing work,

$$P = \frac{W}{t}$$

or, $t = \frac{W}{P} = \frac{260}{10} = 26$ sec

Therefore, the time needed to perform 260 J of work at the rate of 10 W is 26 s.

Hence, the correct option is (C).

63. Given,

Work done $=$ W $= 300$ J

Power $=$P $= 15$ W

Power is the rate of doing work,

$$P = \frac{W}{t}$$

or, $t = \frac{W}{P} = \frac{300}{15} = 20$ sec

Therefore, the time needed to perform 300 J of work at the rate of 15 W is 20 sec.

Hence, the correct option is (C).

64. 1 Unit of electricity $= 1kWh = 1000Watt -$ hour $= 3.6 \times 10^6 J$

1 Kilo-watt $= 1000Watt$

$100W = 0.1kW \quad [\because 1kW = 1000W]$

In 30 days total consumption of the bulb $= 0.1kW \times 30$ days $\times\, 5$ hours $/$ day $= 15kWh$

Given, cost of 1 unit $= 75$ paise

So total expenditure $= 75 \times 15 = 1125$ paise = Rs. 11.25

Hence, the correct option is (D).

65. A decibel is a logarithmic unit used to measure sound level.

- It is also widely used in electronics, signals and communication.
- The higher the decibel level, the louder the noise.
- On the decibel scale, the level increase of 10 means that a sound is actually 10 times more intense, or powerful.
- A whisper is about 30 dB and a normal conversation is about 60 dB.
- Noise above 70 dB over a prolonged period of time may start to damage our hearing and Loud noise above 120 dB can cause immediate harm to our ears.

Hence, the correct option is (B).

66. A vacuum does not allow the sound wave to pass through it.

- A vacuum is a medium through which sound waves cannot escape. A vacuum is basically an area without air.
- Since sound waves are mechanical waves, they cannot propagate through a medium without vibration so sound cannot propagate through a vacuum.
- Sound waves can propagate through solid, liquid, and gaseous media.

Hence, the correct option is (D).

67. As sound waves are longitudinal waves, the air particles vibrate to and from in the direction of the propagation of sound. It is produced by the vibration of it source. It is heard if the frequency is between 20 Hz to $20,000$ Hz. It is a wave of compression and rarefaction. Compression is the region with high air density and rarefaction is the region with low air density.

Hence, the correct option is (B).

68. Hertz is the unit of frequency.

$1\ Hz = 1$ vibration per $\sec = 60$ vibrations per minute.

Hence, the correct option is (C).

69. The current that flows from a point at the lower (negative) potential to a point at higher (positive) potential is called electronic current. Electronic current is produced by the movement of negatively charged electrons.

Hence, the correct option is (A).

70. Incorrect statement about the magnetic field lines is that if magnetic field lines are parallel and equidistant then they represent zero field strength because if they are parallel and are at equal distance then they have uniform magnetic field and doesn't have zero magnetic field strength.

Hence, the correct option is (C).

71. Heating effect produced by current is due to the Collision of electrons.

When a potential difference is applied across the ends of a conductor, its free electrons get accelerated in the opposite direction of the applied field. But the speed of the electrons does not increase beyond a constant drift speed. This is because, during the course of their motion, the electrons collide frequently with the positive metal ions.

The kinetic energy gained by the electrons during the intervals of free acceleration between collisions is transferred to the metal ions at the time of the collision. The metal ions begin to vibrate about their mean positions more and more violently.

The average kinetic energy of the ions increases. This increases the temperature of the conductor. Thus the conductor gets heated due to the flow of current.

Hence, the correct option is (A).

72. Given:

Potential difference $(V) = 220\ V$ and power of the bulb $(P) = 40\ W$

The resistance can be calculated as,

$$R = \frac{V^2}{P}$$

$$= \frac{(220)^2}{40} = 1210\Omega$$

Hence, the correct option is (A).

73. A bar of diamagnetic material placed in an external magnetic field will repel out the field lines and move from high to low field.

Diamagnetic Substances: The substances which are weekly magnetized when placed in an external magnetic field, in a direction opposite to the applied field are called diamagnetic substances.

Example: Copper, lead, gold, silver, zinc, antimony, bismuth, etc.

Properties:

- These substances are repelled by a magnet.
- Atomic orbitals of these substances are completely filled.
- It develops weak magnetization in a direction opposite to the direction of the applied magnetic field.
- As soon as the magnetizing field removed, it loses its magnetization.
- When placed in a non-uniform magnetic field, it tends to move from stronger to weaker regions of the magnetic field.
- When placed in a uniform magnetic field, it aligns itself perpendicular to the direction of the magnetic field.
- Magnetic susceptibility is a small negative value.
- Relative permeability is close to one and always less than 1.
- Magnetic permeability is slightly less compared to free space.

Hence, the correct option is (D).

74. Diamagnetic materials are feebly repelled by magnets. X is negative and very small. Diamagnetic materials are those that some people generally think of as non-magnetic, and include water, wood, most organic compounds such as petroleum and some plastics, and many metals including copper, particularly the heavy ones with many core electrons, such as mercury, gold and bismuth.

Hence, the correct option is (D).

75. A plotting compass is placed near the south pole of a bar magnet. The pointer of plotting compass point towards the south pole.

As you get closer to the magnetic South Pole, the field lines will curve to dive straight into the magnetic South Pole, running perpendicular to Earth's surface. "So quite often, compasses actually won't work," said Tom Jordan, a geophysicist with the British Antarctic Survey.

Hence, the correct option is (C).

76. When a hole is cut at the center of the bar magnet, then the pole strength of the bar magnet will remain unchanged.

- The point on the magnet which has maximum attraction property is called the poles of the magnet.
- The poles of the magnet lie slightly inside from the end.

- When a hole is cut at the center of the bar magnet its end remains unaffected where the poles of the magnet lie.

Hence, the correct option is (C).

77. A farming system in which crop production is combined with livestock production is the mixed farming system.

A type of farming in which the production of crops is done with the rearing of livestock on one farm is known as mixed farming. It is a system of farming in which a farmer conducts different types of agricultural practices together. Mixed farming is done with the view of increasing his income through different sources. Mixed farming is the combining of two independent agricultural enterprises on the same farm.

Hence, the correct option is (A).

78. The nutrients that are required by plants in smaller quantities are considered as micronutrients.

Micronutrients are vitamins and minerals needed by the body in very small amounts. However, their impact on a body's health are critical, and deficiency in any of them can cause severe and even life-threatening conditions.

Example: iron, manganese, boron, zinc, copper, molybdenum, chlorine

Hence, the correct option is (A).

79. Rice fields are preferred for pisciculture because rice grows in water beds.

The artificial reproduction, rearing, and transplantation of fish are called pisciculture. It is also called fish farming. It is the main type of aquaculture whereas other methods can fall within the framework of mariculture. This includes the commercial raising of fish in tanks or enclosures, typically for food. Fish species from fish farms include cabbage, tilapia catfish, and salmon. Fish crop production among rice crops gives off-seasonal occupation to the farmer.

Hence, the correct option is (C).

80. The quality of honey largely depends upon the availability of flowers.

The composition and quality of honey are variable and it depends mainly on the botanical source of nectar from which it is obtained, but also depends upon the pasturage, or the flowers available to the bees for nectar and pollen collection. In addition to an adequate quantity of pasturage, the kind of flowers available will determine the taste of the honey.

Hence, the correct option is (B).

81. Problem of solid waste disposal can be reduced through recycling.

Recycling is the process of converting waste materials into new materials and objects. It is an alternative to "conventional" waste disposal that can save material and help lower greenhouse gas emissions. Recycling can prevent the waste of potentially useful materials and reduce the consumption of fresh raw materials, thereby reducing: energy usage, air pollution (from incineration), and water pollution.

Hence, the correct option is (A).

82. Curd is made from milk which is obtained from cow. Cow is a primary consumer that feeds on producer (grass) and occupies the second trophic level. Consuming the produce obtained from an organism at second trophic level makes Ravi belong to the third trophic level.

Hence, the correct option is (C).

83. In the food web, if we observe the position of mussels with respect to other organisms, we will notice that algae is the primary producer, microscopic animals consume algae and are the primary consumers and mussels are at the next trophic level and are the secondary consumers.

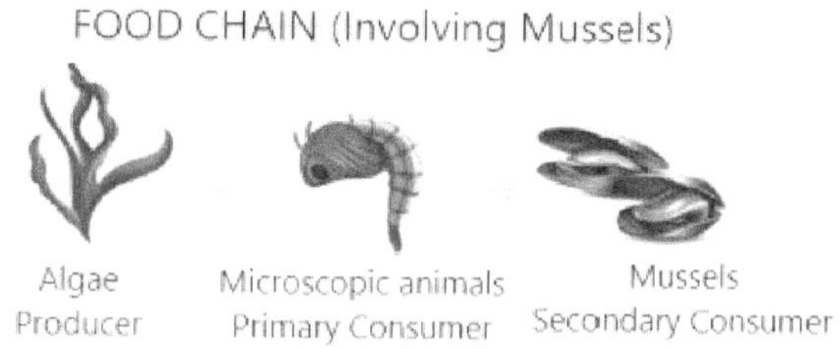

Hence, the correct option is (C).

84. Omnivores - molds, yeast and mushrooms, trophic level is incorrectly defined.

Omnivores consume both plant and animal matter .Molds, yeasts and mushrooms are saprophytes that feed on dead and decaying matter.

Hence, the correct option is (D).

85. A substance has a definite shape as well as definite volume. This substance is Soild.

States of matter:

- Matter exists in nature in different forms, the three basic states of matter are Solid, Liquid and Gas.

Properties of Solid:

- In solids, the particles are closely packed and the gaps between the particles are tiny and hence it is tough to compress them.

Properties of Liquid:

- In a liquid, particles are less tightly packed as compared to solids and less difficult to compress as compare to solid because particles have less space between them to move but more than the that of solid.

Properties of Gas:

- In gases, particles are far apart from each other, the force of attraction between the particles is negligible and they can move freely.

Hence, the correct option is (C).

86. The melting point of ice is 273 K.

- Water can exist in all three forms, i.e., solid, liquid, and gas.
- Solid in the form of ice, liquid in the form of water, and gas in the form of water vapours.

- The melting point is the temperature at which a substance changes its state from solid into liquid.
- For ice, the temperature in degree Celcius is 0 and in kelvin, it is 273.
- Kelvin is the SI unit of temperature and 0°C = 273 K
- The formula for converting °C into K is: K = 273 + temperature in °C
- The temperature at which a liquid transforms into gas is termed as its boiling point.
- For water, the boiling point is 100°C, i.e., 373 K.

Hence, the correct option is (B).

87. Sand does not form a clear solution because it contains minute dust particles on its surface which get mixed with the water, thus making it turbid.

Though the sand gets settled at the bottom of the container the water still will be turbid.

Sedimentation and Decantation:

- These methods are used when one component is a liquid and the other is an insoluble solid, heavier than liquid, i.e. mud and water.
- If muddy water is allowed to stand undisturbed for some time in a beaker, the particles of the earth (clay and sand) settle at the bottom. This process is called sedimentation.
- The partially clear liquid at the top can be gently transferred into another beaker. This process is known as decantation.

Hence, the correct option is (B).

88. In an earthen pitcher, the water remains cold due to the process of Evaporation.

- An earthen pitcher used in summer cools water in it essentially by evaporation of water from its porous surface.
- The walls of an earthen pot are porous, which leads to seepage of water and evaporates from the surface of the pot.
- The heat required for evaporation is taken from the water inside the pot, thus cooling the water stored inside. This is the reason why water remains cool in the earthen pot even on hot summer days.

Hence, the correct option is (B).

89. Quark: A quark is a fundamental particle of matter. It is a type of elementary particle of atoms.

There are 6 types of quark (up, down, strange, charm, bottom, and top)

Quarks combine to form composite particles called hadrons, the most stable hadrons are protons and neutrons.

- The proton is to be composed of two up quarks, one down quark.
- The neutron is to be composed of two down quarks and one up quark.
- Similarly, the positron is composed of quarks particles.
- π-meson: Any of three subatomic particles: π^0, π^+ , and π^- are pi meson.
- Pi mesons are the lightest mesons.

Hence, the correct option is (B).

90. According to Rutherford the radius of the nucleus is about 10^5 times lesser than the radius of the atom.

According to Rutherford, the volume of the nucleus is negligible in comparison to the total volume of the atom. The radius of an atom is about 10^{-10} and the radius of the nucleus is 10^{-15}.

Hence, the correct option is (B).

91. After a chemical reaction number of atoms of each element is same.

- Matter cannot be created or destroyed, according to the Law of conservation of matter.
- So, the number of atoms of each element in the reactants must match the number of atoms of each element in the products in chemical equations.
- In a chemical equation, there are no new atoms formed, and there are no atoms destroyed.
- All atoms of the reactant(s), thus must equal the atoms of the product, according to the Law of Conservation.
- As a result, chemical equations must be balanced.
- This is accomplished by including coefficients into the reactants and/or products.

Hence, the correct option is (C).

92. The chemical name of molecular formula C_3H_8 is Propane.

- Propane, with molecular formula C_3H_8 has 10 covalent bonds in its structure.
- C_3H_6 is called propene
- Covalent bond: The chemical bond formed by sharing of two valence electron between the two atoms.
- There are 8 carbon-hydrogen covalent bonds and 2 carbon-carbon covalent bonds present in the propane molecule. So, the total number of covalent bonds present in propane is (8 + 2 = 10).

Hence, the correct option is (D).

93. When a body is either wholly or partially immersed in a fluid, a lift is generated due to the net vertical component of hydrostatic pressure forces experienced by the body. This lift is called the buoyant force and the phenomenon is called buoyancy.

The Archimedes principle states that the buoyant force on a submerged body is equal to the weight of liquid displaced by the body and acts vertically upward through the centroid of the displaced volume.

Thus, the net weight of the submerged body, (the net vertical downward force experienced by it) is reduced from its actual weight by an amount that equals the buoyant force.

$$F_B = \rho g h A = \rho g V$$

$$F_B = f(V_{\text{displaced}}, \rho)$$

Hence, the correct option is (C).

94. Metacentre is defined as the point about which a body starts oscillating when body is tilted by a small angle.

- The metacentre may also be defined as the point at which the line of action of the force of buoyancy will meet the normal axis of the body when the body is given a small angular displacement.
- The distance MG i.e. the distance between the metacentre of a floating body and the centre of gravity of the body is called metacentric height.
- It is measured along the line BG.

Hence, the correct option is (B).

95. Archimedes principle:

- Any object which is submerged in a fluid is acted upon by an upward force whose magnitude is equal to the weight of the fluid displaced.
- The upward force applied on the object is called as buoyant force.
- If the mass of the object is m then mg is the weight (W) of the object. Weight of any object always act in downward direction
- The boyant force $F_b = \rho V g$.
- Where ρ = density, V = displaced volume and g = acceleration due t
- It does not depend upon height and hence it remains constant.

Hence, the correct option is (C).

96. Archimedes Principle/Law:

- Archimedes' principle states that the upward force which is exerted by an object that is either partially or fully immersed in a fluid is equal to the weight of the liquid displaced by the object. This principle helps to prove the Law of floatation.
- The law of floatation states that the weight of a floating body is equal to the weight of the liquid displaced by it.
- For Example- A ship or submarine in the ocean does not sink until the weight of the water it displaces is equal to its own weight

Hence, the correct option is (D).

97. Rainbow is formed due to dispersion and total internal reflection.

- The phenomenon in which a white light ray when falls on a prism get separated into its component colors is called dispersion of light.
- The band of the coloured components of a light beam is called its spectrum.
- A rainbow is a natural spectrum appearing in the sky after a rain shower.
- It is caused by the dispersion of sunlight by tiny water droplets, present in the atmosphere.
- A rainbow is always formed in a direction opposite to that of the Sun.
- The water droplets act like small prisms.
- They refract and disperse the incident sunlight, then reflect it internally, and finally refract it again when it comes out of the raindrop.
- Due to the dispersion of light and total internal reflection, different colours reach the observer's eye.

Hence, the correct option is (B).

98. The wavelength of Red light is more in comparison to other colours. So, it scatters less than any other colour. That's why red colour is used in a danger signal.

Scattering of light: The phenomenon in which the light ray is redirected in all other directions on passing through particles of dimensions comparable to the wavelength of the light used is called scattering of light.

Hence, the correct option is (A).

99. One cannot see through fog because light is scattered by the droplets in fog.

- It is difficult to see through fog because of the scattering of light by the fog droplets.
- As we know that the molecules of air and other fine particles are suspended in the atmosphere have a size smaller than the wavelength of visible light.
- As the light passes through the fog, the light gets scattered by these particles in all directions and makes it difficult to see.

Hence, the correct option is (B).

100. The scattering of light by the colloidal particle is called Tyndal scattering.

- The Tyndall effect is seen when the light-scattering particulate matter is dispersed in an otherwise light-transmitting medium.
- The Tyndall effect can also be observed when a fine beam of light enters a room through a small hole. This happens due to the scattering of light by the particles of dust and smoke in the air.

Hence, the correct option is (B).

// Notes //

// Notes //